THE
RUSH

ALSO BY EDWARD DOLNICK

The Clockwork Universe

The Forger's Spell

The Rescue Artist

Down the Great Unknown

Madness on the Couch

THE
RUSH

AMERICA'S FEVERED QUEST FOR FORTUNE, 1848–1853

EDWARD DOLNICK

Little, Brown and Company
New York Boston London

Little, Brown and Company
Hachette Book Group
237 Park Avenue, New York, NY 10017
littlebrown.com

First edition: August 2014

Little, Brown and Company is a division of Hachette Book Group, Inc. The Little, Brown name and logo are trademarks of Hachette Book Group, Inc.

The publisher is not responsible for websites (or their content) that are not owned by the publisher.

The Hachette Speakers Bureau provides a wide range of authors for speaking events. To find out more, go to hachettespeakersbureau.com or call (866) 376-6591.

The author is grateful for permission to reprint illustrations as follows:
p. 35, Henry W. Bigler Diary, Jan. 24, 1848. The Society of California Pioneers.
p. 74, The Bancroft Library, University of California, Berkeley.
p. 76, Rufus Porter, *Aerial Navigation* (New York: H. Smith, 1849).
p. 123, *Le Petit Journal,* Dec. 1, 1912.
pp. 147 and 188, Joseph Goldsborough Bruff, Diaries, Journals, and Notebooks, Western Americana Collection, Beinecke Rare Book and Manuscript Library, Yale University.

The map on page 70 created by the author.

ISBN 978-0-316-17568-5
LCCN 2014937565

10 9 8 7 6 5 4 3 2 1

RRD-C

Printed in the United States of America

To Lynn

The planter, the farmer, the mechanic, and the laborer all know that their success depends upon their own industry and economy, and that they must not expect to become suddenly rich by the fruits of their toil.

—President Andrew Jackson, 1837

A frenzy seized my soul; piles of gold rose up before me at every step; castles of marble;...slaves bowing to my beck and call; virgins contending with each other for my love...in short, I had a very violent attack of the Gold Fever.

—James Carson, a soldier stationed in California, 1848

CONTENTS

THE
RUSH

ABANDONED BY HIS COMPANIONS, starving, and trapped by snowstorms high in the Sierra Nevada, even a pathologically optimistic man like J. Goldsborough Bruff found himself fretting. He had thought he could outlast the cold and snow until a rescue party turned up, but months had passed. Now he could scarcely muster the strength to stumble in search of food.

Dinner one night had consisted of candles melted in a skillet, and, another night, boiled woodpecker. A few days later, Bruff found a half-decayed deer's skull; the worms and bugs had left a bit of meat, and Bruff shared it with his faithful dog, a bull terrier named Nevada. (The scraps, Bruff conceded in his diary, "would have been, probably, in different circumstances, quite disgusting!") That was breakfast on April 1, 1850. It marked a step up from another recent meal, coffee grounds with salt. To keep his spirits up, Bruff recited over and over, "I will soon have plenty to eat! Bread and meat, coffee and milk! A house to sleep in! An end of my sufferings!"

Back at home, he had entertained more extravagant fantasies. Bruff was an architectural draftsman from Washington, D.C., with a wife, a houseful of children, a secure job, and a thirst for adventure. In 1849, no one in the East could talk of anything but the gold strike in California. For weeks, Bruff listened and pondered and sat awake late at night studying guidebooks. Finally, his mind made up, he shoved his sharpened pencils aside. Soon he had organized a company of sixty-six men and seventeen mule-drawn wagons. The party sported dashing uniforms, new weapons, and a suitably imposing name.

On April 2, 1849, with Bruff at their head, the Washington City and California Mining Association marched to the White House to meet the president. Then they headed for California and a life of ease and luxury.

Almost exactly a year later, Bruff gathered his strength for a final attempt at escaping the mountains. Staggering his way, falling to the ground every few steps, he inched along. He ate the last of his candles. He gave the wick to Nevada.

PART I

HOPE

CHAPTER ONE

A CRACK IN TIME

IN AMERICA IN THE mid-1800s, everyone knew that two laws governed the world. First, the path to success was long and difficult; the race was not to the swift but to the diligent, who collected their pennies day after day. Second, calamity came in countless guises and swooped down without warning. Jobs, savings, and homes could vanish overnight. In the Panic of 1837, a forerunner of the Great Depression, meat doubled in price; so did flour. Nearly half the banks in the country failed. President Martin Van Buren, who rejected any efforts by the government to ease the crisis as "effeminate indulgence," came to be known as Martin Van Ruin. In eastern cities, one man in three was unemployed, and crowds of rioters shouted, "Bread! Bread! Bread!" Tens of thousands of hungry, homeless New Yorkers wandered the city's streets.

Private disasters struck as broadly and haphazardly as public ones. In an age with no understanding of germs or bacteria or infection, disease ran unchecked. Doctors had little to offer their patients but kind words and dubious potions. Mothers and fathers watched helplessly as scarlet fever or whooping cough or measles picked off one of their children, and then another, and then another. Parents who had not seen a child die were unusually fortunate.

Amputations and other operations were ordeals that looked like scenes from Edgar Allan Poe. Surgeons operated in blood-soaked frock coats and, in the interest of speed, held their knives in their teeth as they switched between cutting and sawing. Every family had seen mishaps turn into calamities. In 1842 Henry Thoreau's brother nicked himself while shaving; in a week lockjaw set in, and spasms and convulsions racked his body; in another three days he was dead. The powerful and prominent were as vulnerable as everyone else. William Henry Harrison, elected president in 1840, delivered a two-hour-long inaugural address on a cold, rainy day, without a coat. He caught pneumonia. The best doctors in the land bled him and blistered him and plied him with castor oil, opium, wine, and brandy. To no avail. Harrison died a month after taking office.

Sanitation was primitive, and diseases like dysentery reigned on a throne of filth. Cholera, the most feared killer of the age, cut down whole swathes of the population at a stroke. Like AIDS in the twentieth century, it seemed to come out of nowhere and to kill gruesomely and agonizingly, with a special taste for young and healthy victims. "King Cholera," the nineteenth century called it, or sometimes simply "The Monster." Victims were "one moment warm, palpitating, human organisms," reported the *London Medical Gazette,* "the next a sort of galvanized corpses, with icy breath, stopped pulse, and blood congealed — blue, shrivelled up, convulsed."

The cholera epidemic that hit the United States in 1832 gained strength all through the 1830s and '40s. In Saint Louis, a major gathering spot for emigrants heading to California to find gold, cholera killed six thousand people in a single year, almost one-tenth the population. In response to the crisis, the government could only declare a national day of prayer "to implore the Almighty in His own good time to stay the destroying hand which is now lifted up against us." People cowered in horror or fled in terror. Many victims had been healthy at breakfast and dead by dinner.

What no one in the 1840s knew—because no one had ever experienced such a thing—was that life-changing, fantastic-as-a-fairy-tale good news could arrive just as suddenly as disaster. Then, in December, 1848, came the most startling message imaginable. In far-off California, the president of the United States proclaimed, *gold had fallen from the sky!* Hesitant to believe at first, Americans eventually gathered their nerve and gave way to hope.

Most people had heard of fortunes won and lost, in commercial investments or in real estate speculation, but only a handful of wheeler-dealers played those heady games. For ordinary Americans, the ecstatic talk of gold and sudden riches was new and shocking and overwhelmingly exciting. They had dreamed and fantasized, of course, but those dreams had always been refuges from real life, not genuine possibilities. Now this!

We can hardly imagine their vulnerability. Today, we have been inoculated with cynicism; our forebears had far less experience of hopes raised sky-high and then dashed. In 1849, when headlines shouted "Gold fever!," the epidemic roared through American cities and villages. Victims fell in droves. In households across the nation, and across the world, the same dreams beckoned and the same debates took place. *Is it real? Can it be? Do we dare?*

For us, it is inevitably a poignant story, for it is a tale of youthful hope and fervor. America itself was young, and so were most of the gold-seekers. We look at them with a mix of envy and condescension, like middle-aged wedding guests contemplating the unlined faces of an impossibly youthful bride and groom.

The goal in 1849 was not so much the prestige and visibility that a fortune would bring as the freedom that a fortune represented. Sometimes the dreamers spoke in flowery language. "Being a shoe-maker," one young man later recalled, "and ambitious to rise some-what over the bench, it is no wonder that the discovery of gold in California excited my fancy and hopes; believing that the cele-brated Golden Age had arrived at last...I joined a respectable com-pany going to the promised land."

Sometimes the language was heartbreakingly plain. "Jane i left you and them boys for no other reason than this to come here to procure a little property by the swet of my brow so that we could have a place of our own that i mite not be a dog for other people any longer."

Always the message was the same: The world could change. Indeed, the world *had* changed. Farmers plodding behind a plow, like their fathers and their fathers' fathers before them, could break free. Clerks locked inside an office, condemned to decades of copy-ing wills and contracts, could win a future as bright as that of any planter's son. At last, astonishingly, for once, there was a way out.

The story is set in America, and it is, in important aspects, the American story. Many of the great themes play out on center stage—the journey west in search of a better life; the collision between races and nationalities; the ingrained faith that tomorrow will vastly outshine today; the focus on material success; the omni-present, taken-for-granted violence; the proud belief that America is the land of the self-made man who rises by virtue of luck and pluck rather than blood or birth.

In the sense that California is like the rest of America, only more so, the gold rush is the American story, only more so.

*   *   *

The news of California's gold, free for all, arrived unbidden in a world that could scarcely make sense of it. America had its rich men in 1848, though they were rare. (A new word, "millionaire," had crept into the language a few years before, to describe the handful of fur barons and real estate tycoons at the peak of the economic pyramid. In the 1840s New York City was home to about ten of these exotic creatures.)* Few who were not born to wealth would ever attain it.

In the mid-nineteenth century, most Americans worked twelve hours a day, six days a week. Life was hemmed in and hard. A factory girl in a cotton mill might earn $2.50 for her seventy-two-hour week, a cook in a restaurant perhaps $2 a day, a ditchdigger $1. In a society still dominated by agriculture, most boys and men labored in the fields, and girls and women cooked, cleaned, and looked after the children. Young men and women who fled home in search of independence and opportunity often found work in mills or factories. A fortunate few made it into offices, where the work was likely just as dull but better paid and less dangerous.

In its early, preindustrial years, American life had inched its way along. When the nation's first newspaper was founded, in 1690, the publisher promised his readers that his paper would be "furnished once a month (or if any Glut of occurrences happen, oftener)." But the first half of the nineteenth century was an era of enormous progress, the newfangled locomotive roaring down the track its perfect emblem. In 1830 the United States had only twenty miles of track; by 1836 that number had soared to twelve hundred miles.

---

*The population of Greater New York today is about forty times larger than in the mid-1800s, but the number of millionaires has grown *much* faster. In comparison with ten millionaires in 1848, the number of millionaires in the New York metropolitan area today is 650,000.

The clang of sledgehammer on railroad spikes rang out in countless fields and valleys that once had known only birdsong. Workmen cleared thousands of miles of roads and carved a vast network of canals. Trains sped between cities, telegraphs flashed news bulletins across hundreds of miles, and flickering gaslights brightened the streets. Posh hotels and wealthy homes boasted indoor plumbing and central heating.

The new nation itself, in the meantime, had grown at a rate scarcely known in history, doubling in size with the Louisiana Purchase in 1803, and then, in the 1840s, tacking on another million-plus square miles in the West and Northwest. A country that at its birth had clung to the Atlantic Seaboard now sprawled across a continent. The population had skyrocketed, too, doubling every two decades and pushing ever westward. The economy had grown even faster than that (though the rich gained ground faster than the poor).

The gold rush took that energy and multiplied it many times over, jamming into a few years events that might have unrolled over the course of decades. In 1848, San Francisco's population numbered a mere 812. By 1851, that village had grown into a rollicking city of thirty thousand, clamorous with the growl and lilt of a dozen languages. "I am among the French and Dutch and Scotch and Jews and Italians and Swedes and Chinese and Indians and all manner of tongues and nations," one new arrival marveled in a letter home.

Change in the 1840s was most visible in New York City, already the biggest city in the United States, and a raucous, filthy, thrilling hybrid of a medieval village and a modern metropolis. Life played out at high speed and high volume—thousands of horse-drawn wagons with iron-rimmed wheels clattered down stone streets, newsboys shouted out headlines promising gore and scandal, pigs squealed, street vendors hawked apples, nuts, eels, and oysters. The subway and Central Park and the Brooklyn Bridge were still decades in the future, but Wall Street and Broadway and Fifth Avenue were already famous. Businessmen hurtled along, elbows churning, intent on the next deal. "A New York merchant," one visitor wrote, "always walks as if he had a good dinner before him, and a bailiff behind him."

Some canny entrepreneurs made fortunes by creating refuges from the chaos. In 1846, on Broadway, Alexander Stewart opened the nation's first department store, a five-story, marble-clad temple to commerce. Light spilled in through plate-glass windows and a domed skylight, caressing two acres of carefully arranged merchandise. Customers marveled at another innovation—all Stewart's goods carried "regular and uniform prices," fixed in advance. In this elegant new bazaar, no one bargained or haggled. Clerks by the dozen stood ready to offer quiet help. Meanwhile, hotels competed to outpamper their clients. Restaurants popped up by the hundreds. The most expensive offered refinements of breathtaking elegance—individual tables, tablecloths, and, most startlingly, menus. In a world of boardinghouses and communal meals, this was splendor.

But not everyone had a place at the feast, and even some who did found their appetites sharpened rather than satisfied by the endless talk of ever-advancing prosperity. ("A few are riding," Thoreau snapped bitterly, "but the rest are run over.") By history's calendar, these transformations took place at lightning speed; but men and women lived day to day or week to week, not generation to generation. They yearned for change, they heard of change all around them, but they did not know if they could find a way to change their own lives.

For black Americans in particular, change seemed not the impossible-to-miss theme of the age but a hoax or a pipe dream. It was slavery, above all other factors, that marked the world of the mid-1800s as unthinkably different from our own. America just before the Civil War was a land in which nearly four million people lived in bondage. In South Carolina and Mississippi, over half the population was in chains.

Behind every such statistic lay a multitude of anguished lives. In April, 1854, in Charlottesville, Virginia, the owners of a seventeen-year-old slave girl named Frances gave her a letter to deliver to a business firm in Richmond. (Frances could not read.) "She does not know that she is to be sold," the note explained. "I could not tell her; I own all her family, and the leave-taking would be so distressing that I could not. Please say to her that that was my reason, and that I was compelled to sell her to pay for the horses that I have bought... and to build my stable. I believe I have said all that is necessary, but I am so nervous that I hardly know what I have written."

Life for whites was vastly better than that, but even for most of them, the sight of progress all around served mainly as a reminder of what they did not yet have. "I have followed that plow more miles than any one man ever did," one Connecticut farmer lamented, and his counterparts in the nation's cities felt their own version of the same anguish.

In New York, in 1844, tailors went on strike to demand a pay raise, to seventy-five cents a day, for their ten to fifteen hours of work. (After five weeks, they won the raise.) In Nashville, Tennessee, in 1847, carpenters called for a shorter working day, a mere ten hours. "We are flesh and blood, we need hours of recreation," they implored. "...Shall we live and die knowing nothing but the rudiments of our trade?" New York swarmed with beggars and ragpickers who scavenged garbage heaps for anything salvageable,

or edible. Hot-corn girls worked the crowds, calling out their
melancholy singsong:

Hot corn! Hot corn!
Here's your lily-white corn.
All you that's got money
Poor me that's got none—
Buy me lily-white corn
And let me go home.

This was a society with scarcely any safety nets. "In 1840," the
historian Andrew Delbanco observed, "the horse pulling a rich
man's carriage down Broadway could expect to sleep that night in
better quarters than the man who knocks on the carriage door
begging for a coin." To fall sick or get hurt or lose a job was to
plummet from a tightrope into an abyss. In such a fast-growing,
fast-changing economy, new opportunities constantly arose and
old certainties fell apart. In the long run, American ingenuity
would enrich the world, and improvements in the plow, the sewing
machine, and the steam engine would create jobs, not destroy
them. In the short run, the price of wheat or whale oil could fall;
new ways of stitching shoes or mining coal or printing news could
render old skills instantly obsolete; lone craftsmen could be steam-
rolled by giant mills employing squadrons of low-paid factory girls.

In this precarious world, fear tended to overshadow hope. The
message that each generation tried to drum into the heads of the
next was to make peace with the grim facts of reality. "All communities divide themselves into the few and the many," Alexander
Hamilton had written at the time of America's birth. The few were
"rich and well born," and the many "the mass of the people." So it
had always been; so it would always be. Who could dispute so plain

a truth? The path of wisdom was not to shake one's fist against fate but to accommodate oneself to it. Through repetition and familiarity, old maxims had long since taken on the power of incantations. *Work hard. Save your money. Pray for the best.* Dreams were a foolish indulgence, distractions in a dangerous world. Dreams of riches were the most foolish of all.

Especially riches pulled from the ground. Two-thirds of all American workers labored on farms, with sweat and muscle the only fuels. "There was no quittin' time and no startin' time," a folk proverb declared. "It was *all* the time." The ancient decree still held: "In the sweat of thy face shalt thou eat bread, till thou return unto the ground." Such was man's lot. Many could not imagine an alternative.

But it had always been hard to banish hope altogether. Though everyone recognized that life was a grim affair best taken one wary step at a time, that was hard to accept. Consolation came in small distractions, akin to purchases of lottery tickets today. In colonial times so many people had spent their time searching for pirates' buried treasure that Benjamin Franklin wrote an essay rebuking them. The way to wealth, he insisted, was to pile coin on coin, steadily and patiently. The earth offered a living, but it was a hard, grudging living. Franklin told a story of a wise father who had given his son a parcel of land: "'I assure thee I have found a considerable quantity of gold by digging there; thee mayst do the same. But thee must carefully observe this, Never to dig more than plow deep.'"

Now the president had announced that Ben Franklin had it all wrong.

———————

Americans had been moving west, in short hops and long jumps, for generations. "If hell lay to the west," the saying went, "Americans would cross heaven to get there." Most of those early settlers had been small farmers seeking better land or bigger holdings than a man could find in the more crowded East. Their new farms looked just like the old ones. So did the new towns that sprung up around them.

That familiarity was the point. These transplanted families hoped to find, in one historian's summary, "not a totally new life but a better old one." The gold-seekers stood that familiar ambition on its head. They'd had enough of the old ways. More than anything else, they *wanted* a totally new life.

Nor was this the only way in which the gold-seekers differed from nearly all the Americans who had ventured west before them. They intended to go thousands of miles farther, for starters. And those earlier travelers had been family men with wives and children in tow, most of them, or else mountain men and trappers, solitary adventurers unfazed by Rocky Mountain snowstorms and desert treks.

The gold-seekers belonged to neither camp. Many had never ventured away from streetcars and gaslights. Most were young, single, inexperienced men, the vast majority still in their twenties or thirties. Their "toil had heretofore consisted," one of them wrote, "in running up a column of figures or counting bankbills."

In an era of dollar-a-day incomes, those who went west before 1848 had hoped simply to prosper as farmers. A few had made it all the way to California before anyone had ever heard of gold. Then the throngs arrived, and the farmers stared at the newcomers in disbelief, as dumbfounded by the commotion as time travelers. "My little girls can make from 5 to 25 dollars washing gold in pans," wrote one of these astonished emigrants, a Missouri man named M. T. McClellan. "My average income this winter will be about $150 per day, and if I should strike a good lead it will be a great deal more."

Letters like that one, to a hometown friend, carried enormous weight. This was eyewitness testimony, and utterly specific. "You know James M. Harlin," McClellan went on. "He has just bought a Mexican ranch, for which he has paid in gold $12,000." Nor was that all. "Jesse Beasley is said to be worth at least $40,000.... You know Bryant, a carpenter, who used to work for Ebenezer Dixon; he has dug out more gold in the last six months than a mule can pack." Harlin's ranch cost a sum that would have taken a ditchdigger back home almost thirty-three years to accrue, even if he'd had no other expenses during those decades. And he had made the money like *that*.

The new arrivals not only passed along these astounding stories but vouched for them with the most solemn oaths they could summon. "The above account and description of matters and things will seem strange to you," McClellan concluded, "but, sir, if you believe Divine Revelations or the sacred truths of Holy Writ, you can believe this statement."

Those first settlers had hoped to stay in one spot and cultivate the land for generations. The gold-seekers wanted to snatch a fortune from the ground and then hurry back home. That was a crucial difference. But it was the sheer size of the gold rush, above all, that set it apart from anything the world had seen since the Crusades. The rush was colossal. In 1849, some ninety thousand young men swarmed to the goldfields (two-thirds of them were American); in 1850, nearly as many more elbowed their way into the scrum, and the throngs kept coming all through the early 1850s. Even if for the moment we focus only on the Americans and not on the crowds from around the world, this was an immense volunteer army, all of them racing toward a goal none of them had ever seen.

In the four years from 1849 through 1852, more than 1 percent of the American population moved to California. To put that number in terms of today's population, picture three million young Americans giving up their jobs, leaving their families, and rushing off to a barely known destination thousands of miles away. Picture them on foot—though few of them had ever slept under the stars—or on shipboard—though few had ever ventured out of sight of land—and all racing headlong to, say, the most distant, least-known corner of South America.

All this was out of the blue. Despite the advent of the train and the steamship, most Americans in the 1840s lived their entire lives inside a tiny circle centered on their hometown. Sailors and whalers aside, a man who had ventured a hundred miles from home was a traveler with tales to tell. For nearly everyone, California was more a name than an actual place, an exotic, half-unreal locale like China or Egypt. It was a name, moreover, that conjured up not simply the West but the farthest edge of the West. That made for extra allure and for a shiver of excitement, too.

In American history, "the West" has always been a moving target. The West began where towns ended and danger began. One worried father in colonial days sent his daughter off to visit relatives who lived fifteen miles away, near Boston. "I did greatly fear for Abigail's safety, as she is gone into Duxbury," he wrote in his diary. "It is her first journey into the West, and I shall pray mightily for her early return."

By the early 1800s the boundary had moved to today's Midwest. (When the New York editor Horace Greeley famously advised young men to "go West," in 1838, he had in mind not empty deserts and soaring mountains but the lush farmland of Ohio and

Illinois.) By 1849 the line had shifted to the western borders of Missouri and Iowa. Cross the Missouri River at Saint Joseph, Missouri, or Council Bluffs, Iowa, and you had entered the West.

California sat at the distant edge of that mysterious and still poorly mapped expanse. (The name "California" came from a Spanish novel, published in 1510, about a faraway land "abounding with gold and precious stones.") Since the mid-1700s it had belonged to Spain and then, since 1821, to Mexico. Neither country had managed to lure many of its citizens to settle the new territory; Mexico, in desperation, had briefly tried sending off convicts as unwilling immigrants. In 1848, California's non-Indian population totaled only fifteen thousand, about one person for every ten square miles. The Indian population was ten times as large.

It was not until 1841 that the first group of emigrants traveled overland to what would someday be known as the Golden State, and not until 1845 that the first wagons managed to cross the Sierra Nevada. In 1848 the number who made the overland trip was only four hundred. Those few travelers inching across a vast continent were, in one historian's words, "as lonely as men left swimming in mid-ocean from a sunken ship."

Then came news of California's gold. One awed '49er looked at the hordes of dreamers all around him. "There seemed to be an unending stream of emigrant trains," William Johnston wrote, in present-day eastern Kansas. "It was a sight which, once seen, can never be forgotten; it seemed as if the whole family of man had set its face westward."

The soon-to-be-rich ran from merchant to merchant outfitting themselves with necessities for the journey. They weighed themselves down with cumbersome contraptions like the "Archimedes

Gold Washing Machine" and the "California Gold Finder." A group of gold-seekers from France bought up a supply of rakes, for the men, and silver tongs, for their wives. The men planned to rake gold nuggets out of the rivers, leaving the flakes and dust behind for those content with such small prizes. The wives, in the meantime, would perch atop stools embroidered in silk and pluck bits of gold from gravel-filled china dishes.

A Rochester, New York, man hired a clairvoyant to accompany him to California, so he could use his partner's psychic powers to learn where the gold lay hidden. In Indiana, buyers lined up for a special salve called "California Gold Grease" that guaranteed a lifetime of wealth. All a man had to do was climb to the top of a hill in gold country, rub his body with the magical ointment, and roll downhill. By the time he reached the bottom and scraped himself clean, he would have a fortune to last the rest of his days. Ten dollars a box.

A young gold-seeker from Ohio put the universal thought into plain words: "The rich for many years have had chances for filling their pockets. Let the poor now have a chance." Nor was it only the young and adventurous who succumbed. Many who were too old or too staid to set out on a long, dangerous journey did the next-best thing—they backed a young miner, or a dozen, in return for a share of the enormous profits certain to come their way.

A week before the gold news hit, a young man seeking a ten-dollar loan would have been slapped down for his extravagance. Now, when he needed $750 or $1,000 for the overland trip or a sea voyage, no one blinked. "The United States was not a rich country in the latter 1840s," the historian Oscar Lewis observed, but "it was absurd to count costs when a sure fortune awaited whoever could contrive to reach the gold fields in the van of the stampede."

The prospect of repaying those loans spurred not anxiety but fantasies of a glorious homecoming. The case of a young Pittsburgh man named George Barclay was more or less typical. Barclay set out with provisions and funds provided by his banker uncle, who also provided several wooden kegs bound with iron hoops. The plan was that he would repay his uncle by returning the kegs filled with gold dust.

If the gold-seekers hesitated, the hardship that preyed on their minds was not failure—for who could imagine returning empty-handed from a land of plenty?—but loneliness and exile. To travel to California and then to dig up a fortune and travel home again would take two or three years at least, and quite possibly five or six. *"What makes you think I won't return, / With lots of gold to adorn you?"* one song asked, *"Dry up your tears and do not mourn, / There's wealth in California."*

While sweethearts wept, parents and clergymen scolded. To leave behind the "wholesome restraints of New England Society" and head to the goldfields, Elisha Cleaveland warned the young men in his New Haven, Connecticut, congregation, would be to join "the filth and scum of society" who had "poured in there to seethe and ferment into one putrid mass of unmitigated depravity." Perhaps the Yale students who made up most of Cleaveland's audience cowered at the thought of participating in such wild goings-on.

But then, on this January morning in 1849, Cleaveland went on to put the case against gold fever in such a way as to make sure that no one heeded a single cautionary word of his sermon. Temptation was natural, Cleaveland conceded, when "within our borders [was] a tract of country larger than New England, underlaid, we know not how deep, with *pure gold*." The gold could be "sifted in immense quantities, from the sands of the rivers, or picked from the rocks, or gathered from the surface of the ground...free to all as the air we breathe."

Parents railed against their children for their foolishness—and this in an era when the young traditionally deferred to their elders. Why did they believe there were shortcuts to wealth? Had anyone ever seen such a thing? And what of family responsibility? Who would make up the income these wayward sons had brought in, or do the work they proposed to neglect? What if the dream-dazed wanderers *never* returned—what would become of their parents when they grew old, with no one to care for them? And even if the gold-seekers did come home, there might be no reunion. California was on the other side of the world. Few people lived into their seventies or eighties; to return after a long absence, it was universally understood, would likely mean coming home too late.

In December, 1848, a young man living in New York City wrote a letter to his sister in Maine, trying out the argument he planned to make to his father. "You know that I am in the prime of life—a good constitution, know how to shovel, can live in a log house or a tent, and build one, too. You know that I always had a desire to travel, to see something of the world. Now, when shall I ever have a better chance?

"I can hardly make a living here," he went on. "We have no capital to carry on business with and it will be a long time before we can get a start. *Labor* is capital out there." A man who could work could grow rich! "I have looked at my chance here and I have made up my mind to go, and I am going if I have to go out as a common sailor." One month later, twenty-three-year-old Franklin Buck was on a ship for California.

*   *   *

The to-go-or-not-to-go conflict pitted not only wary fathers against eager sons but two deeply held beliefs against each other. One was the age-old fear that the world punishes its dreamers, the other the new American gospel that people shaped their own destiny. Was it better to hunker down so as not to tempt fate or to rise up and grab fate by its scrawny neck?

The waverings of a young Vermont couple, Alfred and Chastina Rix, highlight the difficulties of the decision. Both Rixes were schoolteachers in their early twenties. Alfred was square jawed and earnest in appearance, the kind of wholesome young man who, in the popular fiction of the day, was perpetually reviving fainting ladies. Chastina was small and plain, frail looking but feisty and independent minded, more than willing to join the men's debate over such news as the Fugitive Slave Act (both Dixes were vehement abolitionists). They had married in July, 1849, when talk of gold was universal. But life in Vermont was far more taken up with toil than talk. When the number of pupils in their school fell perilously low, Alfred took a second job as a traveling salesman. A baby came along. "We are rather poor now days," Chastina wrote in the diary that she and Alfred kept together. The Rixes stayed in Vermont throughout 1849 but watched one neighbor after another head to California. They lent money to one friend, who headed off "all in a puff for California."

Reluctantly, they stayed put. "Cook, cook, cook, & eat is my business," Chastina wrote bitterly in 1850. "I am just about tired out." In the same diary entry, perhaps significantly, she found time for a brief mention of the friend in California to whom they had loaned money. "Heard from Hale. He is well." Did the curtness of that remark tell a story? Alfred sounded just as irritable and exasperated, worn out by the "stale" wisdom he heard incessantly from the respectable, dull old men of Peacham. They wanted nothing more, he complained, than for "the youth who has just come to the age of feeling & excitability" to bury his dreams and settle down "with a lot of old hard-hearted hypocrites."

Could he bear that cramped fate? Over the course of the next year Alfred worked up his nerve. "A man with gumption goes by it [i.e., goes for it]," he wrote, "one without any goes where his father did." Finally, in 1851, Alfred and two of his brothers, along with a brother of Chastina's, set out to go where their fathers had never been. Chastina stayed behind with the baby, resolved to come out to California as soon as the infant was old enough to travel.

For the rest of their lives, men and women would remember where they had been when they first heard that the world had turned upside down. "One June morning [in 1848] when I was a boy," a gold-seeker named Prentice Mulford recalled decades later, "Captain Eben Latham came to our house, and the first gossip he unloaded was that 'them stories about finding gold in Californy was all true.' That was the first report I heard from California."

Mulford lived in Sag Harbor, New York, in those days a whaling village. In the young boy's eyes, the old ship's captain was an almost mythological figure, and his newest story seemed every bit as thrilling as his other swashbuckling yarns. "Old Eben had been a man of the sea; was once captured by a pirate, and when he told the story, which he did once a week, he concluded by rolling up his trousers and showing the bullet-scars he had received."

Now young Prentice Mulford and old Eben Latham, and everyone else, found themselves swept up in a saga of their own. "All the old retired whaling captains wanted to go, and most of them did go," Mulford wrote. "All the spruce young men of the place wanted to go. Companies were formed, and there was much serious drawing up of constitutions and by-laws for their regulation."

To venture to the end of the earth was to take a monumental gamble. But as more and more people made up their minds to set off for the goldfields, a decision to stay at home came to seem less a display of prudence than a stubborn, almost perverse refusal to hold out your hands when the sky was raining money.

The gold rush offered something for everyone. If you were stuck, you could get free. If you were already moving fast, you could move even faster. If you were a hard worker, what could be better than to work where the reward was buried treasure? If you had an entrepreneurial eye, where better to cash in than in a land of strivers, many of whom would have pockets stuffed with money?

If you craved adventure, this would be an adventure like no other. If you yearned for security, you could set yourself up for a lifetime. If you were on your own and independent, what better time to pick up and go? If you had a family and responsibilities, how better to meet your obligations than by riding home in a wagon full of gold?

And what were the obstacles? The trip would be long and difficult, true, but sailors made longer voyages, and a handful of resourceful emigrants had recently proved that the overland route was doable, too. *Barely* doable, perhaps, but a dash of danger made the notion all the more enticing, in a Boy's Own Adventure way.

In any case, what was the alternative? The Panic of 1837 had proved that the world might collapse without warning, but no one had quite decided on the moral of that story. Was the lesson to lie low, in fear of the next economic blast? The cautious and the elderly might say so, and they did, but the nation was young, and the clamor of eager, impatient voices drowned out the bleak lectures and the dark warnings.*

America in the 1800s was not merely young but young in a double sense. The nation itself had been born almost within living memory, and its citizens were young, too. Take every American in 1850 and arrange them all in a colossal line from youngest to oldest, and the person at the midway point—the typical American—would have been just under nineteen years old. Today, that median American would be nearly twice as old, a shade past thirty-five.

Many of those young strivers felt certain that when an opportunity came along, you grabbed it with both hands. And this was an opportunity like no other, ever. "What would *you* do," asks Gary Kurutz, one of the deans of gold rush history, "if you were a young man today? What would you do if somebody came along and said there was a place you could go and you'd make $10,000 a day, tax-free?

"Well, you can see why there was a stampede to California. The idea was that in one season you'd harvest enough gold to take care of yourself and your family"—here Kurutz's voice rises in high-pitched incredulity—"*for the rest of your life.* You'd be a fool *not* to go."

---

*More than two centuries after America's birth, tourists visiting the United States still find themselves surprised at how deeply optimism is built into the culture. "The palpable sense of newness here creates an odd sort of optimism," according to the 2012 edition of the *Rough Guide to the USA*, "where anything seems possible and fortune can strike at any moment."

CHAPTER TWO

"I BELIEVE I HAVE FOUND A GOLD MINE!"

WHEN AMERICA LOST ITS mind in 1849, and then the rest of the world did, too, the temptation among the historically minded was to think of other examples of mass madness. In the tulip mania of the 1600s in Holland, these skeptics pointed out, men spent more on a single bulb than it would have cost to buy the grandest house in Amsterdam. And that was far from the only economic frenzy the world had seen before the Sierra beckoned.

Today we think of more recent debacles. In the Internet bubble, around 1999, companies that had never earned a penny raised hundreds of millions in stock offerings and then went bust. In the real estate bubble of the early 2000s, Americans convinced themselves that housing prices would climb forever. Anyone could trade up from an ordinary suburban home to a turret-sprouting mansion, it seemed, or buy that mansion for next to nothing down.

But those comparisons do not apply, except in the sense that the world *did* go mad when the gold news broke. Unlike dot-coms built on pipe dreams, California's gold was real and tangible.

Unlike mansions built for imaginary buyers, gold had a ready market. Unlike shares in exotic new companies or suddenly-in-reach new houses, whose value was a matter of guesswork, the value of gold was fixed and settled and public.

The gold rush was not a bubble. California's reality outshone even the most overheated fantasies. In 1849 alone, miners dug up seventeen *tons* of gold. Every pebble in that golden mountain had guaranteed value—$20.67 an ounce in the United States, backed by the federal government—and a similar value around the world. Over the course of the 1850s, miners would unearth a trove of gold worth, in today's money, $12 billion.

The problem with gold had never been that it was merely a fad—mankind had craved gold since before the dawn of writing—but that it was so hard to find. And now it wasn't.

"Neither moth nor rust devoureth it," wrote the Greek poet Pindar, twenty-five centuries ago, "but the mind of man is devoured by this supreme possession." Today gold is used, in tiny amounts, in cameras, phones, and computers, but for most everyday purposes it is too expensive for anything but jewelry.* The result is that gold is never "used up," in the sense that a piece of firewood or a lump of coal is transformed unrecognizably.

Virtually all the gold ever mined can still be found today, perhaps changed in shape but always unmistakably itself. Gold from a goblet that Caesar raised to his lips may now dangle from the ears of a young girl dressing for her prom or glint from the front tooth of a rap star. The very gold that launched the worldwide rush

---

*Eventually, some poor soul kneeling at the base of a mountain of electronic trash will break open those discarded televisions and phones and pluck out the gold.

to California can be examined today, at the Smithsonian Institution in Washington, D.C., almost as if one could look at a court artist's portrait of Helen of Troy. "San Francisco, 1848," the label reads. "This paper contains the first piece of gold ever discovered in the northern part of Upper California."

It is a strange thing, this combination of uselessness and mad desirability. What object other than gold do we covet for such unfathomable reasons? We gaze at *The Girl with a Pearl Earring* and marvel at how Vermeer conjured up beauty from a badger-hair brush and a few hand-ground pigments; we see a jet engine and recognize its power; we look at Lincoln's bloody shirt and feel the tug of history. But how to account for the allure of gold? No less a financial wizard than Warren Buffett proclaimed himself baffled. "Gold gets dug out of the ground in Africa, or someplace. Then we melt it down, dig another hole, bury it again and pay people to stand around guarding it. It has no utility. Anyone watching from Mars would be scratching their head."

For the craftsman, gold's softness and workability are the properties that set it apart. Gold is so malleable that a lump the size of a sugar cube can be beaten into a sheet a hundred feet square. This is gold leaf, beloved of artisans since ancient times. Thin enough to see through, a golden stack five hundred leaves high would be only as tall as a single sheet of aluminum foil. And even at this next-to-nothing thinness, gold will remain forever unchanged by air, water, or nearly any acid.

But it was gold's weight, not its softness, that made the gold rush possible. Gold is nearly twice as dense as lead. If a basketball were solid gold, it would weigh more than three hundred pounds, and only a titan could pick it off the floor. In a river, that heaviness makes all the difference.

Since gold is rare, no one would ever find it if it were scattered randomly, a grain here and a grain there. It is, in fact, *absurdly* rare, a needle in a field of haystacks. Gather up a billion atoms at random from the earth's crust, the geologist Keith Meldahl explains, and only five would be gold. (By way of comparison with more common elements, a billion atoms of crust picked at random would include 470,000 atoms of oxygen and 45,000 of iron.) To find enough gold for one wedding ring, you would have to sift through two hundred tons of dirt.

In California and a handful of other places around the globe, nature has contrived to gather and concentrate those few atoms in the form of flakes and nuggets. The action takes place deep underground, over the course of eons, and the geologic tumult plays out in different ways in different locales. Beneath what would someday be California, plates collided, and the ground cracked, and plumes of superheated, mineral-rich water coursed their way upward through the fractures. What remained were newly lifted mountain ranges striped with quartz veins snaking their way along, mile upon mile. In those stone veins was gold.

Ever so gradually, weather and water ate into those mountainsides and those veins. Bits of gold-bearing rock washed downhill and tumbled into rivers. Those rocks clicked and tapped against other rocks. Eventually—not always, but often—the brittle quartz casing chipped away, freeing the gold within.

Now gold's weight came into play. Gold in a river settles out wherever the current slows, precisely because gold is so heavy. In swirling eddies or quiet spots on the sheltered side of rocks and boulders, the river sheds its burden of golden flakes and grains while still propelling along its load of much-lighter sand and gravel. Day after day, year after year, the river runs its course, and bits of dense, bright gold sink to the riverbed. Someday, perhaps, a grizzled man will shout "Eureka!"

*   *   *

Gold had always belonged to kings and emperors. Those who owned it lived splendid, pampered lives; those who mined it labored their lives away for the benefit of others, scarcely better off than slaves. Those were simple, brutal, eternal facts, as much a part of gold's essence as its color or its weight.

One historian writing before the time of Christ described gold mining in ancient Egypt. Slaves worked the underground mines, wrote Diodorus of Sicily, dragging their shackles behind them. Guards hovered nearby, and to rule out even the possibility of a conspiracy, guards were matched with prisoners whose language they did not speak. No mercy was shown the sick or injured or old, or women. All were worked without letup "until through ill-treatment they die in the midst of their tortures."

Matters had improved only marginally through the ages. Just before the discovery of California's gold, most of the world's gold came from Siberia. The harsh landscape, the bitter cold, and the brutal working conditions had almost nothing in common with sun-baked California. Siberia's miners were not free men hoping to make themselves a fortune but, for the most part, prisoners who had been banished for minor offenses. They worked fourteen hours a day, from five in the morning to eight in the evening every day but Sunday, for tiny wages. Police and Cossacks patrolled the mines; secret police spied on would-be thieves.

The czar, a world away in Saint Petersburg, owned the mines outright or imposed stiff taxes on their wealthy proprietors. Theirs was a good business even so. One dazzled visitor, in 1845, reported on the luxuries with which a Siberian mine owner could ease his isolation. Servants produced "on a plate of Japanese porcelain, oranges imported from Marseilles or from Messina." Costly wines and "inexhaustible springs of champagne" flowed at every meal.

But no one owned California's gold.

The first to race to the goldfields were those who happened to be standing nearest the starting gun. But even these fortunate few dawdled before they ran, sure that the big talk would soon prove empty. No one would have guessed, early on, that the discovery of gold at Sutter's mill would eventually take on the tone of legend. Today the story is as encrusted with myth as the Pilgrims' first Thanksgiving or Paul Revere's ride. By most accounts, it was the morning of January 24, 1848, when a moody, oddball carpenter named James Marshall muttered a phrase destined to become famous. "Boys, by God, I believe I have found a gold mine!"

Marshall's "boys" were a work crew, mostly Mormon, building a sawmill on the American River about forty miles from what would one day be Sacramento. Marshall, a skilled and versatile workman despite his peculiar ways, was the foreman on the job. Work had reached a point where the next task was to divert a stream of water from the river so that it would drive the mill's waterwheel. Marshall's focus was the water itself, rather than anything within it. But as he described his discovery later, on one January day he happened to notice a tiny, yellowish pebble lying a foot deep in rushing water. He snatched up the nubbin—about the size of a pencil eraser—and stared at it. *Could it be?* Marshall knew little about gold, but he knew that it was soft rather than brittle. He set the gleaming pebble down carefully on a flat rock, picked up another rock, and delivered a sharp blow. The tiny nugget flattened a bit, like a lump of clay squeezed between thumb and forefinger, but it did not crack. Marshall ran to find his co-workers.

One of those men left his own account of the discovery. Henry Bigler recalled seeing Marshall run up, a smile plastered on his face and his battered, white hat cradled in his hands. Marshall blurted out that he'd found gold. The men gathered around. Marshall carefully set his hat down. There, in a small dent poked in the crown, sat a few golden pebbles. One of the men reached into his pocket and withdrew a five-dollar gold coin. The others looked back and forth, comparing coin and golden bits. Not exactly alike, they concluded, but close enough.

That night Bigler scrawled an entry in his diary: "Monday 24th this day some kind of mettle was found in the tail race that looks like goald, first discovered by James Martial the Boss of the Mill."

Remarkably, Marshall's men stuck mostly to their assigned jobs over the next few weeks, despite the discovery. (They feared the find would amount to only a few scattered flakes.) In their spare time the most optimistic scoured the river up and down. Bigler, in particular, confessed that he had "gold badly on the brain." He took to dodging his workmates and sneaking off to the ice-cold American River. There he crouched for hours, in February, in the rain and snow, naked and shivering in the river and poking bits of gold out of crevices in the rocks with his knife.

The man best positioned to cash in on the discovery was John Sutter, the biggest landowner in the region. It was Sutter, an eccentric, ambitious, amiable Swiss emigré, who had sent Marshall to build him a mill in the first place. Even before anyone ever whispered a word about gold, Sutter was one of the best-known figures in California. He had fled Europe just ahead of a posse of irate bill collectors fourteen years before, and then had reinvented himself as a New World emperor. Here in America, Sutter was not a small,

> Monday 24th this day
> some kind of mettle was
>
> 177
> was found in the tail race that
> that looks like goald first discov
> ered by James Martial, the Boss of the mill.
> Sunday 30 clean & has been
> all the last week our metal
> has been tride and prooves to
> be Goald it is thought to be
> rich we have pickt up more than
> a hundred dollars woth last
> one week
>
> February. 1848
> Sun 6th the wether has been clean
> and ....

chubby, bankrupt merchant with a wife and five children. He was Captain John Sutter (he bestowed the title himself), an imposing figure with elegant manners, a formal way of speaking, and a taste for ornate military uniforms complete with epaulettes and sword. "I am no ordinary gentleman, no Sir," he was fond of saying. "I am an extraordinary gentleman, yes Sir, I am. I strive to be honored. I will do anything for honor."

In 1839 Sutter had talked the Mexican government into granting

him title to a huge expanse of land—seventy-five square miles—
in the lush Sacramento Valley. Sutter dubbed his kingdom New
Helvetia. At its heart, in what is now Sacramento, he built an enormous structure he called Sutter's Fort, with thick adobe walls
guarded by cannons. A sentry stood watch at the main gate, and
Sutter maintained a private army of some two hundred men, for
protection and pomp.

In the California wilderness, the soldiers in their green-and-blue
uniforms trimmed with red provided just the kind of incongruous
splendor that Sutter relished. The soldiers were Indians, their officers
Europeans. In the evenings they practiced marching drills. Officers
barked out the German commands for "forward, march" and "right,
face" and "about, face." Fife and drum played, and Sutter beamed.

Within the sprawling compound could be found a blacksmith's
shop, a shoemaker's, a carpenter's, a factory that turned out hats
and blankets, a dining hall (though Sutter fed his Indian "employees" outdoors, from a trough). Outside the walls were orchards,
wheat fields, a vineyard, a tannery, a flour mill, and, notably, a sawmill. Sutter reigned proudly over it all like a medieval baron. "I had
at the same time twelve thousand head of cattle and two thousand
horses and ten or fifteen thousand sheep," he would later recall. "I
had all the Indians I could employ."

The Indians, hundreds of them, worked indoors as servants and
outdoors as field hands, for "wages" of trinkets and trade goods.
Their working conditions were as poor as their wages. One startled
observer described the wheat harvest, with "three or four hundred
wild Indians in a grain field armed, some with sickles, some with
butcher knives, some with pieces of hoop iron roughly fashioned
into shapes like sickles, but many having only their hands with
which to gather up by small handfuls the dry and brittle grain; and
as their hands would soon become sore, they resorted to willow

sticks, which were split to afford a sharper edge with which to sever the straw."

Harvesting wheat by hand was an astonishing throwback, and the threshing process—to break up the grain and chaff into small bits—was more primitive still. "The harvest of weeks, sometimes of a month, was piled up in...a huge mound in the middle of a high, strong, round, corral," the same amazed eyewitness wrote. "Then three or four hundred wild horses were turned in to thresh it, the Indians whooping to make them run faster." Finally, on a windy day, the valuable grain and the worthless chaff would be flung high into the air. The light chaff would blow off, the heavier grain would fall into a heap, and a harvest that smacked more of Breughel than of the nineteenth century would be complete.

The town nearest Sutter's Fort was San Francisco, ninety miles away and with a population of about eight hundred. Rumors of a nearby gold strike reached San Francisco in February or March, 1848. The town yawned. People had found gold in California before, and those finds had fizzled. A few people had grown excited; nobody had grown rich.

On March 15, 1848, the newspapers chimed in for the first time, but without much zeal. The *Californian* reported that gold had been found "in considerable quantities" at the sawmill on the American River. The story ran as part of a news roundup, along with such items as "Grizzly Bear" and "Man Drowned," though not quite as prominently placed. Like the others, "Gold Mine Found" rated only a single paragraph and ran buried inside the paper.

A bigger story might have fallen flat, too, for the *Californian* was not a formidable institution. A four-page weekly, the Monterey-based paper had begun printing just two years before. (This made it California's first newspaper.) The editor, a wry, Yale-educated New Englander named Walter Colton, had explained in a brochure promoting his new venture that for a time his newspaper would have an odd look; he had bought a secondhand printing press and could not print the letter *w*. (The previous owners were Spanish, and traditional Spanish has no *w*'s.) "In the meantime vve must use two V's...in due time vvee vvill have something better. VValter Colton."

The *Californian*'s only rival, the *California Star*, paid even less attention to the gold rumors. The *Star*'s editor was a young man named Edward Kemble, just nineteen years old but cynical beyond his years. In April, 1848, Kemble reluctantly ventured out from San Francisco to "ruralize among the rustics" and find out for himself if anything was up at Sutter's mill.

Kemble asked James Marshall where the gold was. Marshall gestured toward the river: "You'll find it anywhere you're a mind to dig for it down there." This reply, Kemble ruefully noted later, was not the brush-off he took it to be but almost the literal truth. Kemble and two companions set out, skeptically, to try their hands at this panning business. They spent the afternoon splashing knee-deep in icy water, sifting sand and gravel. Their labors yielded only a flake or two of gold, and Kemble concluded grumpily that all the talk was only talk. "HUMBUG," he scribbled at the top of his notes.

Back in San Francisco, Kemble hit the same note in the *Star*. "All sham," he wrote. The reports of gold were "a superb take-in as ever was got up to 'guzzle the gullible.'" Nobody but the "superlatively silly" would fall for it. The real story of the week, a glance at the *Star* would have suggested, was a wondrous medicine called Dr. Benjamin Brandreth's Vegetable Universal Pills. These marvelous tablets had the power to banish some three dozen afflictions, from colds and cancers to whooping cough, deafness, nightmares, dysentery, worms, and "a sense of fullness in the back part of the head."

But Kemble had missed an enormous scoop. While he was advising his readers to forget about gold, men in Marshall's crew were exploring new sites and raking in fortunes. Each day brought news of another find. Henry Bigler had found $35 worth of gold on April 21; Alexander Stephens had found $45 worth the next day; Azariah Smith (the man who had pulled the five-dollar gold piece from his pocket) had found a better spot and had panned $95 in a day.

Sutter's mini-state never recovered. What had been a rural enclave largely preoccupied with wheat and cattle suddenly took on the frenetic busyness of a beehive knocked on its side. In ones and twos at first, and then in swarms, Sutter's employees abandoned their work and raced off to find gold. "To all appearances," wrote a gardener caught in the rush, "men seemed to have gone insane."

A young, slick entrepreneur named Sam Brannan—destined one day to be California's richest man—detonated the explosion that grabbed San Francisco's attention at last. Brannan was charming, crooked, tireless, a fast talker and big drinker perpetually in pursuit of another woman, another deal, another dollar. Never satisfied with "enough" when "too much" was an option, Brannan happily put his own twist on Ben Franklin's maxim that "God helps them that help themselves." He was a classic American con man and also a genuine business visionary who saw which way every game was headed before anyone else had done more than scratch his head in bewilderment.

In retailing and real estate, hotelkeeping and newspaper publishing, Brannan seized opportunities, or created them. At a time when San Francisco was only a village and Sacramento barely more than a muddy landing at a river junction, for instance, he snatched up much of the prime real estate in the future metropolises. He paid almost nothing and reaped a fortune when the crowds poured in.

Brannan had arrived in San Francisco two years before the first gold strike, in July, 1846, only twenty-seven years old but already a natural leader. Religion, not commerce, had led him to California. A new convert to Mormonism, Brannan had chartered a ship called the *Brooklyn* and set out from New York as the leader of a party of 238 Mormons in search of a haven from persecution.

From the time Joseph Smith had founded their religion, in 1828, Mormons had been sneered at for their odd views, resented for their "clannishness," and feared for their political clout (they tended to vote as a group). The dislike had turned violent. Vigilante mobs had set Mormons' houses ablaze and tarred and feathered their leaders. At the Haun's Hill Massacre, in Missouri in 1838, seventeen Mormons had been killed and fifteen wounded. In Illinois in 1844, a mob stormed Joseph Smith's jail cell—he had been imprisoned for plotting treason against the United States—and shot and killed him. Missouri had expelled its Mormons, and then Illinois had as well. In 1846 Brigham Young set out to find a refuge for his people. So did Sam Brannan.

California, which seemed about as distant from the United States as you could get, looked promising to Brannan from the moment of his arrival. He made the arduous trek to Utah, in 1847, to deliver the good news, but his picture of California's charms failed to seduce Brigham Young. (California struck Young as *too* enticing, too likely someday to fill up with non-Mormon newcomers; Brigham Young had reached Utah, seen that the desert would scare away the fainthearted, and proclaimed, "This is the place.")

Brannan, undaunted, happily stayed put in San Francisco. Perhaps the Mormons might live in two colonies, with himself as head of the western group? In any case, California needed almost everything, and Brannan set out to provide it, seemingly all at once. He launched a newspaper (this was the *Star*, edited by young Kemble), built two flour mills, opened a hotel, built one store and made plans for more. California was still nearly empty, but Brannan saw at once that the faster it grew, the more his business ventures would thrive. Like a carnival barker talking at double speed to lure the rubes, he took every opportunity to pitch the virtues of Eden on the Pacific.

From the start, he looked beyond San Francisco, and early on he spotted the moneymaking possibilities in John Sutter's fledgling empire. (Sutter himself, "one of the poorest businessmen in the history of capitalism" in the judgment of a recent biographer, would manage to bungle what was truly a golden opportunity.) Sutter wanted mainly to rule his kingdom as he pleased, a pharaoh of the foothills; his fervent hope was that the outside world would keep its distance, so that his private empire could hum along undisturbed and unchanging. It was one of fate's heavy-handed jokes to gather a hundred thousand rowdy gold-seekers from across the globe and send them tramping through his fields.

With its hundreds of employees and remote setting, Sutter's Fort badly needed a store. Brannan built one. C. C. Smith & Company (named for Brannan's partner in the venture) offered blankets and boots, knives and rifles, candles, liquor,* molasses, tea, coffee, everything a man could want, though at prices four or five times what he would pay anywhere else.

The store would play a key role in the gold rush saga. Sometime in April, 1848, one of Sutter's employees, a teamster named Jacob Wittmer, barged into Smith's in need of a drink. He ordered a

---

*Brannan's Mormonism did not conspicuously constrain him; he drank with gusto and happily sold to others what he enjoyed himself, and for a variety of sins would eventually be booted from the church.

bottle of brandy and spilled something from his pocket onto the bar. "What is that?" Smith snapped. "You know very well liquor means money." Drinks were cash only; no credit allowed. Wittmer did know that. "That *is* money," he said. "It's gold."

Then the world knew. So Sutter told it later, at any rate, but the tale was almost surely false. Sutter was one of those cheerful souls who changed his stories to suit the audience and the occasion. Facts were encumbrances best thrown overboard.

Quite likely Sutter himself was the first to spill the secret. Apparently he gave in to temptation on a February evening in 1848, after dinner at the fort. Only a few weeks had passed since Marshall's discovery. Sutter gathered a few of his men around a table and carefully unfurled a rag he'd hidden away. A few flecks of gold spilled out. A moment's doubt gave way to jubilation. "Gold, gold, gold, boys, it's gold!" one man shouted. "All of us will be rich. Three cheers for the gold!" Sutter produced a bottle of wine, and the celebration began.

The world beyond Sutter's Fort had not yet heard the news. In early April, Henry Bigler, still with "gold badly on the brain," visited two friends working a sandbar at a nondescript bend in the American River, about fifteen miles downstream from Sutter's sawmill. Soon that magical stretch of rock and gravel would be famous the world over, known in honor of its discoverers as Mormon Island.*

The men at Mormon Island had scarcely any tools, but those few were enough. Lacking even pans, they scooped up sand and gravel

---

*Many of Sutter's ablest employees were Mormons, ex-soldiers who had fought in the Mexican-American War in the so-called Mormon Battalion. Brigham Young had come up with the idea of the all-volunteer unit, by way of demonstrating Mormons' loyalty to the United States. With the war over, many of the veterans had set out for Utah, but Young had ordered them to wait a bit. Salt Lake City could barely feed the people already there. Forced to linger in California, Bigler and five other Mormon Battalion veterans found work at a spot called Sutter's Fort, and stepped into history.

into willow baskets made by the local Indians and added a little river water. Then, time and again, they swirled the water in gentle circles so that it sloshed over the basket's rim, carrying some of the light grit with it and leaving the heavier contents behind. When a basket was nearly empty, they spread out the residue—which might include bits of gold—onto empty flour sacks to bake in the sun. Many times they did not even have to bother with baskets. With knives, and, astonishingly, with their bare hands, they winkled out pebbles of solid gold.

Mormon Island changed everything. Even a glimpse of gold could start a man daydreaming, and here was gold in such abundance that it set the heart pounding. And that was only part of the story. What was truly marvelous was that this new, rich site had nothing to do with the first one, at the sawmill, except that the two stretches of riverbank looked like each other. More to the point, they looked like countless other spots, too. If there was gold here, why not gold *there?* And *there,* and *there?*

Word quickly reached Smith at his store. Smith wrote to Brannan, his partner. One week later, on May 12, 1848, a one-man parade careened down San Francisco's Montgomery Street. Sam Brannan waved his hat in one hand and brandished a bottle full of gold dust in the other. "Gold!" he shouted. "Gold! Gold from the American River!" (Brannan had prepared for his parade by buying up every pick and shovel in San Francisco, for resale later.)

The city emptied as if a bomb had gone off. "A fleet of launches" left San Francisco, wrote one eyewitness, and headed up the Sacramento River to the goldfields. Within weeks, three-quarters of the houses in town were left empty. Abandoned ships littered San Francisco Bay.

*   *   *

In Monterey, the state capital, no one heard the shouting, or much of anything else. In the East, news traveled by telegraph, at lightning speed; in California the hundred miles from San Francisco to Monterey represented nearly as vast a distance as it had a century before. California in 1848 had no bridges across its rivers, no roads between its towns. The only wagons were carts with solid, wooden, Flintstone-style wheels a foot thick, cut from oak trees. An ax-hewn tree branch jammed through holes gouged in the wheels served as an axle. Every cart carried a pail of thick soapsuds to lubricate the axles, and the shriek of wood on wood pierced the air.

Rumors of gold finally drifted into town on May 29, two weeks after Brannan's parade. Monterey's response was tepid. "The men wondered and talked, and the women too," Walter Colton noted, "but neither believed." Colton served as Monterey's *alcalde,* a kind of mayor/judge hybrid, and little in his small community escaped him. Back in March he'd broken news of the Sutter find in the *Californian,* but now, more than two months later, he found the mood almost unchanged. "Still the public incredulity remained," he wrote on June 5, "save here and there a glimmer of faith like the flash of a firefly at night."

Colton, whose own temperament leaned more to cool skepticism than to fiery passion, sent a scout to the goldfields to investigate. He left on June 6. Two weeks later, on June 20, he returned. A crowd surrounded the messenger and his horse, jostling for a closer view. The man dismounted, reached into his pockets, and withdrew two clenched fists. He opened them to reveal golden nuggets.

The crowd clamored for a touch, and the gold made the rounds. "The blacksmith dropped his hammer," Colton wrote, "the carpenter his plane, the mason his trowel, the farmer his sickle, the baker his loaf, and the tapster his bottle. All were off for the mines, some on horses, some on carts, and some on crutches, and one went in a litter." Colton was mayor of a ghost town.

The *Californian*, which Colton had founded only two years before, declared itself out of business. "The whole country," it proclaimed, "from San Francisco to Los Angeles and from the sea shore to the base of the Sierra Nevada, resounds with the sordid cry of 'gold! GOLD!! GOLD!!!' while the field is left half planted, the house half built, and everything [else] neglected." As a result, the *Californian* declared in its May 29, 1848, issue, "It would be a useless expenditure of labor and material to continue longer the publication of our paper."

Kemble, the young editor at the *Star* who had mocked the gold rumors, held out for two more weeks. Then he, too, closed his newspaper, and set out for the goldfields. The final edition consisted of a single page. "We have done," wrote Kemble, when he saw that there was no one left to print the paper, or to read it. "Let our word of parting be, *Hasta Luego*."

Sailors and soldiers quit their posts without taking the time to shout "So long!" and raced to make their fortune. "Three seamen ran from the *Warren*, forfeiting four years' pay," Walter Colton wrote in his diary in July. "A whole platoon of soldiers from the fort left only their colors behind."

Soldiers and sailors had pledged to do their duty, but they had never imagined a test like this. "The struggle between right and six dollars a month and wrong and seventy-five dollars a day," one soldier noted, "is rather a severe one." In any case, the risk of prosecution seemed nil. "No hope of reward nor fear of punishment is sufficient to make binding any contract between man and man upon the soil of California," lamented the commander of the U.S. naval fleet in the Pacific. The navy gave up on posting men to

California, knowing that anyone near the goldfields "would immediately desert."*

In San Jose, the constable looked on miserably as everyone in
town raced to the goldfields, leaving him to watch over the ten
prisoners in his jail. Unwilling to set the men free (two had been
charged with murder), he resolved his dilemma by marching the
inmates to the goldfields and putting them to work for him.

By the Fourth of July, 1848, great stretches of the once bucolic
American River looked like shantytowns, home to scores of ragged
tents and scruffy men. Two hundred Mormons now worked the
sand and gravel of Mormon Island. Sam Brannan was there, too.
Canny as ever, he was among the first to see that the real money
was in "mining the miners" rather than in hefting a shovel oneself.

Brannan made the rounds of his fellow Mormons, demanding
tithes to support their brethren laboring to build a new Zion in Salt
Lake City. With more and more miners finding more and more
gold, his tax quickly proved more lucrative than even the richest
site along the river. Soon after, Brigham Young sent Brannan a letter bearing curious news. Brannan's tithes had not arrived in Utah!
"A hint to the wise is sufficient," Young advised. Brannan missed
the hint and kept the money.

---

*A sailor's life in the navy was as brutal as on a whaler, making the prospect of gold
and independence all the more appealing. In 1848 naval officers still routinely punished
sailors by whipping them with a cat-o'-nine-tails. In a speech in 1852, one impassioned
senator demanded, "Who, O Senators, is the American sailor, that he is to be treated
worse than a dog?...Let me remind you that he has recently gained for his country an
empire."

CHAPTER THREE

HEADLONG INTO HISTORY

E VERYONE WHO ABANDONED THEIR familiar life and headed west knew they had done something daring. But they never imagined—no one racing to California imagined—that the gold rush would turn out to be, in the words of the historian Kevin Starr, "both Iliad and Odyssey." It would be an Odyssey because California was so remote and hazardous a destination. Travelers risked cholera and death by starvation. They died of thirst in the deserts and froze to death in the mountains. If they chose not to venture across America but to take a shortcut through the swamps of Panama or Nicaragua instead, they faced malaria and yellow fever. If they went by sea, they risked fire and shipwreck.

It would be an Iliad because the reality that slapped the gold-seekers in the face, when they finally reached California, smacked more of warfare than of dreams come true. The war pitted man against nature, which turned out not to be so eager to yield up its riches after all, and man against man, for the goldfields were primitive, violent, and lawless. Murders and lynchings were commonplace, shootings and stabbings even more frequent, disease and drunkenness all but universal. In a land where fortunes were won overnight and squandered just as quickly, men's moods skittered across a spectrum of ecstasy, envy, and despair. Within six months of reaching California, one '49er in five lay dead.

Once they had committed to go to the goldfields, people talked as if they had never had a choice, as if they had been poleaxed by fate. "Gold fever" was the constant refrain, and the tone implied that it truly was a fever that left its victims delirious and disoriented. "I took the fever," a Cape Cod man named Stephen Wing wrote in his diary, "which for a few months was intermittent in its character, but at the close of the year it became seated, and I had it hard."

People had always daydreamed, but words like "adventure" and "wealth" and "choice" had been abstractions. No more. Now fantasy had been made flesh. With the coming of the gold rush, the American Dream took on vivid, pulsing shape.

Even the most sober observers found themselves bowled over. "What seems to you mere fiction is a stern reality," one California official wrote to the secretary of the navy, in Washington, D.C. "It is not gold in the clouds, or in the sea, or in the center of a rock-ribbed mountain, but in the soil of California, sparkling in the sun and glittering in its streams. It lies on the open plain, in the shadows of the deep ravines, and glows on the summits of the mountains."

Better yet, California's climate was easy. Best of all, the territory was wide open—nine days after gold was found at John Sutter's sawmill (and before word of the discovery had leaked out), Mexico handed California to the United States as part of the settlement of the Mexican-American War. With Mexico no longer in the picture and the U.S. government not yet on the scene, California was open to all comers, a free-for-all competition with no rules, no authorities, no taxes, and with prizes beyond calculation.

Nor was that all. Elsewhere in the world, gold finds had been small, confined affairs. In the Sierra foothills, the band of gold-rich quartz veins that the miners dubbed the Mother Lode stretched a breathtaking 120 miles. That meant two things, and each was hugely important. First, there was a *lot* of gold. Second, since the gold was spread so widely, no single man or group could grab it all for himself.

In 1854, near the brand-new town of Melones—named for the melon-shaped bits of gold found nearby—California miners dug up a single hunk of gold that weighed a breathtaking 195 *pounds*. So colossal a find was nearly impossible to fathom. A single ounce, at $20, was as much as a workman in the East might earn in two or three weeks. The original find that had set the whole world racing to California was a nub half as big as a pea.

And 1854 was late in the game. By then every promising site in California had been scoured, every hill tramped by tens of thousands of newcomers, every bed of gravel sifted and scanned. After all that, miners had unearthed the greatest find of all. In the *early* days, especially in the golden years of 1848 and 1849 before the world spilled in, it seemed that all you had to do to make a fortune was open your eyes.

In November, 1848, a father and son working on the Middle Fork of the American River scraped up $3,000 worth of gold from the riverbed in four days. Their only tools were a hoe and spade. In February, 1849, a new arrival sent a letter from Sutter's Fort, near the site of the first finds. "Men here," he wrote, "are nearly crazy with the riches forced suddenly into their pockets."

Sometimes you could make your pile without even setting foot outdoors. Men told tales of barbers who shaved their customers' scruffy beards and then, at day's end, swept up $8 or $10 worth of gold dust from the whiskers on the floor.

With money lying thick on the ground, prices soared. No one minded. Horses went for $200 or $300 apiece, ten times as much as the previous year, but miners would ride from one camp to another and simply set their horses free when they arrived. "It was easier to dig out the price of another," one man wrote, "than to hunt up the one astray."

One dazzled Australian, brand-new to the goldfields and bursting with excitement, ran up to every unfamiliar face and sang out his story. "By me soul, but this is a great country!" he told one startled stranger, in 1849. "Here a man can dig up as much goold in a day as he ever saw in all his life. Hav'n't I got already more than I know what to do with, an' I've only been here a week.... O' Monday I dug nineteen dollars, an' o' Tuesday twenty-three, an' o' Friday two hundred an' eighty-two dollars in one lump as big as yer fist.... Was there ever sich a country in the world!"

In this fabulous new land, a man might find gold without even the most rudimentary knowledge of mining or geology. A newcomer named William Downie, a complete novice, made one of the biggest finds of all. Downie had heard tales of California's gold in a boardinghouse in Buffalo, in 1848, and raced west. He found "gold all along the banks" of the North Fork of the Yuba River. When news of his bonanza leaked out, three thousand miners descended on what had been an empty, anonymous patch of country.

At one tiny bit of ground near what was quickly dubbed Downieville—the claim was scarcely larger than a picnic blanket—four men set to work. Each day, for eleven stunning days in a row, they dug up a fortune worth more than $1,000. Three miners named a nearby claim Tin Cup Diggings; the name honored a pledge they'd made to one another not to knock off work for the day until each of them had filled a cup to the brim with gold.

In the golden age this was a game the rawest amateur could play. One of Downie's companions took a break from mining to fish, caught a fourteen-pound beauty, and threw it into a pot of water to cook. The men ate their fill and then looked into the battered pot. Gold dust gleamed in the cooking water.

By the spring of 1849, rumors of gold had reached every corner of the United States, from its most tumultuous cities to its sleepiest villages. "The gold excitement spread like wildfire," recalled a farmwife named Luzena Stanley Wilson, who lived in a log cabin nestled deep in the Missouri prairie, in the northwest corner of the state. Wilson knew firsthand about fires racing out of control. She knew, too, what life in Missouri likely held in store for her.

The decision to leave that life behind and head for California might faze others. Not Wilson, whose temperament was about four parts briskness and nerve to one part doubt and introspection. "As we had almost nothing to lose, and we might gain a fortune, we early caught the fever."

Luzena Wilson, who was thirty, had been married for five years. Her husband, Mason, wanted to set off at once, and alone, because that would be fastest and safest. Luzena would not be left behind. "I thought where he could go I could, and where I went I could take my two little toddling babies."

Off went the whole family.

*   *   *

In Washington, D.C., an architectural draftsman and amateur artist named J. Goldsborough Bruff rounded up a company of two
dozen young men eager to make their fortune in the land of gold.
Bruff, at forty-four a decade or more older than most of his companions, placed himself at the head of what they'd dubbed the
Washington City and California Mining Association, and sat
down to design suitably grand uniforms.

Outgoing and eager for more adventure than could be found at a
drafting table, Bruff was a handsome man of middling height with
shoulder-length black hair. He carried himself with the erect bearing of the soldier he had almost been (he had attended West Point
but had been kicked out; family legend said he had been caught
dueling). After his stint at military school, Bruff had gone to sea.
He spent three years largely on long hops between South America
and Europe, first as a cabin boy and then a sailor, and developed a
taste for roaming.

He had settled into a quiet life, or so he thought. Then, in 1849,
Bruff found himself assigned to duplicate maps of the American
West that had originally been drawn by John C. Frémont, "the
Pathfinder" himself. Dark-eyed, handsome, reckless, the young
explorer was one of the great authorities on the West and one of the
most famous men in America. (Frémont was hugely controversial.
Lincoln called him "the damndest scoundrel that ever lived, but in
the infinite mercy of Providence . . . also the damndest fool.")

In an era when much of the West was as mysterious as Atlantis,
no dreamer could have resisted the spell of Frémont's drawings of
scarcely known rivers and mountain ranges. Vibrating like a tun-
ing fork, Bruff immediately set about rounding up friends, and
ordering tents, and inquiring after mules, and pricing supplies.

Bruff had energy to spare and an all-embracing curiosity, but he was a man who appreciated proper form. Promises were sacred, friendships permanent, oaths solemn. With this earnestness came a taste for the dramatic. Even in the humblest circumstances, Bruff carried himself as if accompanied by a faint fanfare of trumpets. It was not enough to give his word that he would repay a loan; he would, he declared, "embrace the earliest opportunity to liquidate the pecuniary obligation" he had incurred.

By the time he and his men marched west out of the nation's capital, on April 2, 1849, the Washington City and California Mining Association had grown to number some sixty men. "We go as a body of energetic gentlemen," Bruff announced, "to enrich ourselves, if possible, by every honorable means."

Alonzo Delano meant not only to enrich himself but to heal himself as well. Forty-two years old and a prosperous merchant, Delano seemed an unlikely conquistador. He had spent decades peddling flour, silk, whiskey, and whatever else came to hand in a succession of small towns in Ohio and Indiana. He had finally settled down, in an upstate Illinois town called Ottawa. The tall, slender man had quickly become a local favorite; he had a friendly greeting for everyone and he always had time for a little joke, even if it was only to make fun of his own long, pointy nose. ("A jolly good fellow if ever there was one," one acquaintance recalled, "and, by Jove, he *did* have a big nose.") With a wife and two children, a thriving business, and a prominent role in town affairs, Delano seemed secure.

But in 1848 life conspired to knock him off his perch. First, he contracted a lung illness that threatened to kill him. His doctor recommended a change of climate as the only hope. Even at this early date, balmy California had a reputation as a kind of open-air health spa. One well-known guidebook recounted the story of a California man who had reached the age of 250 — so healthy was California's climate — and finally decided he'd had enough. In order to end his life at last, he had no choice but to leave California. He did, and he died. But as soon as his family brought the body back to California for burial, the corpse revived and leapt to its feet, once again bursting with health and vigor.

No one took such tall tales literally, but on the principle that where there's smoke there's fire, they did not altogether discount them either. The sunny West was surely an improvement on the damp and fever-ridden East. Delano mulled his doctor's advice. And "then, about this time, the astonishing accounts of the vast deposits of gold in California reached us, and besides the fever of the body, I was suddenly seized with the fever of mind for gold." Delano set out to cure both fevers at once. Leaving family and civilization behind, he took to the road, "a nomad denizen of the world."

Mary Jane Megquier — she went by "Jennie" — had grown up on a farm in a small, isolated town in Maine. Even as a girl she had chafed against the confines of her narrow life. From early on she'd felt "no love for the good town of Turner," she declared later, and despite her best efforts she never managed to change her mind. When church elders scolded her for attending a dance, in her teens, her distaste grew.

At age eighteen she married a doctor about a decade older than she was. Thomas Megquier — they pronounced the name *Muh-gweer* — was a Bowdoin graduate and altogether a more conventional character than his young wife. Four years after their marriage, the Megquiers moved to the nearby town of Winthrop. It was, at least slightly, an improvement on Turner. But it proved no place to make a living, even for a doctor who had, as Thomas bitterly recalled, "labored in Winthrop twelve years...day and night" with little but bills and debts to show for it. In the meantime a friend who had moved to far-off Hawaii began sending letters that painted a tempting picture. The Sandwich Islands, as Hawaii was then known, needed doctors, and Thomas made up his mind to go. Then came word of the bonanza in California. Thomas changed his plans. He would start a new life not in Honolulu but in San Francisco. And, remarkably, Jennie could come, too, provided the Megquiers could find friends or family to take care of their three children.

Few women would have taken that leap. Any female in California was a dazzling rarity. In the gold rush era, Jennie Megquier, Luzena Wilson, and other women were outnumbered by men 30 to 1. (It would take another *century*, until the 1950 census, for the number of women in California to match the number of men.) In the diggings, as the goldfields came to be known, women were even scarcer than in town, and miners who encountered a "respectable" woman — not a prostitute — gaped in awe. In those all-male deserts, the merest token of femininity sufficed to knock men sideways. One prospector from New York described the commotion when someone happened to catch hold of a woman's bonnet blowing in the breeze. The miners decided to throw a party in honor of the great discovery. At precisely the spot of the find, they drove a five-foot stake into the ground, set the precious hat atop it, and wrapped the stake in a blanket so that it bore some vague resemblance to a woman's form. Then three hundred celebrants proceeded to dance and drink for two days.

But before the parties came the journey. For gold-seekers from states like Maine, where seafaring was a tradition, the overland route to California was not the obvious choice. Far better to find a ship that would round Cape Horn, at the southern tip of South America, and then sail up the Pacific coast, or to travel by sea to Panama, cross overland to the Pacific side, and catch a second ship to San Francisco.

The Megquiers chose Panama, which was, in 1849, little more than a malarial jungle. (The Panama Canal lay half a century in the future.) No American woman, as far as anyone knew, had ever made the crossing.

Opinionated, impatient, hot-tempered, the grandly named Israel Shipman Pelton Lord lived perpetually at the boil.* Anything—drinking, gambling, young men sporting mustaches or beards—could move him to fury. He rattled off volleys of insults, pop-pop-popping his words like a string of firecrackers, until the rage cooled. "Asses, asses, all." Such was Lord's judgment on his fellow human beings, "and but that their hat crowns were shed long, long ago, their ears would thrust their hats off."

But Lord, who was a doctor, had a compassionate side, too, and it burst forth as unpredictably as did his tantrums. Let a snowstorm hit and it would be Lord who staggered through the drifts to reach a far-off patient. Let an ox falter on the trail west—where such things happened times beyond counting—and it would be Lord who felt obliged to compose a memorial to the poor beast, in countless verses of maudlin doggerel.

---

*Names in the nineteenth century had heft and savor. You could roll them around on your tongue. Emigrant archives are dotted with the likes of Pardon Dexter Tiffany, or Ichabod and Silence Bryant, or Plutarch and Seneca Knight.

They've left me here to starve and die,
Without a lock of hay.
And they've burned my yoke and bows and gone
to Californ-i-a.

Lord kept a travel diary in tiny, meticulous script, and he did his best to note down every river crossing, every hill and trail and plant and bird, he met along his way. He found room for nearly everything except any mention of the reasons he had left his family behind, in Warrenville, Illinois, and set out, at age forty-three, for California.

He did include, almost at the end of his journal, a brief, third-person description of "a Christian man who went to California for gold. He wanted $20,000 [in today's money, $400,000], and he would give the Lord half."

Was this devout, ambitious pilgrim Israel Lord himself?

Thousands of gold-seekers kept journals or wrote long letters to their families or their hometown newspapers, and hundreds of those journals have survived. But most of the emigrants' diaries sound stiff and formal or strained and sentimental. We find ourselves faced with the minutes of an accountants' annual meeting or a long poem in a high school yearbook. Some of this formality was intentional. In the 1840s the use of ornate, circumspect language was a convention, in skilled hands a kind of game. Especially admired was a mismatch between high tone and low subject. Rather than "we were seasick," one emigrant wrote that "the mountainous billows of the Gulf commenced operating on the susceptible frames of the landsmen."

Speech was a different matter. Nineteenth-century voices burst

with life and energy. "There is sometimes in the American metaphors an energy which is very remarkable," an English visitor noted
in 1837, and he gleefully transcribed his favorite examples of over-
heard Americana. "I wish I had all hell boiled down to a pint," he
heard someone say, "just to pour down your throat." Another high-
spirited visitor, the English writer Harriet Martineau, collected her
own favorite American phrases at about the same time. Undaunted
by her deafness, Martineau poked her ear trumpet this way and
that, jotting down tidbits. She eavesdropped on two men disputing
an acquaintance's intelligence. "He!" one man snorted. "He can't
see through a ladder."

In diaries and private letters more often than in formal prose,
that sound of actual life sometimes managed to squeeze through.
"Oh if we could kiss," a woman named Sara Pierce wrote to her
husband, Hiram, in the goldfields, "but alas it will be a long time
before we shall be permitted to embrace one another, but in my
dreams you may depend I have fine times. In one of my night
visions I thought you had come home but you can't think what a
time we had."*

Skilled and unskilled writers alike set down their thoughts. In
contrast with the leading figures in other American sagas — the fur
trappers and mountain men who roamed the American west in the
1820s and '30s, say, or the cowboys who drove cattle across the
plains in the 1870s — most of the gold rushers came from a literate,
letter-writing, journal-keeping segment of society. The trip to
California was expensive, out of reach for those without savings or

---

*This was a prudish age, with strict rules about what could be said outright, but in the
privacy of their diaries and letters some writers veered toward openness. On September
12, 1849, for instance, six weeks into his marriage, the Vermont schoolteacher Alfred Rix
wrote happily in his diary, "This is warm weather and we are pretty well wearied out when
we are done. GUESS."

connections, and many who set out were more familiar with pen and ink than with pick and shovel. More important, the gold-seekers knew they had leapt headlong into history. Like Civil War soldiers a decade later, they assigned themselves the task of recording their impressions of what they sensed would be not only their great adventure but one of America's great adventures.

But exhaustion and sickness tended to erode most writers' vows to keep detailed records. On the trail, it was a rare man who could spend the day staggering under the desert sun, nourished only by a tainted hunk of beef jerky and a mug of warm, soapy water, and then sit down in the evening to record his thoughts. Even the most conscientious, like a young man from Indiana named Elijah Farnham, seldom managed to do more than jot down a few hasty sentences. At times, though rarely, the lack of adornment made for a kind of power. "At 4 this morning," Farnham wrote on May 15, 1849, "a man encamped with us died with the collery [cholera] he had a wife and children they went back."

As weeks stretched to months, letters grew rare and diary entries spotty. Shipboard travelers, too, wrote often at first and then hardly at all, though not because they suffered from overwork. Oppressed by unchanging scenery and endless, empty days, they found themselves unable to summon the energy to take up a pen.

As a result, too many gold rush journals are lifeless recordings of miles covered, illnesses suffered, storms endured — gold spun into straw. Wilson, Bruff, Delano, Megquier, and Lord stand out as welcome exceptions. Somehow all five had mastered the natural, vigorous idiom that one poet would later celebrate as "plain American which cats and dogs can read!"

Yet even such lively eyewitnesses sometimes fell silent just when we would most want to have heard from them. Especially when they were making notes in a diary or writing to relatives, gold rush writers often took for granted what we would love to know. Was the writer skinny or fat, handsome or homely? Why are there no entries for July? When Jennie Megquier referred bitterly to her marriage and "the trials I have endured," what did she have in mind? Why did Joseph Bruff's wife refer to the two of them as "a rather unmated couple"?

Occasionally even those facts we do have are less trustworthy than they appear. Israel Lord's California journal was attributed to "Isaac Lord" for many years, for instance, because that's how he signed the last few pages of his diary, several times over, in large, sprawling letters. Or how someone signed it. The true story behind those bold signatures, it turns out, was that they were written decades after the gold rush and not by the author at all. Sometime in the late 1800s the writer's young grandson, Isaac Lord, found the musty journal and used the blank pages at the end to practice signing his name. We can only guess how crusty, cantankerous Israel Lord would have carried on had he known that posterity nearly assigned his masterpiece to his grandson Ikey.

Israel Lord, Jennie Megquier, and the others knew almost nothing of what the trip west would entail, except that it would mark an end to their old way of life. In the winter and spring of 1849 they took their place in a vast, hopeful procession swarming by land, wallowing by sea, and lurching blindly into the future.

Though they did not know it, these countless travelers were headed to a transformed world. Walter Colton, now without his paper but still mayor of Monterey, found himself marooned with the military governor and one Lieutenant Lanman, a military officer. "Our servants have run, one after another, till we are almost in despair," wrote Colton, "...and this morning, for the fortieth time, we had to take to the kitchen and cook our own breakfast." Colton painted an almost unthinkable scene. Imagine, he wrote, "a general of the United States Army, the commander of a man-of-war, and the Alcalde of Monterey, in a smoking kitchen, grinding coffee, toasting a herring, and peeling onions!"

Colton saw the big picture as clearly as the ludicrous details. "These gold mines have upset all social and domestic arrangements in Monterey," he wrote. "....The master has become his own servant, and the servant his own lord. The millionaire is obliged to groom his own horse, and roll his own wheelbarrow; and the *hidalgo* — in whose veins flows the blood of Cortes — to clean his own boots."

In California the old order had collapsed. Astonishingly, the rest of the United States had done its best to slumber through the revolution. For seven months after Marshall's discovery of gold, newspapers in the East carried not a word about it. When the first mention finally came, it was not an attention-grabbing shout but a mumble of "fire" in a crowded theater. On August 19, 1848, the *New York Herald* ran a long, rambling article with the mundane headline "Interesting Narrative of the Voyage to California, by a New York Volunteer."

The author was a soldier who had enlisted to fight in the Mexican-American War but arrived too late to see any action. He had meandered around California instead. He reported on the sights in San Francisco (a fine harbor but "only a few shantees or camp-like cabins"), the traits of Mexicans ("generally lazy, fond of riding, dancing, and gambling"), and the price of beef and flour. Then, finally, a mention of gold. "I am credibly informed that a quantity of gold, worth in value $30, was picked up lately in the bed of a stream of the Sacramento." The goldfields seemed extensive, the writer went on, and the gold near the surface. Perhaps it was not too much to entertain "golden hopes."

Readers missed the story or dismissed the news. Over the course of the next month, newspapers carried more reports of California's gold, each a bit more excited than its predecessors. More shrugs. "This writer has visited the golden country...in comparison to which the famous El Dorado is but a sandbank," one correspondent told the *New York Herald* on September 17, 1848. "There are cases of over a hundred dollars being obtained in a day from the work of one man. It requires no skill. The workman takes any spot of ground or bank he fancies; sticks in his pick or shovel at random; fills his basin; makes for the water, and soon sees the glittering results of his labor." *Still* no one bit.

A week later, the *Cleveland Plain Dealer* carried an even more exuberant letter from Walter Colton, who was not only the *alcalde* of Monterey but also a U.S. Navy chaplain and therefore an especially trustworthy figure. "I have just been conversing with a man who in six days gathered $500 worth," Colton wrote. "....There are probably now not less than 5,000 persons, whites and Indians, gathering this gold."

Colton, born and raised in the East, had come to know California firsthand, and he could scarcely convey its grandeur to those still stuck at home. "You reckon by acres, and we here by miles and leagues. Your sheep produce one lamb in a year—ours always two, and often four. Your streams have a few minnows in them, and ours are paved with gold!" This was harder to ignore. But while many wavered, few jumped.

One key problem was that the newspaper was the nineteenth century's main source of news, and no one trusted newspapers. For good reason. Editors routinely used their publications as mega-phones to denounce one another or anyone else who happened into view. The tone was personal and vituperative, and a writer's talent for malicious insult was as admired as a fighter's ability to throw a big left hook. Walt Whitman, the editor of the *New York Aurora* before he turned to poetry, showed just how far a writer could go. Whitman described a rival editor, the *New York Herald*'s James Gordon Bennett, as "a reptile marking his path with slime wher-ever he goes, and breathing mildew at everything fresh or fragrant; a midnight ghoul, preying on rottenness and repulsive filth." Ben-nett exercised no more restraint. In an editorial in 1840, he called the pope "a decrepit, licentious, stupid Italian blockhead."

That rowdy, even scurrilous style was new. In their early days, newspapers had been dull affairs that made their money largely from paid subscriptions. Column after dreary column carried transcripts of political speeches, in full, or shipping reports. Then steam power came along, in the 1830s, and suddenly newfangled presses could spit out papers cheaply, quickly, and by the thou-sands. Editors slashed their prices to a penny and fought for street sales. Newsboys shouted headlines of murder and scandal. Reporters competed for scoops, or invented them.

In 1835, for instance, the New York *Sun* reported on page one that the most renowned astronomer of the day, Sir John Herschel, had aimed an enormous new telescope at the night sky and discov-ered life on the moon. And not just *any* life, but herds of miniature buffalo roaming the plains and graceful blue unicorns cavorting on the hillsides (the females could be recognized by their long tails). Most impressive of all, Herschel had seen humanlike creatures, both male and female, equipped with "wings composed of a thin membrane, without hair, lying snugly upon their backs, from the top of their shoulders to the calves of their legs."

The *Sun* presented the hoax completely straight-faced, in the original article and in five followups, and never apologized. Almost a decade later, in 1844, nothing had changed: the *Sun* carried another invented but supposedly true story, this one by Edgar Allan Poe, describing the first-ever crossing of the Atlantic by balloon.

By the standards of the day this was entertainment rather than scandal. Hype was the great American art form. The bigger and stranger the story, the better. At his American Museum, on Broadway in New York City, P. T. Barnum drew enormous crowds who lined up for the chance to see "industrious fleas, educated dogs, jugglers…albinos, fat boys, giants, dwarfs," as well as full-sized wax statues depicting the Last Supper, and "Santa Anna's Wooden Leg, taken by the American Army in Mexico."

Some of Barnum's exhibits had a measure of truth to them — General Tom Thumb was in fact only forty inches tall (though he had been found in Connecticut, not brought "at great expense" from Europe); Joice Heth was an elderly black woman (though she was not the oldest woman in the world, age 161, and had not been George Washington's nurse). For spectators the fun was in sorting out what, if anything, to believe. One of Barnum's greatest draws, the dried-up and lifeless "Fejee Mermaid," turned out not to be a mermaid at all but a fish sewn to a monkey's body. All such spectacles drew breathless newspaper coverage. Against a backdrop of endless hype and hot air, stories of men jabbing randomly at the ground and finding nuggets of gold hardly stood out.

Through September and October of 1848, then, everyone read the news from California, and everyone found some reason to reject it. This was newspaper nonsense, to sell papers. It was speculators' windy talk, to lure hicks to California. It was political hype, to justify the Mexican-American War by talking up the value of the worthless land that Mexico had handed over to the United

States. Over the years people had heard dozens of impossible claims and the excitement never came to anything. Why should this time be different?

But even if no individual newspaper report carried much weight, the dispatches kept coming, week after week, month after month. Every story echoed and re-echoed. Every whisper grew into a shout: someone—*but not you*—was somewhere—*but not here*—and making a fortune.

It was easy to brush aside a rumor or two. Two dozen thrilling rumors made a person think.

———————

The moment when thinking and hesitating came to an end, and a mad, nearly universal desire to hit the road began, can be dated precisely. The East finally woke not to the sound of trumpets or alarm bells but to the rousing notes of a speech by the president of the United States. As rousing, at any rate, as any words could be when spoken by so slight and drab a figure as James K. Polk, "a smaller than life man with larger than life ambitions," in the words of one biographer.

Polk chose the occasion of his State of the Union speech, on December 5, 1848, to proclaim the startling news from California. His leap toward drama fell characteristically short. Well into a two-hour address, he totted up the reasons why the unpopular and recently concluded Mexican-American War had been a good idea. Among "the great results which have been developed and brought to light by this war" were a million square miles of new territory, including part or all of today's Arizona, California, Colorado, New Mexico, Nevada, Texas, and Utah.

Polk painted rosy pictures of each new acquisition. Even sleepy

California would soon hum with commerce. Nor were California's fertile fields and spacious harbors its only virtues. Americans had heard rumors about finds of "precious metals" in California, Polk went on, but they might not have known what to make of the stories.

He proceeded to tell them. "The accounts of the abundance of gold in that territory are of such an extraordinary character as would scarcely command belief were they not corroborated by the authentic reports of officers in the public service." Stiff and stilted language, but that was beside the point. Every listener could translate Polk's words for himself — *It's true! All the rumors you've heard are true*. Polk might as well have flung an arm in the air and waved a golden nugget for all to see.

Two days later, Washington did almost precisely that. Two messengers racing from California reached the capital with a tea caddy containing 230 ounces — over 14 pounds — of new-mined gold. The precious cargo was put on display in the library of the War Department. Crowds rushed to see for themselves and stared, goggle-eyed, at the golden flakes and pebbles. Even reporters, cynics by inclination and training, could only gape. "Any goose who could talk of 'mica' after seeing these specimens would not be worth noticing," the *New York Tribune* declared. "It is no more like mica than it is like cheese."

The headline in the *New York Herald* on December 10 — "*Ho! For California — Gold! Gold!*" — blared out the message that the time for doubt had passed. The *Herald* hammered home the point by retelling the best-known of all stories of foolish skeptics. "When the incredulous apostle saw the prints of the nails in the hands and feet of his master, he believed in his identity. So the skeptic, with regard to the gold stories that come teeming in from Alta California, will have his doubts extinguished in a visit to the library of the War Department." There he would see actual gold from California—gold flecks, gold pebbles, gold lumps—and he would believe. In a religious age, no argument could have carried as much weight as this brief parable.

In Philadelphia, the mint assayed a sample of the haul. Eventually they would prepare a full report, stuffed with numbers and jargon. But in the meantime Philadelphia sent the secretary of war a summary that did not call for a scientific education. The mint's one-word telegram: "Genuine."

The president's speech and the War Department's gold all featured in every newspaper story. "The Eldorado of the old Spaniards is discovered at last," the *New York Herald* exulted on December 9, 1848. "We have now the highest official authority for believing in the discovery of vast gold mines in California...the discovery is the greatest and most startling, not to say miraculous, that the history of the last five centuries can produce."

A minister in Illinois, thrilled almost beyond words by "the official announcement of the astounding facts," likened the impact to the newest force he could think of. The president's speech had "moved the whole Nation, as with an electric shock."

New songs, like "Hurrah for California," captured the euphoria.

O! Won't it be a glorious time
when gold runs down like water,
And nobody won't have to work
and nobody had oughter.

The Declaration of Independence had given Americans the right to pursue happiness. The gold rush promised them the chance to catch it.

PART II

JOURNEY

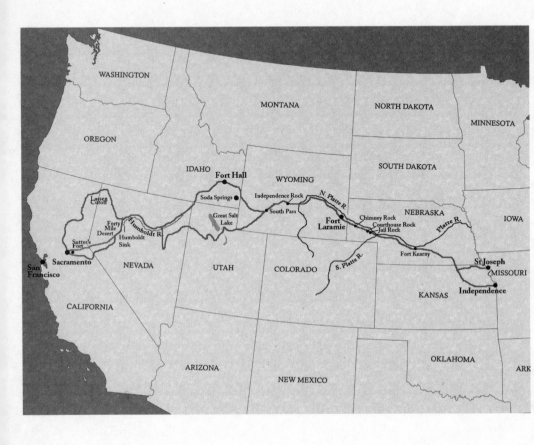

CHAPTER FOUR

SWARMING FROM ALL OVER

O N THE MORNING OF April 2, 1849, "at 9 A.M. sharp, by order," a regiment of young men in splendid uniforms tensed in anticipation of their leader's signal. J. Goldsborough Bruff surveyed his men one last time. All was well. "My Company was paraded, armed and equipped...on the pavement of Lafayette Square, opposite to the White House," Bruff noted contentedly. Now it was time to call on the president.

In hindsight, Bruff's proud words—his talk of orders and precise starting times and his proprietary references to *his* Company— foretold rebellion and trouble down the road. And in time, as the company stumbled its weary way along, dissent would turn to rebellion and then to disaster. But for the moment, all was hope and glitter. Trumpets blared, and Bruff and his fellow gold-seekers broke into columns of six and marched in step to the White House. (In the mid-1800s the White House was open to the public to a degree that is inconceivable today. The era of an ever-vigilant Secret Service lay nearly a century in the future, and Americans took to heart the common description of the White House as "the People's House.") Bruff and his men looked dazzling in their gray coats with golden buttons ornamented with an eagle, gray pants with a black stripe, and caps carefully set just so. Each man carried a rifle, a pair of pistols, a knife, and a hatchet.

The company formed a row, rifles in parade position. Bruff and his fellow officers strode up the steps, where they were granted a brief audience with Zachary Taylor, the president himself. (Polk had served only a single term and then died in June, 1849, just in time to miss the tumult he had unleashed.) Bruff, never a man troubled by shyness, "explained the situation and circumstances" to the president, he wrote later, "and informed him of the strength and character of my Company, its destination &c.

"As we were on the eve of an extraordinary journey, of great extent," Bruff told President Taylor, "and which must be fraught with arduous trials, seasoned perhaps with a due quantum of perils, and that most probably many of us would never again have the pleasure of greeting him, I considered it a duty to make the call, bid him farewell, and [offer] our fervent wishes for his continued good health."

The president "expressed regret that there had been no pre-announcement of our visit," Bruff conceded. If he'd had time, he might have prepared his own speech. As it was, Taylor shook Bruff's hand and wished him and his men well.

Taylor's bemused response did nothing to undermine Bruff's bubbling eagerness. His men all shared it, and so did the thousands of others swarming toward the "jumping off" points for the journey west or clamoring for berths on ships bound for the goldfields. For months, they had debated whether to go or stay put. Now they had leapt into the dark.

*   *   *

Emigrants are always the most hopeful members of their set, the ones willing to leave behind everything familiar on the chance that the new will be better than the old. Those who headed for California, tempted not by vague visions of a better life but by firm expectations of hillsides strewn with golden nuggets, took that customary optimism and multiplied it tenfold. And, in their own minds, they weren't leaving home forever, just detouring long enough to pick up a fortune. That made the picture even rosier.

Every corner of the United States waved farewell to its gold-seekers. More came by land than sea at first, though the numbers in both groups were vast. In 1849 alone, five hundred ships bound for California set sail from Boston, New York, New Orleans, and the other port cities of the United States. Elegant barks with billowing sails, sturdy brigs and swift schooners, hastily refitted whalers and cargo ships, worm-eaten wrecks long since retired, and smoke-belching steamers with colossal paddle wheels all took to the seas. And from tiny hamlets across all thirty states, from Louisville, Cincinnati, Pittsburgh, and every city worthy of the name, emigrants headed overland toward Saint Joseph, Missouri, and Council Bluffs, Iowa, and the handful of other western towns that served as the last outposts of civilization before the trip proper.

Luzena Wilson and her husband, in their log cabin in Missouri, never hesitated. "When we talked it all over," Luzena recalled, "it sounded like such a small task to go out to California, and once there fortune, of course, would come to us." The "of course" was telltale. When she looked back many years later, Luzena shook her head at how heedlessly—almost exuberantly—she and her husband had cast their old lives aside. "We never gave a thought" to

A PASSAGE TO THE GOLD REGION FOR $75 !

FOR SAN FRANCISCO DIRECT.

THE SPLENDID A. No. 1 NEWLY COPPERED

PACKET SHIP APOLLO.

recently in the European trade, having most of her freight engaged, will sail for

SAN FRANCISCO, CALIFORNIA,

and the gold region in that vicinity, from the

Foot of Chambers Street, North River,

WHERE SHE NOW LIES, ON THE SECOND OF JANUARY NEXT.

Passengers will be taken on the following terms ;

Steerage Passage - - - - - -	**$ 75.**
Cabin Passage - - - - - - - -	**150.**
Ditto out and home - - - - - -	**200·**
Ditto with board while there	**250.**

Several Families can be Accommodated.

The advantages offered to passengers by this conveyance cannot be surpassed. The APOLLO is one of the safest and most airy ships in New York, and has few equals in speed. She is destined to sail *directly*, not only for San Francisco, but, if it can be done as is expected, she is to be taken up the Sacramento river thirty or forty miles, into the very heart of the Gold Region, where she is to remain for some time.

The voyage each way, it is expected will be made in about four months.

Persons intending to take passage by this vessel will do well to secure their berths *at the earliest possible moment*, as the ship will, in a day or two be occupied entirely by Carpenters, Stevedores and other Mechanics, busily engaged in fitting up berths, stowing freight, taking in a supply of provisions, and making other preparations for the voyage. Choice of Berths will be given to passengers in the order of the numbers upon their passage tickets.

Freight taken on consignment or otherwise, at the lowest rates.

No Passage secured until paid for.

41042

selling our land, Luzena recalled, "but left it, with two years' labor, for the next comer."*

In New York City, festive crowds gathered at the piers to wave goodbye to the young men who had booked passage to California. Fathers, mothers, and sweethearts cheered and wept and waved their handkerchiefs like semaphores. The adventurers on shipboard shouted till their throats burned. One departing traveler, almost quivering in his excitement, threw a five-dollar gold piece toward shore, shouting, "I'm going where there is plenty more."

All was chaos, the ships' decks a jumble of well-wishers who had shoved their way aboard for one last farewell, passengers struggling under their loads of boots, tents, life preservers, rifles, pistols, and knives, and crew members trying desperately to impose order. On the afternoon of February 5, 1849, hundreds of happy, keyed-up passengers on the *Crescent City* carried on a half-hour-long snow-ball fight. The most enthusiastic combatants climbed high into the rigging, the better to bombard their giddy, giggling rivals.

Every scheme to reach the goldfields, no matter how absurd, found believers. An inventor named Rufus Porter offered tickets on his "AIR LINE TO CALIFORNIA," an eight-hundred-foot-long, steam-powered, cigar-shaped "aerial locomotive." Passengers would ride within a large compartment suspended beneath a hydrogen-filled balloon, flying "from New York to California in Three Days." Two giant propellers would do all the work; passengers had only to sit back and sip their wine. The fare was $50, and parachutes were free. Two hundred people bought tickets.

---

*That kind of wanderlust-on-hyperdrive had marked Americans as different almost from the nation's birth. "In the United States a man builds a house to spend his latter years in it, and he sells it before the roof is on," Tocqueville wrote in amazement, in *Democracy in America*. "He plants a garden, and lets it just as the trees are coming into bearing; he brings a field into tillage, and leaves other men to gather the crops."

BEST ROUTE TO CALIFORNIA.

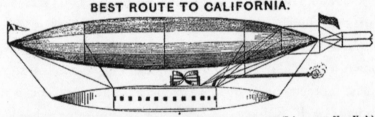

R. PORTER & CO., (office, room No. 40 in the Sun Buildings,—entrance 128 Fulton-street, New-York,) are making active progress in the construction of an Aerial Transport, for the express purpose of carrying passengers between New York and California. This transport will have a capacity to carry from 50 to 100 passengers, at a speed of 60 to 100 miles per hour. It is expected to put this machine in operation about the 1st of April, 1849. It is proposed to carry a limited number of passengers—not exceeding 300—for $50, including board, and the transport is expected to make a trip to the gold region and back in seven days. The price of passage to California is fixed at $200, with the exception above mentioned. Upwards of 200 passage tickets at $50 each have been engaged prior to Feb. 15. Books open for subscribers as above.

On the island of Nantucket, thirty miles off the coast of Massachusetts and a full continent's breadth from the diggings, one-fourth of all those of voting age set out for California. In Chicago, one newspaper reported, it looked as if "nearly half the city was bound for the Gold Regions." In New York, a young lawyer who stayed behind wrote that it seemed "as if the Atlantic Coast was to be depopulated."

A cartoon in the New York *Atlas* tried to capture the mood of thrilling chaos. Above the title "Ho! For California," a gigantic crowd formed a stampede. Muscular toughs in work clothes, young swells in tailored coats, pudgy parsons, men of affairs in top hats, all shoved and elbowed their way along, as if California lay only a block or two ahead.

Hayseeds and Harvard professors joined the exodus, and Cherokee Indians and Wyandots, and planters and lawyers and preachers. Young men whose lives had scarcely begun swarmed alongside old-timers whose best days were hazy memories. "From Maine to Texas," wrote one nineteenth-century historian (who joined the rush himself), "there was one universal frenzy." Northern abolitionists made uneasy company with Southerners who brought their slaves to do the digging for them. Free blacks who had parents or children still in chains joined the throngs, hoping to earn enough money to buy their families' freedom. "I saw a colored man going to the land of gold prompted by the hope of redeeming his wife and seven children," wrote an emigrant from Ohio. "Success to him."

Money could literally mean freedom, but it also meant self-respect. One Ohio gold-seeker wrote to his wife about his dreams, and the bitterness leaps from the page. He could bear any hardship, wrote David DeWolf, if only he could manage "to make enough to get us a home & so I can be independent of some of the Darned sonabitches that felt themselves above me because I was poor cuss them I say...Darn their stinking hides." (DeWolf did prosper in California and returned home after two years with enough money to buy a large farm. He died fighting for the North in the Civil War, at the battle of Corinth, in 1862.)

The historian Hubert Bancroft, who saw gold rush California with his own eyes, compiled a famous list meant to convey the variety of people swept up in the torrent. He started his tally with "the trader [who] closed his ledger to depart" and "the farmer yoked to endless mortgage payments."* Then, as if caught up in the flood himself, Bancroft sped up. Here were "the briefless lawyer, the starving student, the quack, the idler, the harlot, the gambler, the hen-pecked husband, the disgraced; with many earnest, enterprising, honest men and devoted women." Finally Bancroft paused to catch his breath. "These and others turned their faces westward, resolved to stake their all upon a cast."

---

*One gold-seeker composed a song that captured the same theme in rhyme. "Oh, I'm going far away from my Creditors just now," it began, "I ain't the tin to pay 'em and they're kicking up a row." James Pierpont would go on to write "Jingle Bells," but he managed not to make any money from one of the best-known of all American songs and not to find any gold in California either.

*　　　　*　　　　*

Not everyone was as enthralled with the gold rush multitudes as Bancroft. Every aspect of the spectacle—the size of the churning crowds, the gold-seekers' ambition, their unpreparedness, their willingness to leave their families—offended someone. The wealthy condemned the gold-seekers as troublemakers out to topple the social order. Ministers (those who stayed home) lambasted their congregations for putting riches ahead of family. High-minded Ralph Waldo Emerson focused on the gold-seekers' crassness. "All of them," he complained, "[shared] the very commonplace wish to find a short way to wealth."

So they did. Worse yet, they did not trouble to hide it. The emigrants belonged to a striving, commercial society; in America, as horrified visitors from abroad and homegrown idealists like Emerson had long noted, the one true value was getting ahead. The upstart Americans did not know their place, and some went so far as to reject the notion that they *had* a fixed place. (One feature of everyday life that made well-to-do Europeans cringe was the American custom of shaking hands; unlike bowing or taking off one's hat to a superior, joining hands highlighted the presumptuous notion that one man was as good as another.)

Americans delighted in their forwardness. They gleefully recited a poem written in 1840 that heaped praise on their homespun virtues:

[An American] would kiss a Queen, till he raised a blister,
With his arm round her neck, and his old felt hat on;
Would address a king by the title of "Mister"
And ask him the price of the throne he sat on.

In the uncouth United States, one English writer remarked after a visit, "Any man's son may become the equal of any other man's son." This was not praise. Now the news from California had drawn together hordes of young men whose fevered dreams were the stuff of English nightmares.

The gold-seekers set off jauntily, like soldiers when war has first been declared. "There was scarcely one," wrote a journalist who accompanied them, "who did not feel himself more or less a hero." Few would sustain their high spirits as they clattered along in their slow-motion caravans or rolled across endless seas. But no matter how exhausted and mud-spattered they grew, or how queasy and restless, the emigrants consoled themselves with the thought that they were participants in a grand and sweeping epic. They made no mention of Homer or Achilles, but they took immense pride in styling themselves "argonauts," counterparts of the brave adventurers who had set out with Jason to pursue the Golden Fleece. In their hearts, they knew that they did not cut figures as imposing as savvy Jason and mighty Hercules and the other men of the *Argo*. In place of kings and warriors stood farmers and teachers, clerks and shopkeepers, and dewy-cheeked dreamers of all stripes.

"What an innocent, unsophisticated, inexperienced lot" the gold-seekers were, one of them recalled many years later. "Not one of them then could bake his own bread, turn a flapjack, re-seat his trousers, or wash his shirt. Not one of them had dug even a post-hole. All had a vague sort of impression that California was a nutshell of a country and that they would see each other there frequently and eventually all return home at or about the same time."

Virtually all the ideas and expectations that filled the travelers' minds would soon prove irrelevant. But if they had guessed wrong about the shape of their adventure, they had got one big thing right. Farmers and merchants they might have been, but now they had left those roles behind. "Few could conquer with Pizarro or sail with Drake," in the words of one historian, "but the California gold rush was the great adventure for the common man."

Guidebooks spelled out the food and gear the emigrants would need. Overland travelers would spend about five months on the road, with no dependable places to resupply along the way. One well-regarded volume—unlike many rival authors, Joel Palmer had actually made the journey he described—recommended two hundred pounds of flour per person, seventy-five pounds of bacon, twenty-five pounds of sugar, ten pounds of salt, ten pounds of rice, half a bushel of dried beans, and five pounds of coffee, among other items, and ropes, shovels, saws, and skillets, but "no useless trumpery."

This was bare-bones travel, or it should have been; it was vital to pare weight in order to spare the animals. Emigrants in earlier generations had traveled in roomy Conestoga wagons, but those were large and intended for shorter jaunts on better roads. Mules or oxen struggling across deserts and mountains would die in their traces— thus condemning their owners to death as well—if yoked to anything so big. Instead, the gold-seekers traveled in small, everyday, working wagons straight off the farm; they bore no more resemblance to "prairie schooners" than pickup trucks do to limousines. These were sturdy vehicles, but they had never been tested under conditions anything like those they would confront on the trail. Nor had their drivers.

A typical wagon was roughly four feet wide and ten feet long, about the dimensions of a large closet. The bed of the wagon was essentially a wooden box with sides about two feet high. Many wagons had a false floor a foot or so above the bottom side of the box; the space beneath the floor provided out-of-the-way storage. A piece of canvas stretched over wooden spokes bent into an upside-down U served as walls and roof. Headroom was about five feet. Everything essential for life — tools, food, clothes — had to be crammed inside. Many of the emigrants found a place for a stash of whiskey. Ostensibly this was a precaution in case anyone needed an all-purpose medicine or a snakebite remedy, but at the end of a hard day many a gold-seeker dipped into the first-aid kit.

Emigrants sometimes made room for a mirror or a chest of drawers, or a banjo or fiddle, or books. Dickens, Dumas, and Scott were favorites. Alonzo Delano packed a volume of Shakespeare, Oliver Goldsmith's *Vicar of Wakefield*, and a book on geology. But what had been precious in Ohio or Illinois was often thrown away as junk or burned as firewood after a few hundred miles on the prairie.

The quarters were cramped, but nearly everyone walked rather than rode in any case, to preserve the animals' strength. There were exceptions. Small children sometimes rode, and so did pregnant women and the injured and the ill. But the wagons had no springs (or brakes); for a man feverish with dysentery or white-faced from the pain of ribs he'd broken while trying to ford a river, or a pregnant woman, the constant lurching and jolting was a torment.

The diet on this endless journey was monotonous — a perpetual round of beans, bacon, biscuits, and coffee, as if the emigrants were sailors on a transoceanic voyage — but dullness was only one of its drawbacks. (Luzena Wilson threw most of her pots and skillets away after only a few days' travel, to save weight, in forlorn recognition that "on bacon and flour one can ring but few changes.") The emigrants ate almost no fruit or vegetables; they sipped pepper-mint oil to soothe their stomachs and forced down castor oil for what they called "intestinal inertia." Scurvy was widespread, and the sight of men bent double by the pain a commonplace; at Fort Laramie, in Wyoming, in the winter of 1849, one-fifth of the sol-diers were on crutches on account of the disease.

Most emigrants funneled through Missouri, and for many of them, it was the sight of bustling, rowdy Saint Louis that first made clear just how grand an adventure they had embarked on. With a prime location at the junction of the Missouri River and the Mississippi, and a population of nearly eighty thousand, Saint Louis was one of the biggest cities in the nation and by far the biggest in the West. Thousands of gold-seekers buying supplies and jabbering in excite-ment added to the hubbub. So did the voices of guides and trappers pitching their services to companies of greenhorns wary of ventur-ing out on their own. Seventeen-year-old Lucius Fairchild thrilled to the "noise and din" all around him. "Every street is crowded with busy men and teams all intent on his own business taking care of No. 1." With his head spinning, Fairchild marveled that Saint Louis must be "the largest town of its size in the world."

Whoops of excitement could not quite drown out the moans of the sick and dying. The hordes of newcomers had reached Missouri at the worst possible time, with the cholera epidemic in full force. "Nothing to be seen but one funeral after another," one Saint Louis man wrote in his diary. Local people took to signing their letters "Take care, and don't take the cholera."

For the gold-seekers, this was far worse than a bad omen at the outset of what they intended to be a glorious adventure. Unbeknownst to them, cholera was a disease of crowds and contaminated water.

Both would be defining features of their marathon journey. The emigrants trembled at the thought of Indian raiders hunting them down, but it would be microscopic, never-yet-imagined bacilli that truly represented danger on the route west.

Israel Lord's journey began with a short jaunt, by steamboat, from his home in northern Illinois to Saint Joseph, Missouri. Lord was crabby and suspicious from the start, but then he usually was. "The towns on the river," he wrote, "are miserable, dull, ill-built, unpainted, wretched looking affairs." Saint Joseph struck him as a bit less shabby than the others, though most of its buildings were "not very well done." For Lord this counted almost as a rave.

Worse than the towns were his fellow gold-seekers. Where was their self-respect? Who these days gave a thought to dignity? These greenhorns had no knowledge of the West, no skills, no experience. All they had were brand-new outfits and, dangling from their waists like ornaments on a Christmas tree, as many weapons as they could find a home for.

"Imagine to yourself a biped five feet four inches high," Lord sputtered, "with big whiskers, red mustachios, steeple-crowned hat, buckskin coat done up with hedge-hog quills, belt, pistols, hatchet, bullet pouch, bowie knife twenty inches long, red shirt, spurs on left heel eight inches long, with a burr as large as a small sunflower." Like the members of every older generation (he was forty-four), Lord looked with bewilderment and scorn at the fashions of the young—their hair, especially. "The boys take considerable pains to make themselves ridiculous," he complained. "The most disgusting feature is the hair on the upper lip."

Lord had history on his side. By the time of the gold rush American men had been clean-shaven for about a century. Beards had been so rare for so long that one Philadelphia woman noted in her diary on an April day in 1795 that she had seen "two bearded men." (Soon after, she noted with scarcely more wonder that she had seen an elephant.) Every signer of the Declaration of Independence was clean-shaven, and so was every president until Lincoln. Even Uncle Sam was always portrayed without a beard.

The '49ers would help change that. A gold-miner "neither shaves nor shears," one young man wrote proudly. "He has no use for either razors or scissors. The tonsorial art is, in his estimation, a most reprehensible and unmanly innovation." The boys swanning around Saint Joe, proudly displaying their new-grown whiskers, would soon become the grizzled prospectors of a thousand drawings and daguerreotypes. Israel Lord would have been furious had he foreseen that they would help start a new fashion and that generations to come would think of these ludicrous, scruffy, unshaved men as emblems of freedom and masculinity.

The mustachioed bipeds who so irked Israel Lord had no patience for tut-tutting killjoys. Like schoolboys waiting for a bell that would set them free, they milled about Saint Joe and the other border towns in a state of jacked-up eagerness and frustration. "As far as we could see," Joseph Bruff wrote on May 7, 1849, "over a great extent of vallies & hills, the country was speckled with the white tents and wagon-covers of the emigrants." Desperate as they were to get on their way, they found themselves literally waiting for the grass to grow. No grass for their animals meant no fuel for their journey. Making matters worse, spring came late to the prairie in 1849.

So the gold-seekers did their best to kill time and anything else that happened in view. Any deer or rabbit that showed its head drew a fusillade of shots. When they weren't firing their new weapons, the emigrants tilted their hats, shined their boots, and marched off to pose for photographs. These were early days for photography, though, and the gold-seekers' rowdy good cheer seldom came through in their pictures. Subjects had to keep still for so long that everyone looked stiff and miserable, like prisoners girding themselves before a firing squad. Holding a smile for minutes on end was nearly impossible, too, though many people kept their lips clamped shut for the camera anyway, to hide missing or blackened teeth.

Talking, in the form of endless speculation, proved the greatest diversion for the would-be adventurers. At any lull in the conversation, someone was sure to jump in with yet another story of California's riches. One favorite tale related the sad fate of a miner who had found a lump of gold that weighed 839 pounds. The nugget was too heavy to budge but too valuable to leave, and its discoverer had last been seen sitting astride his treasure and offering $27,000 to anyone who would bring him a plate of pork and beans.

Many such yarns had originally been the creation of inspired newspapermen. *Did you hear about the diamond that rolled down a hill in California and killed five men? It was so large that it took two ships to carry it off.* (The *Cleveland Plain Dealer* had carried the story, deadpan, on March 5, 1849.) In California, the *Boston Herald* reported, nails and bolts were made of solid gold, and golden frying pans hung in every kitchen. Hunters shot buffalo with golden bullets, and lumberjacks felled solid-gold trees using saws with diamond teeth.

Newspapers weren't alone in providing misinformation. Emigrants waiting to get under way pushed into crowded auditoriums to hear experts give talks on how to melt gold into brick-shaped ingots. The process required heavy cast-iron molds — *Lecture Fee Does Not Include Price of Molds* — that would prove useless in the goldfields, if they had not been thrown out long before. In a pinch, one rueful buyer wrote later, they might have made "a capital weapon to kill a bear with." Con men and fast-talking merchants peddled large, complicated assemblages of gears and sieves that promised to take the labor out of separating gold from gravel. For those who bought, the swindlers offered the perfect followup— iron safes to store their gold in.

Hoping to dodge trouble, the gold-seekers clutched their guidebooks like tourists in Paris or Rome today. They had bought gleaming new outfits—"many a man whose legs never crossed a mule stalked along with most terrific spurs clattering at his heels," one gold-seeker griped—but their gear only marked them as rubes.

"The markets are filled with broken down horses jockeyed up for the occasion," lamented a California-bound lawyer passing through Saint Joseph, "and unbroken mules which they assure you are handy as sheep." Farmers, accustomed to sizing up livestock, had a better idea of what they were looking at than did lawyers and clerks, but the debate over which animals to purchase was endless and nerve-racking. A few travelers opted for horses, which were fast but poorly suited to months of hard labor on a grass-only diet. Mules and oxen were better at living off the land and therefore a far more common choice, oxen especially. But how to decide? Mules were hardy and sure-footed but expensive and infuriatingly obsti-nate. Oxen were stronger and cheaper but prone to hoof ailments and distressingly slow. The expense was serious. A mule cost roughly $75 (about as much as a wagon) and an ox $25, and emi-grants needed four or six animals to pull their wagons, plus a few spares in case of trouble.

Decisions, once made, were final. This, too, was new. East of the Missouri River, all the familiar features of life prevailed. "West of that stream," one emigrant wrote, "were neither states, counties, towns, villages, nor white men's habitations." So they had heard, and for once the rumors were largely true. The East was a land of trains, towns, and timetables, with well-traveled roads and well-stocked stores. The West, in one historian's words, was "the place where civilization ended and the Middle Ages began."

For many of the gold-seekers, that step back into an earlier age would prove a shock. They had studied their guidebooks, but they had not truly grasped what they had read. They had no idea what it would mean to travel thousands of miles with scarcely any sources of food beyond what you could carry or shoot, no access to water if the river you were following dried up, no recourse if your oxen sickened or your mules died. No idea, above all, what it would mean to cross a vast continent on foot. For no matter its name, the rush was a race run at a crawl. Two miles an hour was a standard pace, fifteen miles in a day good progress.

The guidebooks did provide useful information about the route itself, if not about its hardships. Emigrants knew they would follow the Platte River and then the North Fork of the Platte westward across the Great Plains in what is now Nebraska; then cross the Rocky Mountains at South Pass, in Wyoming, which would mark the halfway point in their journey; then cut across Idaho or the Utah desert—here the maps grew vague—and then trek across Nevada.

Finally, they would climb the Sierra Nevada into California and descend to the goldfields on the mountains' western slopes. (The first overland party, in 1841, had not been so well informed. "Our ignorance of the route was complete," one emigrant recalled. "We knew that California lay west, and that was the extent of our knowledge.")

The gold-seekers knew they had to stick close to water, for themselves and for their animals, and they knew that the calendar would squeeze them hard. They could not start before May, when grass came in on the prairie, and they absolutely had to reach the continent's far side by November, when snowstorms might block the mountain passes across the Sierra Nevada. (Storms could hit as early as October.) The Donner Party had been trapped in the winter of 1846, less than three years before. The gruesome fate of those California-bound emigrants had horrified the nation—newspapers had wallowed in "the awful truth" about the party's descent into cannibalism and who had eaten bits of her father's body or seen her husband's heart cooked—and the miserable details were still fresh in every traveler's mind.

But the emigrants did *not* know that the farther they managed to struggle, the worse the obstacles they would confront. (Nor had the Donner Party: "We are now on the Platte," Tamsen Donner, the wife of one of the group's leaders, had written to a friend on June 16, 1846. "We feel no fear of Indians. Our cattle graze quietly around our encampment unmolested.... Indeed if I do not experience something far worse than I have yet done, I shall say the trouble is all in getting started.")

The endless prairies early on, the first ordeal, would come to seem benign in retrospect. By the time the gold-seekers reached Nevada the trail would be lined with abandoned wagons, dying animals, and a scattering of human skeletons. Buzzards would circle overhead and coyotes skulk just out of reach. Then they would have to drag their wagons up some of the most formidable mountains in North America, tackling jagged peaks and sheer drops beyond the imagination of those who came from parts of the country where a hill a few hundred feet high qualified as a landmark.

Nor did the emigrants have any way of knowing that their very presence would add to the hazards on the trail. In pre–gold rush years, so few travelers had headed west that there was grass and water for all. In post-rush years, trading posts and other amenities would give the journey some of the trappings of routine. But in 1849 and for a few years afterward, the crush was at its peak and conditions were at their worst. Grass was sparse because thousands of animals had devoured it, water was filthy because crowds of humans had contaminated it, and help along the way was almost nonexistent.

No one could have imagined how quickly the West would change. Twenty years after the gold rush, the transcontinental railroad would span the nation. Roads, cities, and factories would rise out of nowhere. A boy born into a world where a galloping horse represented the fastest speed imaginable might one day cruise down a highway in a convertible with the radio blaring. Bronco Charlie Miller, who claimed to be the last of the Pony Express riders, lived to see gas stations and all-night diners where once he had clung to his pony's neck while dodging Indian arrows. An emigrant named Ezra Meeker, one of the first white settlers in the Northwest, traveled overland to Oregon Territory in 1852. In his old age, he flew in an open-cockpit airplane over the same route he had once inched along in an ox-drawn wagon.

But those changes would come too late for the '49ers, who found themselves in a predicament too strange to have a name. They had been catapulted ahead in time, to a brand-new world where for the first time a person could get rich overnight. But it *was* true, too, that they had been flung backward into an ancient, pretechnological era akin to the Middle Ages, a world powered not by coal and steam and machines but by tensed animals and straining muscles.

When the gold-seekers called themselves argonauts, they meant the term as a literary flourish. It was more than that. Prepared or not, they had left behind the familiar features of the nineteenth century. Modern mundanities like bills and shopping errands were irrelevant on the road, and life was reduced to age-old, almost mythic priorities—survival and starvation and the quest for hidden treasure.

CHAPTER FIVE

A DAY AT THE CIRCUS

THE GOLD-SEEKERS AT THE jumping-off towns set out eagerly, shoving their way into line for a ferry across the Missouri. "The crowd at the ferry is a dense mass fighting for precedence to cross," Joseph Bruff wrote on May 5, 1849. "Two teamsters killed each other on one of these occasions, with pistols, at the head of their wagons."

Once they had made it across the river, the travelers looked around to get their bearings. With the United States and all its comforts now behind them, they confronted for the first time just what they had volunteered for. "Our first campfire was lighted in Indian Territory, which spread in one unbroken, unnamed waste from the Missouri River to the border line of California," Luzena Wilson wrote. "Here commenced my terrors."

Wilson's terrors, like those of nearly all the emigrants, had mostly to do with Indians, who would no doubt swoop down in the night, tomahawks clutched in their teeth. "I had read and heard whole volumes of their bloody deeds," Wilson wrote, "the massacre of harmless white men, torturing helpless women, carrying away captive innocent babes." Tales of Indian depravity had been a staple of American literature from the earliest colonial days, as popular as crime thrillers today or pulp novels a few generations ago. Readers shivered at first-person narratives of kidnaps, desperate escapes, and tortures. "Gracious God! What a scene presented itself to me! My child scalped and slaughtered...my husband scalped and weltering in his blood," Mary Kinnan wrote in one of countless similar narratives, in 1795.

As the years passed, the tales grew less earnest and more lurid, the blood and gore ever more explicit. By the 1840s, readers across America put their work aside at day's end, sank into a favorite chair, and settled down with *Captivity and Sufferings of Mrs. Mason, with an Account of the Massacre of her Youngest Child* or perhaps *Indian Atrocities: Affecting and Thrilling Anecdotes.*

No sooner had Luzena Wilson begun her journey and crossed the Missouri River than she found herself surrounded by two hundred of the red fiends. Darkness fell and she cowered in fear. "I felt my children the most precious in the wide world, and I lived in an agony of dread that first night.... I, in the most tragi-comic manner, sheltered my babies with my own body, and felt imaginary arrows pierce my flesh a hundred times during the night." Finally the sun rose, and the Wilson party set off through Indian country. "I strained my eyes with watching, held my breath in suspense, and all day long listened for the whiz of bullets or arrows."

The second night proved as harrowing as the first. Wilson saw a wagon train camped nearby and begged her husband to ask if they could all travel together, for protection. The train had a grand name—the Independence Company—and a splendid appearance, with sturdy, mule-drawn wagons, banners flapping in the wind, and a brass band tootling away.

Mason Wilson pleaded on his wife's behalf. No dice. "They sent back word they 'didn't want to be troubled with women and children; they were going to California,'" Luzena recalled years later, still indignant at the memory. "My anger at their insulting answer roused my courage, and my last fear of Indians died a sudden death. 'I am only a woman,' I said, 'but I am going to California, too, and without the help of the Independence Company!'"

Luzena and Mason and their small wagon train trudged along, on their own. The Independence Company raced ahead, their speedy mules vastly outpacing the Wilsons' oxen. Luzena watched them vanish in the distance.

They would meet again.

No attack came. The Indians turned out to be "friendly, of course," Luzena remarked later, and had nothing more dire in mind than trading ponies for liquor and tobacco. (This would not always be the case. In the 1840s, Indians could still look at the tiny trickle of westward-moving whites as more a novelty than a threat, and as a source of trade goods besides. By the 1850s, the trickle of outsiders had grown to a flood, and Indian indifference had shaded into hostility. Even so, the emigrants killed more Indians than the other way round. By the tally of the historian John Unruh, a renowned scholar of westward migration, Indians killed 362 emigrants in the years between 1840 and 1860, and emigrants killed 426 Indians.)

The emigrants' terror drained away when they saw they would not be attacked. No longer in a panic, they found themselves perplexed and intrigued instead, adrift in an unfamiliar landscape. The long, open, empty views lured them but spooked them, too. "The timber continued four or five miles," Alonzo Delano wrote, "when it ceased, and the eye rested on a broad expanse of rolling prairie, till the heavens and earth seemed to meet, on one vast carpet of green."

They had yet to reach the true prairie, but this blankness was dismaying enough. Delano scanned the horizon for something familiar to grab onto. Nothing. "In vain did the eye endeavor to catch a glimpse of some farmhouse, some cultivated field, some herd of cattle cropping the luxuriant grass in the distance; yet no sign of civilization met the eye. All was still and lonely, and I had an overwhelming feeling of wonder and surprise at the vastness and silence of the panorama."

Nearly all the emigrants, used to forests and fields, struck a similar bewildered note. "Now that we are over [the Missouri], and the wide expanse of the plains is before us," wrote a woman named Margaret Frink, "we feel like mere specks on the face of the earth." After another five days' travel, her awe began to shift toward distaste. Other eyes might have found the vista enticing—rolling hills, a dozen varieties of grass in countless shades of green, darting birds, flitting butterflies, wildflowers—but the emigrants saw only emptiness. "We left all forests behind us at the Missouri River," Frink went on. "Here the whole earth, as far as the eye can reach, is naked and bare except that a thin growth of grass partly hides the sandy ground."

The panorama soon grew oppressive. The worst feature of the trip's first several hundred miles was that the scenery scarcely changed, and the prospect of crossing that infinite expanse came to seem a mockery. The emigrants found themselves in the predicament of swimmers who had never seen the ocean but had nonetheless vowed to cross it.

Some lost heart and turned around. "Gobacks," as they were called, numbered perhaps several hundred altogether. Emigrants on their way west routinely ran into their discouraged, eastbound counterparts. Joseph Banks, part of an Ohio company of gold-seekers with the jaunty name Buckeye Rovers, noted in his diary that he had met a man who had decided to head back home. "Says he can't go all the way," Banks wrote. "Has money enough; loves his wife more than gold."

Still, considering the hordes heading west, the number of those retreating was minuscule. For most travelers, life at this early stage of the journey retained a quality of cheerful chaos that reality had not yet managed to undo. Wagons carried brash names like *Wild Yankee* or *Gold-Hunter* or *Helltown Greasers* painted on the canvas, or high-toned ones like *Pilgrim's Progress — California Edition*. So many wagons flew the Stars and Stripes that, in camp at night, the emigrants looked more like an army than a party of civilians.

But no army had this improvised, helter-skelter feel. "Every mode of travel that ever was invented since the departure of the Israelites has been resorted to this year," one gold-seeker wrote, and the mood in the early days on the road was more akin to that of a parade than an expedition. "Some drive mules," Israel Lord wrote, "some oxen, some horses. All kinds of vehicles are en route for California — buggies, carts, boats on wheels, arks."

One man set out on foot from Saint Joseph, alone, trotting behind a wheelbarrow that contained all his possessions. He covered twenty-five to thirty miles a day, whistling "Yankee Doodle" as he ran. Three hundred miles into his trip, the Scottish-born Wheelbarrow Man turned down an offer to join a wagon train. "Na, na, mun, I ken ye'll all break doon in the mountains and I'll gang along myself." He did continue by himself, all the way to California. When he returned home to Pennsylvania in 1852 (still on his own), he brought with him a fortune of $15,000, some $300,000 in today's money.

Wheelbarrow Man had no monopoly on unfounded optimism.

From the nation's birth onward, the historian Simon Schama has pointed out, Americans were never more pleased than when they were in motion. To stay at home was not to put down roots but to rust in place. "Happiness for Voltaire was cultivating one's garden," Schama observed. "Happiness for Thomas Jefferson was rolling across the continent, gathering the millions of acres needed to make the American homestead."

Now the gold-seekers had begun rolling their own way across the continent. They were young and on their way to riches, and, mostly, they were happy. As untroubled by their ignorance as campers on their first overnight trip, they reveled in the newness of every sight and experience. A twenty-year-old New Englander named Kimball Webster wrote excitedly, on May 3, 1849, that he and the rest of his company had pitched their own tents, and cooked their own suppers, and slept outdoors. All these were firsts.

So was waking in the middle of that first night, drenched, under sopping wet blankets. Webster and his companions had made camp at the bottom of a hill in a rainstorm. No one had seen how that might not be a good idea, and certainly no one had thought to dig a trench to divert the water that came streaming down the hillside. Webster good-humoredly chalked up the mistake to "our own innocent ignorance." For nearly all these boisterous young men, such mishaps weren't warnings of trouble ahead but opportunities for gleeful teasing of anyone who had blundered even more badly than you had. Everyone was in the same pitching, rocking boat, after all, everyone struggling to master the same skills.

The more ludicrous the pratfalls and the more elegant the victims' outfits, the better the entertainment. "There is another company from Virginia who are dressed in uniform," wrote a gold-seeker from Wisconsin. "It is fun to see them breaking mules being, most of them, clerks & mechanics who never had any thing to do with animals. They make awkward business of it and a good deal of sport for the bystanders."

Mules had a special talent for taking advantage of greenhorns. Anyone foolhardy enough to try riding a mule, rather than strapping a pack to its back or harnessing it to a wagon, quickly regretted his decision. Kicking and bucking, the mules sent would-be riders spinning into the air and then crash-landing, in the words of one observer, "Hell, west & crooked." They were as "wild as the deer on the prairie," wrote Kimball Webster, and the emigrants had scarcely any idea how to tame them. "It took as many men to pack a mule as could stand around it," Webster noted, "and we were obliged to choke many of them before we could get the saddle upon their backs."

The mules fought gamely and managed to kick many of their would-be packers into submission. Improvised strategies proved no use. "We tried in vain to break our mules by putting large packs of sand on their backs and leading them about," Webster went on, "but it availed very little." On their first day on the road, Webster's company woke at sunrise to pack the mules. After a full day's futility, they finally took their first steps out of camp at five in the afternoon.

Even stolid oxen proved nearly impossible for the novices to manage. On the day they set out on their journey to the goldfields, Samuel Rutherford Dundass and the rest of his party of Ohio greenhorns rose early, the better to make a fast start. "Owing chiefly to some difficulty in yoking" the oxen, first minutes and then hours slipped by. The animals ran into trees, collided with other teams, and set off determinedly in the wrong direction. In their delight at finding themselves in the hands of "total strangers to driving," the oxen nearly flipped their wagons.

Other newbies had an even harder time. A glamorous, much-envied outfit called the Pioneer Line would prove one of the great fiascos of the whole gold rush saga. The Pioneer Line was a for-profit venture that offered to take all the work and worry from the overland journey. For a bargain rate of $200 per traveler, the company would provide wagons, animals, and meals for a quick dash to the goldfields. The "gay and festive" passengers, the promotional literature declared, would have only to sit back and enjoy the scenery. A Pennsylvania man named Bernard Reid, a schoolteacher turned surveyor, was one of 125 gold-seekers who quickly plunked down his money.

The entrepreneurs who had organized the Pioneer Line purchased three hundred mules, but only one had ever pulled a wagon. Breaking the mules turned out to be immensely difficult, Reid noted, since the mules "had not given their consent to the ceremony." When the wagon master, named Mose, tackled one especially formidable mule with his bare hands, the startled animal burst into a gallop "with Mose's body streaming through the air like a ship's pennant in a high wind, and so they went, mule and man, round and round the ring, the spectators cheering wildly."

The Pioneer's Mexican cowboys were experts with their lassos, but even they were outmatched by the mules. "A vaquero would single out a victim and throw his lasso. If it missed, it sent the whole herd galloping around the arena," Reid observed. "If it caught, the galloping went on the same, or faster if possible," except this time with the vaquero lashed to the runaway and doing his best to hold on. "Half a dozen circuses combined in one would have been tame in comparison," Reid wrote happily.

The circus ran late on the first day of what had been advertised as a sixty-day sprint to California. By the time the last Pioneer wagon in line set out, the first wagon had already pulled up to make camp for the night. This first night's camp was one mile from the starting point.

*   *   *

These misadventures would have delighted many stay-at-homes, who envied and mocked the gold-seekers in roughly equal measure. The genteel and hugely popular *Godey's Lady's Book*—the magazine's editor was the author of "Mary Had a Little Lamb"—spoke for many who could scarcely abide the '49ers. Thousands were going to California, scolded *Godey's,* "who have never dug a rood of garden in their lives, and never slept out of the home."

To spoof the gold rush greenhorns, *Godey's* created a character named Jeremiah Saddlebags and made him the star of one of the first comic strips. A city dweller to his core, Jeremiah has not the least notion of what life on the road and in the mines will demand. He prepares for the journey by carefully selecting the white gloves and silk tie that best set off his appearance. (He spoils the effect somewhat by shaving his head, to thwart any Indians who might be after his scalp.) His palms are soft, his muscles puny.

And, as if he were not already ludicrous enough to make *Godey's* readers roll their eyes, Jeremiah was a "low-paid clerk." So were a great many of his real-life counterparts on the road to California. Small wonder. In the mid-1800s, a clerk's work was excruciatingly dull. The most soul-sucking cubicle job in today's world hardly compares. Offices had no typewriters, no adding machines, and, worst of all, no carbon paper or copiers. What they had were clerks with quill pens. Men in the nineteenth century wore out their lives in paperwork, copying towers of wills and mortgages by hand in duplicate and triplicate. (In his great story "Bartleby, the Scrivener"—a scrivener was a human copying machine—Melville describes poor, forlorn Bartleby "copying by sunlight and by candlelight...silently, palely, mechanically.")

Any spirited person sentenced to such a fate would yearn to

break free. The main virtue of "the servile trade of quill driving," as one clerk described his job, was that most of the alternatives were just as bad. In Wisconsin, teenaged Lucius Fairchild could hardly bear to think that he was stuck behind the counter of his father's store, "showing rags to the ladies of Madison." Rural life was no better. In Mark Twain's Hannibal and in countless towns like it, "the day was a dead and empty thing," despite all the era's talk of progress. The sun beat down, a fly buzzed against a window, the town drunk rolled over, life drowsed on.

Even without the lure of gold, countless young men would have filled their days with dreams of adventure and a change of scenery. But there *was* gold, and it proved almost irresistible. No one has ever matched Mark Twain in capturing his peers' desperation to get away. A few years too young to venture off to California himself, he watched, yearningly, as gold-seekers on their way west poured through Hannibal in 1849. More tantalizing still, eighty Hannibal residents joined the exodus and set off, too. For young Sam Clemens and thousands of young men like him, the notions of travel, and the West, and striking it rich set the head spinning.

"I was young, and I envied my brother," he wrote later, when Orion Clemens finagled a job as secretary to the governor of the newly created Nevada Territory. "He was going to travel! I never had been away from home, and that word 'travel' had a seductive charm for me. Pretty soon he would be hundreds and hundreds of miles away on the great plains and deserts, and among the mountains of the Far West, and would see buffaloes and Indians, and prairie dogs, and antelopes, and have all kind of adventures, and maybe get hanged or scalped, and have ever such a fine time, and write home and tell us all about it, and be a hero and he would see the gold mines and the silver mines, and maybe go about of an afternoon when his work was done, and pick up two or three pailfuls of shining slugs, and nuggets of gold and silver on the hillside. And by and by he would become very rich, and return home by sea, and be able to talk as calmly about San Francisco and the ocean, and 'the isthmus' as if it was nothing of any consequence to have seen those marvels face to face. What I suffered in contemplating his happiness, pen cannot describe."

Envied by nearly everyone and still half astonished at their own nerve, the emigrants could not help strutting a bit. And who could blame them? One day they had been drones trapped in an office or stuck on the farm, and the next they were free, independent men, roaming the wilderness, sleeping under the stars, and destined for fortune.

So they told themselves, at any rate, and in hard times they bucked one another up with tales from the land of gold. But their visions of roaming free collided almost at once with the mundanities of traveling in a vast, sluggish procession. We think of the gold-rushers as lone adventurers—solitary prospectors crossing an empty continent in search of fortune—and they had entertained similar ideas themselves. Many of them did write early on, as Alonzo Delano had, about their solitude and loneliness. They quickly learned better.

Since the grass set the schedule, everyone had started west at the same time, and even the vast prairies did not swallow up the multitudes. The topography, especially in the early stages, funneled all travelers into a narrow channel. "As we wended our way up the valley of the Platte," a gold-seeker wrote, "one could look back for miles and miles on a line of wagons, the sinuous line with vari-colored wagon covers resembling a great serpent crawling and wriggling up the valley."

The wagons crept along at a slower-than-walking pace, with seldom a chance to pass. ("Once in line you stayed in line all day," one emigrant groused.) Drivers shouted at one another to get moving; whips cracked; interlopers who had stopped for a repair or a meal angled to cut back in line, and their rivals maneuvered to squeeze them out. Trains sometimes drove deep into the night, straining to see in the darkness, so desperate were they to get ahead of the rivals who had hobbled their progress all day.

On one occasion a group of emigrants found themselves stuck behind a company of some fifty wagons, "and we either had to stay poking behind them in the dust or hurry up and drive past them." The impatient travelers passed the caravan, continued a good distance, and stopped to eat lunch. Wrong call. The slow group had continued plodding along. "While we were eating we saw them coming. All hands jumped for their teams, saying they had earned the road too dearly to let them pass again." Road rage at two miles an hour, with two thousand miles to go.

The spur was not simply the urge to be first in line, for bragging rights at day's end. The farther back in line, the more the dirt and grit flung in your face. This dust was a great scourge and, incidentally, another sign of just how crowded the trail had grown. "Our train consisted only of six wagons, but we were never alone," Luzena Wilson wrote. "Ahead, as far as the eye could reach, a thin cloud of dust marked the route of the trains, and behind us, like the trail of a great serpent, it extended to the edge of civilization."

Pulverized by wagon wheels and then kicked up by countless hooves, the dirt and dust hung in clouds like fog. (Perhaps the image of a wagon train as a snake turns up in so many diaries not just because the trains wound their way along but because the emigrants found themselves condemned to creep in the dirt.) On many a bright, sunny day, one emigrant remarked, he had walked next to his wagon and been unable to make out the oxen in the murk just a few paces ahead. When the wind kicked up, it hurled dirt and sand "like fine hail." The travelers choked on the grit and stumbled along red-eyed, some of them in makeshift goggles made from window glass jammed into leather frames.

When the rains came, the dirt turned to mud. This was not a relief but simply a change of hardship. The animals, who had struggled to drag heavy wagons through thick sand and deep ruts cut into the dry ground, now slipped through heavy, sucking, squelching muck that tugged at their hooves and grabbed at the wagon wheels. Wagons sunk to the axles, immobile. Mules and oxen flailed. Drenched, exhausted, and frustrated, the emigrants unharnessed animals from one wagon and yoked them to the mired one. Animals pulled with all their might; humans leaned their shoulders into the work and shoved. With enough pushing and heaving, the wagon would lurch free, and the animals could be yoked back where they belonged. Then the train would move ahead a few paces and run aground again.

If the rain kept up, camp was a grim affair. With a downpour making it impossible to build a fire, dinner at the end of a grueling day would be beef jerky and hardtack washed down with muddy water, while squeezed into the wagon or cowering beneath it. Come nightfall, sleeping space was hard to find. The wagons were small and cramped and, in any case, the covers leaked. Tents were no better. The best alternative was to bed down under the wagon, on a piece of canvas or a blanket, and hope for sleep to come quickly.

In these first weeks on the trail, there were not even any landmarks to serve as beacons. Even today, driving through Nebraska at eighty miles an hour following the emigrants' route, you can scarcely tell you're making progress. The landscape is flat to the horizon, and the view is grass in all directions. (The novelist Willa

Cather moved to Nebraska as a child, from the East, and never forgot her initial shock. Nebraska was "the end of everything," she'd moaned, and "as bare as a piece of sheet iron.") Tooling down the road in a car, breathing cool, clean air and sipping an icy drink, a driver covers as much distance in an hour as a gold-seeker did in a week's hard walking.*

———

There was no good way to travel to California, but there was a choice of bad ways. Those who lived inland immediately thought of wagons drawn by animals. Near the coast, thousands upon thousands opted for travel by ship. Newspaper editors and guidebook authors hurried to lay out the options. Maps showed the various sea routes from New York to San Francisco and explained their pros and cons.

To travel by way of Cape Horn, around South America, was fairly safe but maddeningly slow. The route covered nearly fifteen thousand miles—five times the overland distance—and took five months. Passengers suffered through a long, storm-racked passage around the Horn and then a mind-numbing stretch of motionless torpor in the tropical heat off the west coast of South America, where the sun beat down and the winds failed and ships wallowed in place.

To go by way of Panama was faster but riskier and more expensive. You sailed to Panama, then traveled some sixty miles overland,

———

*On May 27, 1849, Israel Lord noted that the rough going did offer one consolation: no one needed to churn milk into butter. All you had to do was put milk or cream into a closed container and tie it on the wagon in the morning. The day's jouncing ride "throws the milk from one end of the churn to the other," Lord wrote delightedly, and by day's end "the butter gathers in lumps of the size of a walnut, and may be poured from a small hole."

and completed your journey on a second ship. The land leg was the hardest. One mapmaker remarked matter-of-factly that "the swamps, stagnant waters, reptiles etc. render walking across next to impossible." To sail to Mexico instead, and then cross overland to the Pacific coast, was faster still but even less inviting, especially bearing in mind the lingering hostility from the just-concluded Mexican-American War. "To prevent danger of being attacked by robbers through Mexico," the same mapmaker advised, "persons should go in parties of 50 or more."

A journey by sea had considerable advantages over a trip by wagon, though both took about five months. A shipboard traveler could start at once, for one thing, rather than wait for spring to come to the prairie. In a race, this was no small factor. And, as a fare-paying passenger, you would have little to do for much of the journey but pass the time while someone else carried you toward your goal. The overland emigrants, trudging their way along step by weary step, could only dream of such luxury.

Shipbuilders and shipowners raced to capitalize on gold fever. With hordes of passengers thrusting their money at anyone who would carry them westward, California-bound ships jammed every port. A few were elegant affairs, like the new and roomy *Edward Everett* out of Boston, named for Harvard's president, which boasted a library and a troupe of musicians who performed each evening.* Many were converted whalers whose opportunistic owners saw more profit in hauling gold-struck passengers than in hunting fifty-ton beasts with hand-flung harpoons. A fair number were ancient, barely seaworthy relics that had been built to carry cargo. Passen-

---

*It was Everett, a famous orator, who was the featured speaker at the dedication of the national cemetery in Gettysburg in 1863. The ceremony was postponed for three weeks to give Everett time to prepare. He spoke for two hours and was followed by Abraham Lincoln, who delivered his Gettysburg Address in two minutes.

gers shoved their way aboard these floating wrecks only to find themselves crammed into the dark, dank space between decks. There they slept in makeshift bunks and gulped for fresh air at hastily cut hatches.

Ships that plied the Panama route were especially shoddy, because shipowners gambled that nearly any tub could survive the short haul. "Nine men occupied a space of but six feet square," wrote a dismayed passenger on the steamship *Crescent City*, newly embarked on his first sea voyage. "The farmers in bringing into our villages dead hogs for market, dispose of them with as much regard to their comfort, as dictated the arrangement of our sleeping accommodations." Crammed belowdecks, 160 men fought for elbow room and groaned in misery in a stinking slosh of bilgewater and vomit.

On such hulks, safety was no sure thing. One singularly unlucky traveler, a ship captain's wife named Dolly Bates, sailed on three different California-bound vessels, and all three caught fire or sank at sea. She left Baltimore in July, 1850, "with bright hopes and glowing anticipations," but did not reach San Francisco for a full nine months.*

————————

Jennie and Thomas Megquier, setting out from Maine, scarcely gave a thought to inching across the continent in a jolting wagon. They would travel by ship, but by which route? Everyone had opinions, and every opinion was contaminated with rumor and guesswork. Newspapers warned that to sail round Cape Horn would mean week after week squeezed tight against your fellow

---

*Danger followed Bates ashore. Within weeks of her arrival, San Francisco itself burned nearly to the ground.

passengers belowdecks and tossed by towering waves. Panama or Mexico would mean heat and disease and dugout canoes and churning rivers. "You must not believe half you hear," Jennie noted crossly, as she pondered the gloomy alternatives.

On December 17, 1848, her last day in Maine, Jennie wrote a letter to the friend who would be watching over her children. Angie, at seventeen, was the oldest (and only nineteen years younger than her mother); John was fifteen, Arthur nine. Jennie's decision that the best thing she could do for her children was to leave them and travel to the far side of a broad continent, perhaps for years, tore at her. And yet she could see no other path to financial security.

"Sunday night, lonesome as death," she began her letter. It had been a bleak day, and she had spent it dutifully. "I have been to church all day to please the Deacon"—this was a reference to her father, deacon of the local Baptist church—and she resented the "sacrifice" of her time. She had cried, she admitted, but she made sure that no one saw her tears. "I thought it best to keep them back for my own amusement when I am alone."

The reluctance to display emotion was simple good manners, as practiced in New England, but the wry, aloof tone was something more. That was Jennie all over, and it was an act of will as much as a matter of style. Her preference was to tame a predicament not by denying its existence but by holding it at a distance and viewing it with a cool, ironic eye. In the trials that lay ahead, she would draw strength again and again from the same tactic. Melancholy had its temptations, but yielding was unthinkable.

The Megquiers opted for Panama. They would take a steamer from New York to the village of Chagres, on the Atlantic side, then find a way to cross the isthmus, and then take another ship to San Francisco. "It is a long route and a dangerous one," Jennie wrote a hometown friend in Maine on February 18, 1849, just before setting out from New York, "but I have not regretted for one moment that we left your peaceful village."

Nor would she.

The Megquiers left New York City on March 1, 1849, in a "splendid steamship" called the *Northerner*. Almost at once, "a fine northeast storm" hit the ship, and for three days the passengers took to their beds in misery. Then the skies cleared and the mood lightened. "There is about two hundred gentleman and I am the only lady," Jennie wrote cheerfully, "and in that case I receive every attention." She had, she went on, "plenty of company all to myself."

Life at sea was a new experience for Megquier and her fellow passengers. She marveled at the sight of flying fish and ran to look whenever anyone spotted a whale, but she never arrived in time. Nearly all the gold-seekers, at least those not felled by seasickness or trapped in steerage, discovered wonders of their own. In April, 1849, after seven weeks at sea, one Maine farmer touched land at an island off Brazil. He described an exotic fruit he had just seen for the first time: "We found benaners growing wild in the clearing & et our fill you eat only the core first peling off the skin which is bitter & contains little nurisshment."

Early on, even humdrum events stirred the travelers to gleeful anticipation. Aboard the ship *Duxbury* one winter morning, a young Massachusetts man named William DeCosta wrote eagerly about the delectable treats the cook had prepared. "Duff, plum duff for dinner this day!" he wrote in his diary on February 28, 1849. "Duff" was dough, flour mixed with salt water and pork fat, then dotted with raisins or sugar or meat, tied in a bag, and boiled for four or five hours. It tasted no better than it sounds, and the texture was worse still. (The names of shipboard dishes often hinted at their quality. Dandy funk and fruit grunt were desserts, for instance, consisting mainly of bread dough and broken-up biscuits.)

For the moment, though, DeCosta and his new shipmates were thrilled. "The cry has gone through the ship," he exclaimed, "and the echo is still ringing in my ears. What a treat it will be—every man's eyes sparkle, one would suppose we had heard the cry of 'Land ho!'"

The gold-seekers would learn soon enough that food at sea was bland at best, unspeakable at worst. Duff, which was meant to be light and spongy, usually emerged from its long bath as a leaden mass or a pasty blob. "Mine were generally of the hardened species," recalled one man who had worked briefly as a ship's cook, "and the plums evinced a tendency to hold mass meetings at the bottom."

One traveler described shipboard meals as an endless succession of "wormy bread, putrid jerked beef, musty rice, and miserable tea." Another described the dreadful fare in verse:

It might be mule
or the leg of a stool
Or the horn of a mountain sheep
Or a Spanish hide
or cork chips fried
Or a swordfish from the deep.

To dream of plum duff was a beginner's mistake, as if a college freshman today were to chortle in glee at the prospect of tuna casserole in the cafeteria. But on February 28, William DeCosta had been at sea only seventeen days, and visions of sugarplums danced in his head. A month later, he wrote sadly that "Sunday has become 'Duff day,'" and "to eat it is like brick-laying."

*   *   *

As weeks turned to months, the excitement of life aboard ship gave way to ennui. Days consisted of long episodes of squalor and excruciating boredom when nothing at all happened, punctuated by bouts of terror when everything happened at once and storms tossed the ship about or fire burst out in the cargo bay. Mostly, it was changeless, enervating tedium. Young men nodded over their card games or placed bets on how many miles the ship would cover in the course of the day. They gathered in groups for halfhearted contests to see who could jump farthest. They retreated on their own to write in their journals or strum the banjo.

The prospect of riches and adventure at journey's end—if their journey ever did end—only heightened the frustration. One traveler, becalmed five days, found it "oppressive almost beyond endurance." With the sun beating down and the sails barely fluttering, he felt trapped, as if "the ship and all that is in it are chained to one particular spot of the vast ocean, and all human exertion is futile."

———————

From around the world, ships bound for California carried hordes of passengers every bit as hopeful, and as ignorant and frustrated, as Jennie Megquier and her fellow Americans. The gold rush was primarily an American story, but no nation found itself indifferent to California's news. Gold-seekers from Australia, Chile, Mexico, France, England, and China swarmed to the diggings, pouring into California as though spilled from a giant scoop. The Americans and the foreigners had overlapping but not quite identical motives. By and large, Americans felt *pulled* to California, drawn by dreams of freedom and riches. Foreigners felt *pushed* from home, shoved out the door by war, hunger, and economic hardship.

In 1848 and 1849 the world was falling apart. Australia had been hit by a depression, China by famine and seething political unrest, Europe by a series of devastatingly bad harvests. Europeans had dubbed the decade the Hungry Forties, as they watched the price of bread and potatoes, the staple foods of the poor, soar out of reach. "The old year ended in scarcity," a Prussian minister wrote in January, 1847, "and the new one opens in starvation." Food riots broke out in France, Italy, Germany, and Holland. Angry peasants broke into granaries and attacked merchants, landowners, and tax collectors. As the cost of food shot ever upward, people had little or no money left to spend on nonessentials, and the economy spiraled farther and farther downward. Thousands upon thousands of workers and small craftsmen lost their jobs, in an era when government help for the poor scarcely existed.

For a brief time, it looked as if the grim story in Europe would have a glorious outcome. Democracy would supplant monarchy; freedom and equality would overcome feudalism and oppression. The year 1848 saw revolution break out in one European country after another, most dramatically in France. In February crowds of demonstrators barricaded the streets of Paris with cobblestones. Shouting "Vive la réforme!" and singing "La Marseillaise," they brandished looted rifles and waved shards of iron wrenched from gates and railings. The king's soldiers opened fire; the revolutionaries fought back. Within weeks, King Louis Philippe fled to England. Ecstatic crowds swarmed into the abandoned palace and jostled for a turn sitting on the throne. In the same month, February, 1848, Karl Marx published his *Communist Manifesto*. "Let the ruling classes tremble at a Communist revolution," he thundered.

It was not to be. The revolutions of 1848 first raised hopes and then dashed them, as if a brief, giddy spring had suddenly transformed itself into a long, gray autumn. Across Europe reformers and radicals found that they had succeeded mainly in shaking the old regime out of its complacency. The economy continued to stagger, the same tired leaders clung to power, and the heady talk of liberty and workers' rights vanished into memory. With few prospects at home—even worse, with yesterday's jubilant visions turned to ash—countless Europeans clutched at the news of gold and made their way to California.

Desperate as the times were, the gold-seekers did not come from the worst-off classes, who could not afford the fare to a distant land. The story took on the same shape abroad that it had in the United States—the poor could not afford to leave home in search of gold, and the rich had no reason to take the risk. The gold rush was a mass exodus of the restless, dissatisfied middle. The truly destitute found themselves shut off from this enticing possibility, as from so many others. In famine-racked Ireland, for example, in the five years between 1846 and 1851 a million people died of starvation and diseases brought on by malnutrition. With a chunk of bread an unattainable luxury for so many, a voyage across the ocean was as unimaginable as a trip to the moon. Men died with mouths stained green from grass. But in those miserable years a million slightly better-off emigrants did leave Ireland; in the year 1849 alone, ten thousand made their way to California.

France played on the craving for a better life in an especially cynical way. After the French deposed their king, in 1848, they put a republican government in place. The newly elected president was a small, goateed, erratic figure named Louis Napoleon whose sole credential was that he was the nephew of the great Napoleon. Soon he named himself emperor.* Partly to move radicals and trouble-makers safely out of the way, the government and a private firm helped organize a lottery, the Society of the Golden Ingots. Tickets cost one franc, roughly $3 in today's money. First prize was 400,000 francs, and, what was even more exciting, five thousand lucky ticket holders would win a free trip to California to make their fortune.

Karl Marx railed against the scheme, out of fear that the lottery would lure the working class away from socialism. Rather than fight for revolution, Marx warned, France's radicals would find themselves seduced by golden dreams. And so they were. Crowds of gawkers shoved against one another at 10 Rue Montmartre in Paris, lottery headquarters, jostling for a view through the window. Inside, a pile of gold ingots gleamed in the light. Eager buyers grabbed up millions of tickets, not only in France but also in England, Spain, and Italy. In the end, the Society of the Golden Ingots sent seventeen shiploads of emigrants to California to pan for gold.

In England, even without a lottery to stir people's dreams, hopes soared. This was the era of Dickens's *Hard Times,* when grim factories swallowed dispirited workers who "went in and out at the same hours, with the same sound upon the same pavements, to do the same work, and to whom every day was the same as yesterday and tomorrow, and every year the counterpart of the last and the next." No wonder so many grabbed onto the dazzling news. In Liverpool, an observer marveled at the ever-rising buzz of gold talk. "The gold excitement here and in London exceeds anything ever before known or heard of," he wrote in January, 1849. "Nothing is heard or talked about but the new El Dorado."

---

*It was this move that inspired Marx's famous observation that history repeats itself, "the first time as tragedy, the second time as farce."

And not only talked about. A new song, to the tune of "Yankee Doodle," caught the rollicking mood. The casual bigotry was age-old, the jaunty optimism brand-new:

Now's the time to change your clime,
Give up work and tasking;
All who choose be rich as Jews,
Even without asking.

Go! Go now!, the song proclaimed, and it built to a rousing final chorus:

Every one who digs or delves,
Stout, and tough, and brawny,
Buy a pick and help yourselves—
Off to Californy.

In Norway, in 1850, a newspaper printed a letter from a gold miner who wrote that in California he was making fifteen dollars a day; back home in Bergen his daily take had been all of ten cents. So many ships set off for California that one Norwegian newspaper pleaded with would-be gold miners to stay home. "Nothing in Norway's condition—economic, political, or religious—makes emigration necessary."

In Hawaii the exodus began the moment the first rumors wafted ashore. (Rumors crawled by land and sped by sea. With the settled portions of the United States cut off from California by two thousand roadless miles, Honolulu had quicker access to California's news than Saint Louis did.) Between June and October of 1848, before most of the world knew what was up, nineteen ships crammed with gold-seekers had left Hawaii for California. Few blamed them. Maybe California wasn't the land of milk and honey, wrote one newspaper editor in Honolulu, in 1848, but "it abounds with wine and money, which some folks like better."

Versions of the same story played out across the globe. In Canton (now Guangzhou), China, ships' brokers cast for passengers with leaflets baited with promises. Throughout the 1840s China had been pummeled by drought, flood, and famine. Against that backdrop, even a journey across the Pacific to an unknown land and an unknown fate beckoned temptingly.

Chinese travel brokers had no need to remind potential emigrants of the horrors at home; they concentrated instead on fantasies of luxury. America was *Gum Shan—Gold Mountain*—and life on the far side of the ocean was soft. "Money is in great plenty and to spare," one leaflet proclaimed. "There will be big pay, large houses, and food and clothing of the finest description." Not only could you grow rich; just as amazingly, you could walk free. "It is a nice country, without mandarins or soldiers. All alike: big man no larger than little man." For those who could not read, cartoon leaflets told the same enticing story in pictures.

Twenty thousand Chinese borrowed the fare and bade goodbye to their families. They squeezed their way aboard old, run-down ships; steerage was so overcrowded that some passengers held "standee" tickets and had to sleep in shifts. The trip took six weeks if wind and weather cooperated, twice that long if storms blew up. The number of newcomers peaked in 1852. In a single two-day span that summer, two thousand Chinese men clambered ashore in San Francisco and walked into a new life.

CHAPTER SIX

AN ARMY ON THE MARCH

ON MAY 5, 1849, Alonzo Delano noted contentedly in his journal that he and his companions were making good time. Fifteen miles a day was impressive, especially because every day seemed to bring another gale. Nobody from the East had seen windstorms like these. (On Nebraska highways along the same route today, high winds can spin cars and flip tractor-trailers onto their sides.) Delano's men battled their way through the buffeting, their task made all the harder by a mistake in the wagons' design. The canvas sides rose too high; as the wind howled across the prairie, it flung the wagons about like tiny sailboats in a storm. Delano saw the threat—"the force of the wind made the labor much harder on our cattle"—but he pooh-poohed it. Surely a bit of rejiggering the canvas would set things right.

On the same day that he remarked on the gusting winds, Delano shrugged off the discovery that his wagon train had been scammed in Saint Louis. The bacon they had bought, he wrote, "began to exhibit more signs of life than we had bargained for." The mild reaction was characteristic of the man. Delano was cheery in all but the most dire circumstances, a novice in the outdoors but

willing to try anything, constantly wandering off on his own to
scout for shortcuts or to survey the scenery (and nearly always man-
aging to lose his way). In the same diary entry in which he brushed
aside gale winds and moldy food, he noted matter-of-factly that
"We found this morning...that one of Mr. Greene's oxen had
become too sore to travel."

Nearly all the next day was wasted chasing a runaway pony. It
raced off while its dismayed owner ran behind shouting "Whoa!"
The pony did stop after a minute or two, surprisingly, and the
out-of-breath owner staggered up and reached out a hand to grab
its bridle. Close, closer, and then...the escapee wheeled around
and, in Delano's words, "kicked up his heels like a dancing master." After a few yards, the horse halted again, and the game
resumed. The chase continued for several miles until finally the
pony, "like a coy maiden suffered his resolute follower to put his
arm around his neck, and bring him in."

Travelers of a more fretful frame of mind might have been disheartened by mishaps like these, but, then, they might not have
started in the first place. More than optimism was involved, more
even than optimism compounded by inexperience and youthful
resilience. The gold-seekers seemed almost to *welcome* misfortune.
They had to, because they could not permit themselves to think of
their venture to California as an enormous bet, though in truth it
was. Instead, they framed all the difficulties of the journey—and
later the harsh labor of mining itself—as evidence of their own
good faith. They weren't gambling, which would have been indulgent and immoral; they were taking on a challenge that demanded
hard work, stamina, and persistence, the very traits their culture
valued most highly.

So Delano's company dismissed their missteps and decided to
find a shortcut across the plains, the better to speed their way to

California. Setting off on their own, they promptly headed in the wrong direction; eventually, they sorted out their mistake; by day's end, they had managed to return to their starting point. Delano's diary entry for May 8 concluded, "Distance gained, nothing."

Nearly all those who headed west endured similar misadventures. Every hurdle these novices encountered, no matter how low, posed a challenge. Delano and his companions could not cross a stream without someone careening into the water. (When one man fell in twice in a single day, the group proclaimed him the best marksman in the group, "for without firing a shot he had got a brace of ducks—certainly two duckings in one morning.") The company's most experienced hunter spotted an antelope and galloped after it, rifle at the ready. By the time he abandoned the chase, both the antelope and the wagon train had disappeared. A search party set out after the lost hunter. The search party disappeared. A second search party managed to rescue the rescuers.

To make up for their meanderings, the company decided once again to find a shortcut. They lost their way again. Delano noted wearily that the whole procession had wandered the plains as lost as "the children of Israel in the wilderness." Even so, they looked on their mistakes as mere blunders rather than disasters. "Fifty able-bodied men...were not to be easily discouraged," Delano wrote proudly, in mid-May.

Look how far they had come, and not only in miles. In what already seemed the remote past, before he had even reached Saint Joe, Delano had nearly been undone by the task of repairing his wagon. That should have been a routine job, the nineteenth-century counterpart of changing a tire. But "being unaccustomed to labor," as he put it, Delano had struggled for a time and then collapsed into an exhausted heap.

Now, after a bit of seasoning in the outdoors, he could pitch a tent in the rain and wake up dry! He could take a turn as a night guard, rifle at the ready. He could shoot a raccoon, skin it, gut it, and cook it over a fire. "While it is roasting, walk ten miles, fasting, to get an appetite," Delano wrote proudly, "then tear it to pieces with your fingers, and it will relish admirably with a little salt and pepper, if you happen to have them."

The other companies crawling over America's sea of grass felt the same glow of accomplishment. Several weeks into their journey, the emigrants had begun to grow confident in their know-how. The rituals that marked each day—the 4 a.m. wake-up, the cooking of breakfast and boiling of coffee, the break at midday, the setting-up of camp in the evening—had grown familiar. Reality was hard, with its storms and mud and dust, but the gold-seekers had come to feel they had made it through their growing pains. They could manage. They no longer looked like "a company of Christians bound on a business excursion," one greenhorn wrote proudly. Instead, he and his companions were "sunburnt and bearded, with belts full of bowie knives and revolvers." When a "perfect tornado" hit, these swarthy buccaneers reveled in the chaos. The sight of flying tents and tumbling wagons, one traveler wrote, "would have made a parson split his sides with laughter."

In most minds the sight of countless wagons all streaming in the same direction made the spectacle all the more exciting. The emigrants reveled in their numbers, early on, like revved-up fans today pouring into a football stadium or a concert. It looked "as if a mighty army was on its march," Alonzo Delano noted proudly, "and in a few moments we took our station in the line. . . . Although we were strangers, yet there was a fellow-feeling in having one pursuit in common, and we drove merrily along." At night, around the campfire, the gold-seekers picked out tunes on their banjos and sawed away at violins or smacked tambourines and danced a step or two. Some had even more energy. "Love is hotter here than anywhere that I have seen," one emigrant confided to his diary. "When they love here they love with all thare mite & some times a little harder."

Most emigrants found, as Luzena Wilson had, that the Indians who had loomed so large in their nightmares proved less frightening in the flesh. Now letters home made studiedly casual mentions of Sioux and Cheyenne warriors with guns, bows and arrows, and bloody scalps dangling from their saddles (from raids on other tribes). The tone implied that such sights were all in a day's work. "Many a Green 'un trembled with fear," noted one correspondent, himself a proud veteran of several weeks on the road.

Even the landscape seemed to grow less forbidding. Israel Lord, of all people, felt moved to praise the scenery. "We passed over the most beautiful prairie I ever saw," he noted about sixty or eighty miles after crossing the Missouri, though he hastened to point out that there was "sometimes no timber in sight and scarcely any elevation worthy the name of hill."

Cheerier souls than Lord waxed positively effusive. "To see it and feel it in all its beauty," wrote Eleazer Ingalls, a forty-year-old emigrant from Illinois, "one must be hundreds of miles from civilization, out on those great ocean-like prairies…where the sight of a tree is as welcome to the traveler as the sight of a sail to the mariner when he has been for a long time traversing an unknown sea. He must be there on a balmy sunset eve, after a long and wearisome march over arid plains, destitute of water, and suffocated with the dust. Then when he can find a camping ground combining all the blessings of grass, good water and beautiful groves…no description would give a life-like picture of such a scene."

*   *   *

Day after day the emigrants plodded on, cursing the wind and dust, clambering down gullies and across creeks, totting up the miles they had covered. (They relied on odometers, store-bought or jury-rigged, that estimated distance by counting wheel revolutions.) Now the weather revealed a new trick. Sudden and furious hailstorms added to the miseries of gusting wind and pounding rain.

On the treeless plains, the wagon trains were more vulnerable than mobile homes today. "All the storms which I ever before experienced were as nothing compared with the one we endured this day," one traveler wrote on June 8, 1849, in Nebraska. "The rain fell in torrents accompanied by a whirlwind and by hail the size of hickory nuts. Two of our carriages were overset by the gale and one of them crushed to atoms. Mules and loose stock were stampeded and ran for hours." When the barrage ended, the ground lay buried under three inches of hail.

Caught by surprise in a storm the same week, Israel Lord could do little but try to ride it out. No one had managed to tie up the cattle in time. Panicky, bellowing, still yoked to their wagons and threatening to capsize them at any moment, the spooked animals only added to the bedlam. "The thunder and lightning were continuous for at least an hour," wrote Lord, "and the hailstones as large as an ounce bullet, or larger." The next time a storm blew up, Lord noted, the first priority should be securing the cattle.

Lord had begun learning the basics, like Alonzo Delano and all the other greenhorns, but he was by nature less sunny than Delano, and the more he learned, the more he worried. Delano would have seen the question "What could possibly go wrong?" as reassuring. Lord would have made a list.

"It is necessary to rouse every man as soon as it is light enough to see to work," he warned in his journal on June 2, "else we get a late start.... We have already passed a considerable number of teams which have not the remotest chance of reaching the mountains by November even, and those who are thus belated must either remain in the plains or perish in the mountains." The most common problem, he went on, was "too heavy loads" in the wagons. Wooden chests and boxes were "worse than useless," because they weighed too much. Cloth sacks were far better. "Many of the wagons look much as though they put in all they could think of, and hung everything else on the outside." Newspaper cartoons had tried to convey the absurdity of these overburdened travelers, Lord snapped, but the reality was worse than any drawing.

By June 6, Lord's company had traveled some two hundred and fifty miles, following a river called the Big Blue as it wandered westward across Nebraska. They topped a hill and spotted the Platte River, which they would cling to for the next five weeks and five hundred miles. So far, so good, but Lord did not let down his guard. On June 8, he noted that "our cattle have been lame with cracks in the hoof."

But of the thousands of travelers on the road, few shared Lord's foresight.

———————

The very first words in Israel Lord's journal had sounded a dark, foreboding note, as if spoken by a nineteenth-century Philip Marlowe: "May 6, 1849. We left a dead man by the name of Middleton on the levee at St. Louis, and thought that we had left all the cholera with him."

They had not. As he traveled westward, Lord took to copying

down the inscriptions carved into roadside grave markers. On a single day, May 27, he recorded ten names.

On June 2, Lord's company happened on a man lying on the ground near a dry gulch, still alive but alone and helpless. His head rested on a bag stuffed with clothes. Nearby lay a hunk of bread and a battered tin cup. The sick man gasped out his story in a couple of dozen words. "He called himself T. R. Waring from Andrew, Iowa," Lord wrote. "He had the cholera and was abandoned by his company." For two days Waring had been hoping that an eastbound company would come along and bring him home. Lord and his companions did their best to make the sick man comfortable, but they could not truly help. We "filled his cup with coffee," Lord wrote sadly, "and went on our way."

For the emigrants, such encounters were doubly horrifying. Cholera was a gruesome disease, which was bad in itself, and now it seemed to be stalking them as they traveled, which was worse. "Every steamer was impregnated" with the disease, wrote a gold-seeker named George Thissell, who set out from Ohio on March 16, 1849. "We had scarcely steamed a hundred miles when we landed at Louisville, Kentucky, and put off four of our dead. . . . No pen can describe the scenes on board the steamer for the next twenty-four hours. The dead and dying were in every berth. When within twenty miles of St. Louis, in the night, we landed and put off nine more dead. All were buried in one large grave. Not even a stake was driven into the ground to mark their last resting place."

The emigrants thought of cholera as a disease of cities, crowds, and poverty rather than of open, sprawling vistas. Once in the sparsely settled West, they had felt sure they would be safe. That faith arose from what seemed indisputable fact. Everyone knew— no one could help knowing—that cholera preyed on cities, and on the filthiest, most squalid sections of those cities above all. *Why*

Le Petit Journal

ADMINISTRATION
61, RUE LAFAYETTE, 61

Les manuscrits ne sont pas rendus

On s'abonne sans frais
dans tous les bureaux de poste

5 CENT. SUPPLÉMENT ILLUSTRÉ **5** CENT.

23me Année — ❧❧ — Numéro 1.150

DIMANCHE 1ᵉʳ DÉCEMBRE 1912

ABONNEMENTS

	SIX MOIS	UN AN
SEINE et SEINE-ET-OISE	2 fr.	3 fr. 50
DÉPARTEMENTS	2 fr.	4 fr. »
ÉTRANGER	2 50	6 fr. »

LE CHOLÉRA

that was, no one knew. Was cholera a judgment of God, who was fed up with the sinful, self-indulgent ways of slum dwellers? Was it caused by some poison in the air seeping out of the muddy, slimy earth? For anyone in the mid-1800s to suggest that the disease was caused by organisms invisible to the naked eye would have been dismissed as superstition, a throwback to outmoded doctrines of possession and evil spirits.

The wealthy leapt to embrace the notion that the poor had brought the disease on themselves. As soon as cholera had burned through "the scum of the city," one well-to-do New York merchant assured his daughter, it would die out for lack of fuel. Not until 1883 would the disease be fully understood. The poor were indeed killed out of all proportion to their numbers, it turned out, but morality and character had nothing to do with it. Neither did the foul air and sickening stink of the cities, plausible though that theory was. Instead, the culprit was a bacterium called *Vibrio cholerae* found in sewage-contaminated drinking water or on dirty, uncooked fruit or vegetables.

In this same year of 1849, an English doctor named John Snow published an article in the *London Medical Gazette*. Snow rejected the leading theory of cholera's origin—that it was a "miasmatic" disease caused by poisonous vapors in the air—and proposed a new explanation: cholera came about when a person drank water that had been contaminated by sewage. Snow did not know about "germs" and bacteria. No one did, in 1849, but he showed how his theory explained a number of long-mysterious observations. How could it be, for instance, that a doctor could treat a cholera patient and never fall ill himself, while the patient's whole family sickened and died? Snow's work on cholera would eventually make him one of the great figures in the history of medicine. At the time, no one paid any attention.

In *Ghost Map,* his brilliant account of Snow's achievement, the writer Steven Johnson explains just how the micro-organisms undo their host. Once a person has swallowed contaminated water or food, Johnson writes, *Vibrio cholerae* "converts the human body into a factory for multiplying itself a millionfold." The cholera victim expels those millions of bacteria in a foul, watery gush. If some of that tainted liquid happens to seep into a well or a river that other people depend on for drinking water—perhaps when someone rinses dirty clothes or bedsheets, or when a cesspool leaks, or a sewage pipe discharges too near an intake pipe— the disease will claim new victims, who in turn will spread it to others.

This is one reason that the threat of cholera did not soar until fairly recent times, when people first crowded into enormous, teeming cities. By good fortune, *Vibrio cholerae* organisms cannot make people sick unless they swallow them; it is impossible to inhale cholera germs or to "catch" them by touching a sick person's skin. Nor can animals carry cholera from place to place, as rats and fleas carry plague. *Vibrio cholerae* can travel only inside a human host. (It can live contentedly in contaminated water, but unless a person comes along to drink, it is stuck in place.)

So cholera needs large numbers of people if it is to explode into a full-fledged epidemic. In particular, it needs people who live crowded together and drink one another's contaminated water. Early in human history, when people lived in small, scattered bands, cholera remained merely a local threat. With the rise of giant, filthy, slum-infested cities pouring tons of sewage into rivers and streams, it roared to life.

And now the gold-seekers, gathering by the thousands, had created a traveling slum. "The gold rush was to cholera," one medical historian observes, "like wind to fire."

*   *   *

Travelers' accounts from the 1800s routinely talk about the water supply in a way that makes a modern reader cringe.* The effect is akin to overhearing someone in lion country remark, "Such a lovely evening. Who's for a stroll?" Gold-seekers knew instinctively not to drink filthy water, of course, but they had no way of knowing that an innocuous-looking dipper of water might teem with toxins.

In any case, Americans in the nineteenth century were accustomed to drawing water directly from rivers and wells, and they had never heard of such things as filtration and chlorination. On steamboats, for instance, buckets were used both to throw slops over the side and to draw up drinking water. A woman named Eliza Steele, on a pleasure cruise along the Ohio River in 1840, saw that her glass of water had half an inch of mud in the bottom, and put it aside. A companion complained that the water was *not muddy enough,* and took a swallow from her own glass. "Dear me! What insipid water! It has been standing too long. I like it right thick." Whereupon, Eliza Steele continued, the woman called a chambermaid over and ordered her to "Get me some water fresh out of the river, with the true Mississippi relish."

If James Marshall had spotted his glint of gold a few years later, cholera might not have done in so many of the emigrants. They might, at least, have boiled their drinking water. Certainly they would have been better off than in 1849, when one gold rush physician could give no better anticholera advice to his patients than to protect themselves with a diet of bacon covered in cayenne pepper and washed down in whiskey. But the gold rush fell just on the

---

*"The past is a foreign country," observes the anthropologist Gregory Cochran. "Don't drink the water."

wrong side of the divide that marked the beginning of the modern age of medicine.

John Snow's breakthrough came too late for "J. J. Hardy, Winchester, Ill., age 33," whose name Isaac Lord copied down from a marker stuck in the ground. "Have passed a great many graves," Lord noted solemnly on June 10, 1849. "The cholera is only a few days ahead of us."

A race for riches during an epidemic was a strange thing, like a scavenger hunt in a graveyard, and the gold-seekers' moods veered erratically. "Passed a number of graves as indeed we do every day," Lord wrote on June 30, but now the travelers had begun to encounter new, exciting sights as well. Lord tasted antelope for the first time. "The meat is better than venison, something like lamb. They are the size of a small deer." Even prairie dogs rated an enthusiastic mention. "One of the oddest little creatures we found in our journey of two thousand miles was the prairie dog, about as large as the poodle dog," wrote one emigrant (without the aid of any nearby poodles, apparently, to provide scale). "As they sat up on their hind legs, all over the prairie, they resembled a miniature kangaroo."

But it was buffalo, the emblem of the plains, that all the emigrants had dreamed of since before they left home. They had strained their eyes for weeks, transforming every dark spot on the horizon into a wild creature they could gallop after. Buffalo herds in late spring were smaller than they would be in another month or two, but even now a group might number in the hundreds or thousands. A single animal, in that vast assembly, might stand six feet at the shoulder and weigh close to a ton. Soon now, very soon, the gold-seekers boasted, they would dine not on beans and bacon but on delicious slabs of buffalo steak, sputtering straight from the fire.

Israel Lord saw his first buffalo on the morning of June 13, 1849. "In a moment all was excitement. Sixty wagons were in full view, and when the word *Buffalo!* was passed, the men seized their guns and started hot footed for the scene of action, or for some more elevated ground to get a better sight." Soon two hundred men had gathered along a low hill, their eyes fastened on two hunters in pursuit of a single buffalo. "There he turns...and now he comes. How black he seems. Harder and closer they press him, and now he turns directly back and towards us. Hurrah! Hurrah!" More men joined the chase, riding and whooping. Half a dozen were in at the kill, but when another buffalo suddenly appeared, they abandoned their first prize and raced to bring down another.

The Plains Indians had long since mastered the buffalo hunt in all its varieties, from the stealthy, ever-so-slow slither along the ground to the heart-pounding dash on horseback into the midst of a racing, ground-shaking herd. Most of the emigrants had more trouble. A '49er from Massachusetts, a young carpenter named Reuben Shaw, wrote a detailed account of his first buffalo hunt. He and some companions spotted a large herd of buffalo grazing quietly. They rode in pursuit but the buffalo saw them, or smelled them, and scattered. Soon the hunters had lost sight of the hundreds upon hundreds of immense, hairy beasts, who were somewhere in the sandy hills, and they'd lost track of one another as well. Shaw wandered lost in a cloud of dust.

Suddenly, to his astonishment, part of the herd materialized not more than twenty yards away. In a frenzy of excitement, Shaw picked out a victim, aimed, and fired. His horse, as unaccustomed to gunfire as was his rider, reared up, and Shaw crashed to the ground. The buffalo ignored the commotion. Shaw limped back to camp, body aching, clothes torn, canteen crushed. His horse had made it back before him, and so had two other hunters, also newly horseless and newly bruised. No buffalo were injured.

Many hunters fared even worse. "The casualties of buffalo hunting are very common," Joseph Bruff noted in his diary, at nearly the same time. "Men charg'd by wounded bulls, unhorsed & many badly hurt—the horses generally running off with the band of buffaloes, for the Indians to pick up hereafter."

But with emigrants streaming west by the tens of thousands, all of them armed, all of them intent on buffalo, this was a contest certain to end badly for the animals. Badly, too, for the Plains Indians, whose way of life depended on the presence of herds that for centuries had numbered in the millions and turned the prairie black. The Indians relied on buffalo meat for food; they made clothing and moccasins and tepees from its hide, cord from its sinews, soap from its fat, and fuel from its dung.

The end would come a generation later, when railroads crossed the plains and professional hunters could send thousands of hides and tons of meat to distant markets. But already, in this first gold rush year of 1849, one emigrant remarked that "the valley of the Platte for two hundred miles presents the aspect of the vicinity of a slaughter yard, dotted all over with skeletons of buffalos." Careless and in a hurry, the emigrants killed their prizes, cut off a steak or two, and left the rest. "We frequently see half-eaten corpses by the road side," Isaac Lord wrote on June 17.

For the Indians, the gold rush sped up a story that already seemed headed toward a dark end. One side held all the power, and the other stood in its way. The white population of the United States was enormous, ever-growing, hungry for land, and disdainful of "savages" who stood in the way of progress. And white settlers and traders brought devastating diseases, like smallpox, that feasted on populations who had never confronted such killers. Lacking all immunity, Indians died by the thousands.

The first white emigrants, tiny in number and intent on Oregon or California, had done comparatively little damage to the Indians whose territory they passed through. But the gold-seekers and those who followed close behind would destroy the buffalo herds, strip the grass, foul the water, and bring disease. "The locusts of Egypt could scarce be a greater scourge than these great caravans," wrote one stunned '49er, "as grass and whatever else is green must disappear before them."

In July, 1849, a U.S. Army captain on his way to an assignment in Utah stopped to visit a Sioux camp along the Platte. He walked into a village of the dead. "We found the bodies of nine Sioux, laid out upon the ground, wrapped in their robes of buffalo-skin, with their saddles, spears, camp-kettles and all of their accoutrements." All had died of cholera, from drinking water that emigrant trains had contaminated. In a tepee lay the body of a dead girl about sixteen years old. She wore her finest outfit, embroidered buffalo robes adorned with porcupine quills, scarlet leggings, and new moccasins. Not far off were two more Sioux encampments, the larger numbering around 250. Cholera had struck there, too, the captain wrote, and those who remained alive were "fearfully alarmed by this, to them, novel and terrible disease."

Most of the emigrants had been following the south bank of the Platte River, traveling on a nearly straight east-to-west path. The route had been smooth and more or less level, at least compared with what lay ahead. Now, after several hundred miles following the Platte upstream, the emigrants had reached the junction where the South Fork and the North Fork met to form the Platte proper. The two forks formed a V lying on its side, with the junction toward the east; the emigrants found themselves on the south side of the South Fork. From here almost to the Continental Divide, they knew from their guidebooks, the trail followed the North Fork. The only way to get there was to cross the South Fork. That was trouble.

All river crossings were dangerous. Men had drowned trying to cross the Missouri, at the very start of their westward journey. More would perish at every river they came to, drowning in a parched and arid landscape where dying of thirst seemed a likelier fate. Travelers seldom tried crossing the Platte, which had a reputation as "the worst river to ford in the west." A river as strange in the emigrants' eyes as the prairie itself, the Platte spread into countless braids as it meandered over a nearly horizontal landscape. (French fur trappers had named the river *Platte,* for "flat.") A mile or more wide but rarely more than waist- or chest-deep, it posed a hard choice to anyone who would take it on—the swift current and quicksand bottom made the river dangerous to cross in a wagon or on horseback, and its countless sandbars and channels made it unsuitable for ferries.

The forks of the Platte were narrower than the Platte itself, but they were challenge enough. In a landscape prone to sudden storms, a river might surge and tumble one day and mosey the next. At any instant the bottom could give way, and a horse or a man who had been stepping confidently could suddenly find himself swimming for his life. The South Platte was "fearful to look at," recalled the gold-seeker Margaret Frink, "rushing and boiling and yellow with mud, a mile wide and in many places of unknown depth." Everywhere you turned you saw teams of mules or oxen plunging into the water, or men on foot, struggling ahead, falling, tumbling. Animals bellowed, men shouted and cursed. One moment the water reached only to the men's knees, the next they were neck-deep and fighting the current.

It looked fairly calm on the day Luzena and Mason Wilson prepared to cross. The Wilsons and their companions tinkered with the wagons, improvising wooden risers to lift the bed a foot or so higher than usual, and then pushed their way into the water. Some men perched on the oxen's backs. Others waded. The river swept into the wagons and carried away some of their contents, but the Wilsons made it across. Luzena looked back. The oxen in the team behind her were in midstream, stuck fast.

"The frantic driver shouted, whipped, belabored the stubborn animals in vain, and the treacherous sand gave way under their feet. They sank slowly, gradually, but surely. They went out of sight inch by inch, and the water rose over the moaning beasts. Without a struggle they disappeared beneath the surface. In a little while the broad South Platte swept on its way, sunny, sparkling, placid, without a ripple to mark where a lonely man parted with all his fortune."

Joseph Bruff saw a wagon caught in a similar predicament, and this one contained a sick man. The trapped man was only fifty yards from shore but marooned. One good samaritan did his best to help. "It looked queer to see a man wading downstream, waist deep in the rapid river," Bruff wrote, "with a pot of coffee in one hand and a plate of bread and meat in the other, going to the wagon, to the relief of his comrade." Bruff, who had a weakness for dogs, took note of "a pointer dog, at the water's edge, howling for his lost master." The story had a happy ending, with the stranded man's companions eventually able to harness a dozen mules to the trapped wagon and drag it to land.

Safely across, Bruff took the time to climb a hill overlooking the forks of the Platte. He admired the "beautiful prospect" and noted down the inscriptions on two graves. For weeks now, scarcely a day had passed without a grave marker—on many days, scarcely an hour had passed—and Bruff had copied down the message on every one. He would continue, grave after grave, to journey's end.

Few sights struck the emigrants as sadder than a hasty burial in a makeshift grave. "No loved one near, no tolling of the church bell, no marble slab to mark his last resting place," lamented twenty-four-year-old George Thissell, as he watched the burial of a friend who had been shot to death by accident. Even in a devout age, it was hard to find consolation in thoughts of eternal rest. In a land without wood, there would be no coffins, and the emigrants had learned that wolves and coyotes could dig up a body regardless of how many rocks and stones were piled on top of it. "It was not an uncommon thing," Thissell wrote, "to see a leg or arm dragged from the grave."

Best not to dwell on such things. Callow young men and grumpy old-timers alike squeezed back a tear or two, at first, but death quickly came to be part of the daily routine. Within weeks many emigrants deemed it hardly worth mentioning. The tone of one young emigrant's letter home, written on June 5, 1849, captured the prevailing mood. "Another of our company died at 12 o'clock of the Cholera he belonged to Monroes mess and was at the point of death when they joined our company we buried him while nooning I will give you a description of our daily life which is pretty much the same all of the time."

Was this indifference? More likely, it had less to do with callousness than with a kind of resignation—*what is there to say?* Even kindhearted Joseph Bruff, despite recording every grave inscription he passed, quickly grew matter-of-fact about death on the trail. On July 12, still fairly early in the trip, his journal entry included a curt sentence: "Passed a camp of 5 wagons, one of the party was in a tent dying of Cholera." In the next line Bruff recorded the day's weather. "Clear & very warm."

"What can't be cured must be endured," the proverb had it, and the emigrants had no choice but to be stoical. Like cops or emergency room doctors today, they witnessed a relentless parade of grim sights. As a matter of self-protection, they could not weep over every tragedy. "Custom made us regard the most unnatural events as usual," Luzena Wilson would recall many years later. "I remember even yet with a shiver the first time I saw a man buried without the formality of a funeral and the ceremony of coffining." She did not bother to spell out the melancholy truth that many such unnatural events had followed that first one.

On the burial morning, Wilson had been eating breakfast by the campfire, idly watching two men dig in the ground. Until they retreated into a tent and emerged with a body wrapped in a blanket, she'd had no idea why they were digging. Ten minutes later the men covered the grave over. Half an hour later they rode on, "leaving the lonely stranger asleep in the silent wilderness, with only the winds, the owls, and the coyotes to chant a dirge." None of his friends had written the dead man's name on a piece of wood or even left a stone to mark his grave. "There was not time," wrote Wilson, "for anything but the ceaseless march for gold."

CHAPTER SEVEN

LET US GLORY IN OUR MAGNIFICENCE

ALMOST AS SOON AS they staggered ashore on the far side of the South Platte, the emigrants confronted new obstacles. They were still traversing the plains, with hundreds of miles to go before they reached the mountains, but now deep gullies and steep bluffs cut across their path. "The worst hills this side of the Missouri," Israel Lord noted on June 17, and this was an understatement. At a spot later named Windlass Hill, the gold-seekers had to unhitch the animals from their wagons, attach ropes to the rear axle, and then lower the wagons down the bluff inch by lurching inch. This was a precarious business, roughly akin to easing a piano down a ski slope. A team of men at the front of each wagon tried to maneuver around the rocks in the way. Higher up the hillside, another sweating, cursing team clung to the ropes, fighting the wagons' weight and playing out slack a few inches at a time.

But the trail soon eased, and then, to the gold-seekers' delight, the scenery at last began to change. Today everyone around the world knows the austere beauty of western landscapes from countless movies, but the emigrants had no such grounding. The prairie had been new; this was wondrous. Treeless seas of grass had struck the emigrants as a mere absence. Now they found themselves entranced by the sight of cathedrals carved in stone, and towering, eroded pinnacles, and sandstone fortresses.

"Here you saw the minarets of a castle; there the loopholes of a fort; again, the frescoes of a huge temple; then the doors, windows, chimneys, and columns of immense buildings appeared in view, with all the solemn grandeur of an ancient yet deserted city," Alonzo Delano wrote, as he approached Scotts Bluff, in present-day western Nebraska. "It seemed as if the wand of a magician had passed over a city, and like that in the Arabian Nights had converted all living things to stone."

More important than the beauty of the setting was the incontrovertible proof that they had made headway on their journey. Guidebooks had listed the milestones on the route west—huge and looming Courthouse Rock and Jail Rock; beckoning Chimney Rock; Fort Laramie, where the travelers hoped to resupply themselves. Now, at last, they could begin to cross them off their list. Chimney Rock, a towering natural pinnacle visible from a distance of forty miles, quickened their steps. A pyramid more than three hundred feet tall from ground to tip, topped by a hundred-foot-plus spire, the stone formation awed even the most jaded travelers.* "No conception can be formed of the magnitude of this grand work of nature until you stand at its base & look up," wrote an Ohio gold-seeker named Elisha Perkins. "If a man does not feel like an insect then I don't know when he should."

But the great stone monuments seemed to mark milestones for grumbling and dismay, too. The emigrants' moods lurched wildly, their spirits buoyed one moment by the majestic views and cast down

---

*Chimney Rock was an American name. The Sioux called it Elk Penis.

the next by their endless labors. Only a few weeks before, in May, the men in Alonzo Delano's company had been so high-spirited that at day's end they ran footraces in camp, for the joy of it. Now, in June, the mood in the evening was often bleak. On the same night that Alonzo Delano marveled at sights worthy of Scheherazade, a storm swept in, and the rain beat down. "The evening was wet, cold, and cheerless," Delano wrote, and the mood in camp turned so dark that even "the scenery around us could not dispel" the gloom. Morning came too soon and brought with it "the vilest oaths, and the most profane language, and frequent quarrels and feuds."

It was erosion that had made these landscapes, over inconceivable spans of geologic time, and now, on a human scale, erosion set in, undermining the emigrants' spirits. Worn out by all they had already done, surly and bad-tempered at the prospect of how much still lay ahead, the emigrants began to snap at one another. "If a man has a mean streak about him half an inch long," one of Delano's traveling companions remarked, "I'll be bound if it won't come out on the plains."

Accidentally bump a man and spill his coffee, on what Delano called "this long, weary, and vexatious journey," or launch once again into a too-familiar story, or whistle one more tuneless melody, and you were liable to find yourself in a shoving match or a screaming argument. "Perhaps there is no situation so trying upon the infirmities of human temper as a long trip like this," wrote Bernard Reid, who was traveling in the supposedly luxurious and carefree Pioneer Line.*

In Israel Lord's company, the quarreling took the form of sulking

---

*A wagon train in 1849 presaged many of the miseries of a family vacation in a hot, crowded car today. "Grown men are apt to become children again and make mouths at one another on very slight provocation," Reid complained. On one summer night he had been forced to step in as peacemaker in the Battle of the Sugar Sack—the supply of sugar had begun to run low, and some of the Pioneers accused others of taking more than their share.

and griping. "If I ordered a halt at 5 o'clock, they grumbled—we ought to drive till sundown," Lord wrote to his brother. "If we drove till sundown we ought to have stopped at 4 o'clock. If we turned to the right for feed, we should have gone to the left, if to the left, nothing but the right would answer. If we went away from the road to camp I was a dam'd fool and a d—der one if I camped on the road. If I halted at noon it was a dead loss of time, if I kept on till night I should kill the cattle."

Angry and impatient, the emigrants could scarcely believe that once they had thrilled at the sight of the crowds all around them. Now the constant bumping up against one's neighbors, and the mere fact that they were *always, always* there, gnawed at even the mildest souls. And what was merely miserable on the plains was agonizing on shipboard, where overcrowding and lack of privacy drove the emigrants nearly mad. On the journey around Cape Horn—half a year at sea, and covering a distance more than half the globe's circumference—the storms and waves proved scarcely more of an ordeal than the close quarters.

"At home I saw my neighbors not oftener than two or three times a week," lamented a passenger on the *Edward Everett,* out of Boston. "Now I have them about me at every hour of the day and night." Another sea traveler, a gold-seeker from Maine who found himself trapped in what was essentially an overcrowded, down-at-heels boardinghouse, took refuge in fantasy. "One of the first things I plan to do when I get home is to take my gun and a sack of provisions and go up and camp out on the west side of Mount Baldy. I'll stay there a month and maybe longer and if I don't see a single human being I won't be disappointed."

From here on, the emigrants' mood would ratchet downward, each new hardship sapping their spirit as well as their strength. Eleazer

Ingalls, an Illinois lawyer, noted in his journal on June 20, 1849, that he had passed the grave of a man who had killed himself. He had evidently been traveling on foot, carrying a meager store of supplies, and had finally lost hope. Somehow he had managed to cut his own throat. "Poor fellow," wrote Ingalls. "He had become discouraged in prosecuting one long journey, and had entered upon another longer journey, with, perhaps, less preparation than upon the first."

The team spirit that had marked the early miles gave way under the pressure of weariness and bad weather. Some travelers used their last reserves of energy to make sure that others would suffer as they had. Alonzo Delano stopped to examine one of the heaps of abandoned cargo that gave the road to California the look of an enormous yard sale. Nearly everyone had packed too much. Iron stoves, featherbeds, pillows, quilts, chests of drawers, knives, forks, food, dress shirts, pots and pans lay in discarded heaps. To his horror, Delano found piles of sugar that had been soaked in turpentine to render it useless, heaps of flour purposely sullied with dirt, wagons chopped into pieces, clothes torn into shreds, "simply because the owners could not use it themselves, and were determined that nobody else should."

Not always, though. Delano did find that sometimes a generous soul had abandoned a wagon and left it intact or set out neat mounds of unadulterated bacon, flour, and sugar, with a note inviting travelers to help themselves. But these good deeds stood out, Delano noted, as "occasional honorable exceptions."

The route followed the North Platte river valley west across present-day Nebraska, and the emigrants trudged on, already inclined to discount the cliffs and castles that had been a novelty only days before. The next milestone, to their delight, was not a natural wonder but a man-made refuge. This was Fort Laramie, in

what is today eastern Wyoming, a large, square, thick-walled adobe
structure of no particular distinction but, to the weary emigrants,
an oasis in the desert. The fort was not merely a landmark but a
place to purchase supplies (at inflated prices) or to drop off letters
(though the letters seemed simply to vanish, it turned out later,
rather than to make their way back east).

For the merchants in charge, a store on a stampede route in the
middle of nowhere, and without a single competitor for hundreds
of miles, was itself a gold mine. Eager entrepreneurs from Saint
Louis had finagled contracts to sell flour and lanterns and liquor
and tobacco and almost everything else. The emigrants made easy
marks. After "nothing but the huts of savages for more than 500
miles," in one gold-seeker's words, the fort made a welcome sight.
The weary travelers squawked at the prices and then, with no
choice, paid up.

"Oh, what a treat it does seem to see buildings again," wrote an
emigrant named Lucy Cooke. "My dear husband has just been
over to the store there to see if he could get anything to benefit me,
and bless him, he returned loaded with good things." When they
pushed on again, Lucy had a can of preserved quinces, some chocolate, "and a big packet of nice candy sticks."

Soon after, the road turned bad again. Israel Lord had been
admiring the scenery—"some of the hills look like a mine of Spanish brown, others rose pink, others salmon, chocolate, flesh color,
cream"—but his mood darkened as the route worsened. "The road
is up hill and down and down and up...and backing and whoaing
and stopping, and yelling and (I am sorry to say it) cursing, from
beginning to end."

There was no longer any grass, Lord noted, "but plenty of grass-
hoppers, and wild sage and crickets and horned toads." Blessedly,
though, there were no longer any mosquitoes. "The hum of their

departing wings sounded a welcome jubilee to us, Lord wrote. "They followed and stuck by us faithfully to the last, but even musquitoes seem to have some sense, and cannot stand everything. I reckon they knew too much to come up here."

The reference to mosquitoes sounds like commonplace grousing, but it was far more important than that. Short-tempered though he was, Lord was not one to fuss. For him and the other gold-seekers, mosquitoes were not just a nuisance but a scourge. They swarmed "thick as snowflakes," one emigrant wrote, and another reckoned them at "more than forty bushels to the acre, and of a very large breed."

Even gold rush diaries that skimmed by other miseries depicted mosquitoes as a special torment. "The mosquitoes swarm by the millions," wrote George Thissell, a carriage-maker from Ohio. "They were nearly as large as Italian bees, and their bills more than a half inch long; with these they bored right through our blankets. The cattle could not feed or rest, and the captain called out a double guard." Covered with bites that made them look as if they had measles, emigrants stumbled along under cheesecloth veils or smeared themselves with vinegar or oil or other concoctions in the hope it would serve as a repellent. Mostly they scratched and bled.

Israel Lord, for once, kept his temper. "They are very great pests," he noted simply, "and have caused me, at least, more trouble and suffering" than anything else on the trail. "Hunger, thirst, cholera, cold and heat may be endured or cured, musquitos never."

It was actually far worse than anyone in 1849 imagined, since no one then suspected any connection between mosquitoes and the diseases they carried. (Mosquitoes were not linked with yellow fever until 1881, nor with malaria until the 1890s.) Until the late 1800s, malaria in particular was all but universal throughout the middle band of the United States, all along the Mississippi River and its tributaries, from warm states like Louisiana to cold ones like Ohio and Illinois and Wisconsin.

Ague or "intermittent fever," as it was called, afflicted its victims with fevers, chills, and shivering fits. When he was a boy growing up in Missouri, Mark Twain would recall, everyone took bouts of sickness for granted. "Bear Creek...was a famous breeder of chills and fever in its day. I remember one summer when everybody in town had this disease at once. Many chimneys were shaken down, and all the houses were so racked that the town had to be rebuilt." When Alonzo Delano met another gold-seeker, the two men quickly established that they both had lived in Indiana. "What part?" Delano asked. "Oh, from down on the Wabash, where they have the ague so bad it shakes the feathers off all the chickens."

The jokes were a brave response to what was deemed an unavoidable reality. "Chills and fever were believed part of frontier life, like hard work," one historian observes. "Housewives learned to hurry through their work before sitting down to wait the daily attack; ministers scheduled their sermons for times when they would not have the shakes."

Gold rush diarists often skimmed by what was too commonplace to record, but Joseph Bruff, Israel Lord, Alonzo Delano, and nearly all their fellow emigrants wrestled with what Delano called "my old companions, chill and fever." The only escape *was* escape, and part of California's appeal, even in the years before anyone had heard of gold, was that it offered a refuge from disease.

In 1840, Missourians had gathered eagerly around a fur trapper named Antoine Robideaux, newly back from the West. "There was but one man in California who ever had a chill there," the trapper told his starry-eyed listeners, "and it was a matter of such wonderment that the people of Monterey went eighteen miles into the country to see him shake."

This alone was a prize worth a march across a continent. A land so blessed was almost as unimaginable as a land strewn with gold. When, later, it turned out that a single locale offered *both* health and wealth, Americans took it as tantamount to proof that they truly were God's favorites.

The notion that America had been chosen by God to carry out a special destiny was repeated endlessly in the 1840s, in every pulpit, lecture hall, and magazine. The United States was the most democratic of nations, the most egalitarian, the most open to talent and ambition, the fairest and freest, a light unto the world. The doctrine of manifest destiny—the term was coined in 1845 by a magazine editor named John O'Sullivan—spelled out the proud message. "For this blessed mission to the nations of the world, which are shut out from the life-giving light of truth," thundered O'Sullivan, "has America been chosen."

The discovery of gold mere days after Mexico had signed a treaty handing California to the United States only confirmed this bone-deep faith. In California, God had ordained an Eden of sunny days, gentle breezes, mild winters, rich soil, and, lately, treasure. All these gifts He had set aside for his special pets, the Americans. What else could explain the timing of the gold discovery?

From the beginning, that message of gold-rush-as-moral-fable spilled out from every venue. How was it, the Reverend Samuel Worcester demanded in a January 14, 1849, sermon at the Tabernacle Church in Salem, Massachusetts, that the Spanish, "so ferocious and bloodthirsty in their search and rage for gold," had never found California's gold? "It must certainly be that God had a purpose," and plainly that purpose was to preserve this treasure for the Americans. A decade later, Abraham Lincoln would frame the startling news from California in a similar way. The discovery of gold was not happenstance or good fortune but testimony to Americans' superior ways, proof that they possessed uncanny alertness and sharpness. "Why," Lincoln asked, in an 1859 speech on inventions and discoveries, "did Yankees, almost instantly, discover gold in California, which had been trodden upon, and over-looked by Indians and Mexican greasers, for centuries?"

That faith in America's special place imbued gold-seekers with a virtuous glow. (Yes, foreigners swarmed to the goldfields too, but their motives were no doubt low and merely mercenary.) Just as it was manifestly the destiny of the United States to expand from the Atlantic across the continent to the Pacific, so it was indisputably the destiny—almost the duty—of the bold and ambitious to better their station in life as quickly and dramatically as possible. To do otherwise was to reject a gift from God.

This emphasis on material success was new. In colonial America a self-made man had been a figure to admire, but "self-made" was not yet a synonym for "well-off." Early on, the term had more to do with a man's character than with his finances. A self-made man had succeeded in improving *himself*, by the exercise of piety, thrift, and discipline. He was "self-made" in almost a literal sense, as if he had sculpted the raw material of himself into a more attractive shape. If in time his social standing happened to rise as well, that was pleasant but not really the point.

In the nineteenth century, "self-made" took on new overtones. The self-made man remained the American ideal—the presidential election of 1840, the "Log Cabin Campaign," turned on the humble background of man-of-the-people William Henry Harrison—but now a "successful" man was a worldly success as well as a spiritual one.* Prosperity was a sign of virtue, because it served as proof of drive, vigor, and determination. To call an American "self-made" was to honor him; the sneer implicit in the French "nouveau riche" was entirely absent. In the land of opportunity, praise went to those who saw their chance and grabbed it.

And if prosperity was the goal, what better way to prosper than to head west to find gold? In California, Americans would do well for themselves and would, at the same time, bring the values of hard work, enlightened Protestantism, and modern ways to a land encumbered by sloth, benighted Catholicism, and rural backwardness. "The farm boy who embarked on the California adventure was more than a mere seeker after wealth," writes the gold rush chronicler Ray Billington. "He was a white knight riding forth in the service of humanity."

This was the era of "America's national adolescence," in the phrase of the historian David Kennedy, and America was no more appealing than most teenagers. Americans walked with a strut and shouted their virtues at every opportunity. ("In the States," one visiting Scotsman observed, "to blow your own horn, and to make as much noise as possible with it, is the most fundamental principle of all business.") As with adolescents, some of the bravado perhaps hinted at doubts beneath the surface—the Panic of 1837 was only a few years in the past, after all, and who was to say it could not return like a bad dream?—but few confessed to any such subversive thoughts.

So throughout the 1840s, the Fourth of July—a more important holiday than it is today and seldom an occasion for modesty or doubt in any era—was greeted with an extra dose of back-slapping

---

*Harrison was in fact the son of a prominent planter who had signed the Declaration of Independence and served as governor of Virginia, but never mind.

gusto. All the more so when celebrated by emigrants on their way to the goldfields. "Let us glory in the magnificence of our great inheritance," proclaimed a Fourth of July orator in 1849, aboard the California-bound bark *Sylph,* "as one star after another takes its place in our glorious Union, and one ocean after another enlarges the area of freedom, and one banner after another trails in the dust before our stripes and stars."

Overland travelers observed the Fourth with similarly rapturous speeches. Israel Lord celebrated Independence Day in the company of about one hundred other gold-seekers but characteristically gave short shrift to the bluster. He endured "any quantity of speeches, and sentiments, and firing of guns" and noted curtly that "one man had a thumb shot off."

For emigrants traversing the continent, the date had an additional significance. If they had reached a landmark called Independence Rock by the Fourth, in what is today southwest Wyoming, they were on pace to reach the far side of the continent before snow blocked the passes through the Sierra Nevada. Any later and they might share the Donners' fate.

Alonzo Delano arrived at the huge, smooth, granite hillock ahead of schedule, on June 22, Israel Lord a few weeks later, on July 13. Joseph Bruff, a man hard to rattle and impossible to hurry, would not arrive for another two weeks. On the Fourth of July, he was still in Nebraska, in the vicinity of Chimney Rock. He made a careful sketch of the towering formation, complete with a tiny figure on horseback at its base, for scale.

Even after weeks on the trail, Bruff found nearly everything of interest. He made careful drawings of "the singular and romantic bluffs" and took cheerful note of the cactus flowers, which came in

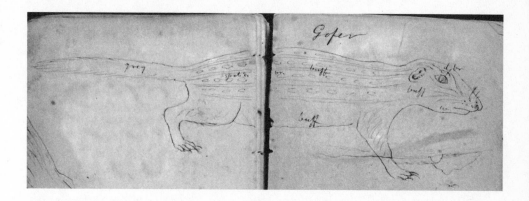

both red and white, and fields of poppies, in orange. On one occasion when he had wandered off on his own to explore, his men sent a messenger with a note imploring him to "hurry up."

Only days after they had scolded him for dawdling, Bruff paused once again. He had spotted a "small animal of the Lemur genus with cheek pouches filled with grass-seed." Surely this curious creature—Bruff learned that it was called a "gofer"—deserved to be recorded. Bruff made a color-coded drawing.

Weightier events made for longer delays. On July 8, Bruff's company lost its first man to cholera. The death was "sudden and astounding," Bruff wrote glumly, and he organized a formal funeral. A sentimental man despite his military bearing, Bruff composed a long poem in honor of his fallen companion. *"The adventurer's train, / On the Platte river plain / Was halted at an early hour; / For a comrade was ill, / Whom no medical skill / Could save from a Higher power!"* the opus began, and it concluded, many verses later, *"And a tear did trace / Each sun-burnt face."*

The dead man was sewn into a blue blanket and carried on a bier of tent poles to a newly dug grave hundreds of yards off the trail. Bruff spent three hours carving a headstone and filling in the engraved letters in black (with grease normally used to keep the wagon wheels lubricated). The company donned their uniforms and marched to the graveside two by two, to the accompaniment of a dirge played by bugle, flute, violin, and accordion. A prayer was read aloud, the Stars and Stripes placed atop the body, and a contingent of men, holding reins as coffin straps, lowered their companion into a rock-lined grave.

On March 13, 1849, Jennie Megquier wrote her daughter a letter from Chagres, the port town in Panama where her steamship had just docked. "It is the most beautiful spot I ever saw. The shores are covered with a thick growth of trees and in front of us rises one of those old castles that we read of."

Her enthusiasm was genuine, not put on to lift her daughter's spirits. Thrilled with her first peek at life in the tropics, Megquier reveled at the unfamiliar sights. Here were marvels that one saw only in drawings—palm trees, coconuts, huts covered in palm leaves. The next day, when she and her companions began their journey upriver into the jungle, Megquier grew even more excited. "The air was filled with the music of the birds, the chattering of the monkeys, parrots in any quantity, alligators lying on the banks too lazy to move unless you went very near them." It was, she exclaimed, "the most romantic scene I ever beheld."

Few visitors to Panama shared her enthusiasm. Horrified from the moment they stepped ashore, even experienced travelers shuddered as they looked around them. Panama was muddy, dangerous, and disease-ridden, not a tropical garden but a festering swamp. "Probably there was not in all the world a more loathsome spot," wrote Hubert Bancroft, who passed through Panama on his way to California in 1852. The "most beautiful spot" that Megquier had ever seen was, in the historian's view, "a bed of slime and decaying vegetation reeking pestilence, alive with crawling reptiles, given over of nature to the vilest of her creations."

In prose as overripe as the jungle itself, Bancroft catalogued Panama's defects. "The very ground on which one trod was pregnant with disease, and death was distilled in every breath of air." In the swamplike humidity, furniture sprouted mold and fell apart before your eyes, and iron rusted overnight. Panama might boast "the finest vultures on the planet," Bancroft observed, but it could claim no other superlative.

The writer Frank Marryat, also bound for California's goldfields, was another who failed to see the beauty that Megquier detected in Chagres. "It is composed of about fifty huts, each of which raises its head from the midst of its own private malaria, occasioned by the heaps of filth and offal, which putrefying under the rays of a vertical sun, choke up the very doorway."

Marryat's condemnation of Chagres differed from Bancroft's in only one particular. The town *did* boast a distinction besides vultures. Just as some villages were famous for hats or baskets, and every visitor left with a souvenir, so all visitors to Chagres carried away a memento of their visit. In the case of Chagres, the local, not-to-be-missed specialty was tropical fever, and many travelers on their way to California "acknowledged the superiority of this malady by giving up the ghost a very few hours after landing."

The journey across Panama was a two-stage affair, about sixty miles in all, starting with a forty-mile excursion up the Chagres River to a village called Gorgona. From the moment they landed in Chagres, travelers clamored to get away, not so much because of the squalor as because of their eagerness to get rich before all of

California's gold was gone. With every day's delay, there would be less treasure left to find and more men hunting for it. When newly rich, homeward-bound travelers paraded through Chagres displaying their wealth, the tension spiked to almost unbearable levels. "A returning Californian had just reached the place," wrote a journalist covering the gold rush for the *New York Tribune,* "with a box containing $22,000 in gold-dust, and a four-pound lump in one hand." The town lost its mind. "Life and death were small matters compared with immediate departure from Chagres," the *Tribune* reported. "Men ran up and down the beach shouting and gesticulating."

The only way out was by dugout canoe up the river. But the boatmen who poled the canoes knew that new steamers crammed with frantic passengers arrived every day. They took their time and raised their fees. (In the early days boatmen charged $10 a passenger. Within months the rate had climbed as high as $50.)

On March 20, 1849, Jennie and Thomas Megquier and a companion set out upriver perched atop their luggage in the middle of a hand-hewn canoe, barely above the rushing water. The canoe was two feet wide and twenty feet long, propelled by one man in the bow and one in the stern. Each boatman wielded a long pole, thrusting it against the shallow river bottom and then pushing off, every muscle tensed, like a pole-vaulter working in slow motion. The boatmen were "naked or [wearing] nothing but a bit of cloth about their loins," Jennie wrote, "the perspiration pouring off them in torrents." (The nonchalant tone is noteworthy. Nakedness was a charged topic in the mid-1800s; faced with the boatmen of the Chagres, even so rough a character as the future general Ulysses Grant resorted to joking euphemism. The men, Grant wrote, were "not inconveniently burdened with clothing.")

At night, in camp, Megquier scribbled her observations in an unpunctuated ecstasy. "Would to God I could describe the scene. The birds singing monkeys screeching the Americans laughing and joking as they pushed us along through the rapids was enough to drive one mad with delight."

The stopovers, in villages of a few huts, were not luxurious. Chairs and tables were not to be seen, nor forks or spoons. Megquier reveled in it all. "To eat soup with a jackknife is no small job," she observed happily. Pigs, hens, dogs, cats, and ducks all clustered round the diners, hoping for scraps. Megquier, who prided herself on gulping down whatever was put before her, managed nearly everything except "stewed Monkeys and Iguanoes." She might try them eventually, she wrote a friend back in Maine, but her "appetite has not been quite sharp enough to relish those yet."

Come dark, someone found the Megquiers a bed (rather than the standard hammock), but sleep was next to impossible. Villagers streamed in throughout the night, eager to clap eyes on their strange guests. Jennie, a bit of a ham even at four in the morning, reveled in the attention. "They would come and look at me as one of the greatest curiosities in the world," she boasted to her daughter.

Many travelers bound for the goldfields confronted similar conditions, though rarely with such equanimity. A gold-seeker named Mary Ballou, who would later prove feisty enough to run a boardinghouse in a rowdy mining camp in the diggings, found herself nearly undone by Panama. At a stopover much like the Megquiers', she tried to sleep, but "the monkies were howling, the Nighthawks were singing, the Natives were watching." Exhausted and miserable, "I laid myself down on the ground a weeping," Ballou wrote, "and I thought if I had wings how swiftly I would fly to my Home."

Bold, swashbuckling men fared no better. Heinrich Schliemann, who would later win fame as the archeologist who discovered

the site of ancient Troy, made his way across Panama to California's goldfields in 1851. The very image of the archeologist-as-
adventurer—he was one of the real-life models for Indiana
Jones—Schliemann blanched where Jennie Megquier exulted. His
woes began with his first glimpse of Panama. "Among all the miserable places I have met with, and it happened to me to see many in
different parts of the world," he wrote, "I must give the palm to
Chagres."

This terrible spot was "the most horrible imaginable," and even a
brief stay was a torment scarcely to be endured. In Chagres,
Schliemann wrote, "our sufferings increased every moment."
Drenching rain poured down endlessly, mosquitoes descended in
swarms, and meals consisted of nothing but "the raw meat of
lizards, monkeys, turtles, mules, and crocodiles." At these dismal
meals, the only consolation was that portions were ample, because
the wild creatures in Panama grew to Jurassic proportions. "The
lizards called here 'Iguanas' exceed the ordinary size of the alligators and crocodiles," Schliemann informed his readers, "and I have
seen the former to the length of 40 feet."

Premature death was the all-but-universal fate of visitors to Chagres, Schliemann went on, and the only question was just what
form it would take. "Many of my fellow-passengers were killed by
the bite of scorpions and snakes (particularly rattlesnakes) which
abound in these regions." Schliemann soon grew inured to such
grim scenes. "In this horrible situation all human feeling forsook us
and we sunk below the beast. We became so familiarized with
death that it lost for us all its terror. . . . Thus it came that we laughed
and amused ourselves at the convulsions of the dying and that
crimes were perpetrated among us; crimes so terrible! that now at a
later date I cannot think of it without cold and trembling horror."

Once out of Chagres and headed toward Gorgona, matters

improved ever so slightly. But even here the "poisonous climate" left Schliemann as weak and miserable as if he were "lying in a Russian steambath." Temperatures during the day soared to 110 degrees, and at night grunting pigs and restless children made too much noise for him to sleep. So humble a pleasure as a cool glass of water was unattainable. "The water is as warm as the air," Schliemann wrote, and full of insects besides.

In passage after passage Schliemann's narrative takes on the tone of a Gothic thriller. Though no travelers in Panama would dare venture out without pistol and dagger, he tells us, they are at risk even so. What, he wondered, was that horrible, rotting smell that is all-pervasive in Panama? Could it be the stink of a dead mule, fallen on the trail, or a giant lizard lying mangled in the jungle? Perhaps, "but alas, [the stench came] much more frequently from the decomposition of travellers murdered on the road by the hand of the natives."

One of the locals' favorite tricks was to capsize their boats on purpose, Schliemann warned; the unprepared passengers would drown, and the crew would help themselves to their belongings. "Often," he continued glumly, "when they are unsuccessful in their attempts to drown their passengers, they stab or shoot them to death and throw them over the banks of the river in the thicket, where the corpses are consumed by insects and by buzzards, which can be seen in myriads on the way from Chagres here."

Nothing with any resemblance to Schliemann's overheated night-mares turns up in Jennie Megquier's journal. Panama was not quite heaven on the half shell, but Megquier found it a grand adventure. The view upriver was "the most delightful in the world," with "most splendid trees" all the way to the water's edge in every shade of green, and beautiful flowers in bright red and "the most brilliant hues that could be imagined." Murdered travelers indeed!

Gorgona, the town that marked the end of the river leg of the cross-Panama route, was "a scene for a painter." Here, too, Megquier basked in the spotlight. "I had a great number of callers. The natives would come and stand in the door and look at me with perfect astonishment." She toured the town, which consisted of little more than a few huts (for the locals) and some shabby hotels (for the out-siders). Gorgona did boast a church, though it was so run-down that animals wandered inside during the hymns and prayers. "A mule took the liberty to depart this life within its walls while we were there," Megquier noted, "which was looked upon by the natives as of no consequence."

The last leg of the trip, from Gorgona to Panama City, was a journey of some twenty miles overland. Travelers proceeded on muleback on a narrow trail that wound across the mountains, with "just room for the beast to put his feet," Megquier wrote, "which if he should make a mistep, we should be tumbled down in a lagoon an hundred feet deep."*

Megquier reached Panama City unharmed except for a head-ache from the bright sun. The city was not much to look at — "there are a great number of churches each having quite a number of bells which they contrive to keep someone thumping most of the time" — and Jennie and Thomas found a hotel. The walls were rid-dled with holes, but Jennie had grown hard to faze. "Cats, dogs, and rats trooped through our room every night," she wrote to her daughter, "but they take a bee line from one hole to another not stopping to make our acquaintance."

For Heinrich Schliemann, Panama was hell incarnate, an infer-

---

*Schliemann took the same route, but he focused more on the human threat than on the danger of a fall. Here, away from the river, outsiders had to fear not drowning but mugging. "On the way from Gorgona to Panama they equally shoot or stab them, and throw them down in the abyss, where never a living human being has put his foot."

nal region where "hundreds of us were attacked by the isthmus-fever, diarrhoea, dissentry & ague and died after a day or two of cruel suffering." Jennie found it all a thrill. "I presume you will hear a great many stories" about the horrors of Panama, she warned her daughter, but pay no attention. "We have not suffered for any thing," Jennie wrote, "and if we were rich, I should not grudge the expense at all, if we did not make one cent, to see what we have seen and heard."

On the Pacific coast at last, Jennie and Thomas Megquier waited for a ship to carry them to California and riches. Along with two thousand others from around the world, they spent their days gazing anxiously out to sea. Most days passed with nothing but false sightings and dashed hopes, and in the meantime, Chagres and Gorgona spilled out, every day, a new batch of dirty, exhausted gold-seekers. At rare intervals a ship did arrive, and a thousand emigrants fought for a hundred spots. Some waved tickets they had purchased in New York or New Orleans. Others, who had anticipated ships in abundance, tried to fight their way aboard. Most failed.

"The town was overrun," Jennie wrote, its beaches converted to shantytowns, its few hotels crammed with angry, restless men with little to do but quarrel and exchange rumors. Where was the *California*? When was the *Oregon* due? Who was sick with yellow fever? Who had died of cholera? "Every nook and corner is filled," Jennie wrote, "and many of them I think would not be recognized by their friends." Grubby and unshaven, in filthy shirts and muddy pants, the wretched men who spent their days forlornly staring at the empty ocean "looked less like civilization than the natives."

Hope both tortured and seduced the stranded travelers. When

ships from California came in, the gold-seekers peppered the returning adventurers with questions. "The news from the gold fields far exceeds our expectations," Megquier wrote, in an agony of expectation. "Every man that goes to the mines picks up a fortune." Cabin boys had grown rich, Megquier marveled, and she herself had held "a lump of pure gold, weighing two pounds, in my hand, just as it was dug."

Megquier did not envision herself swinging a pick, but she might cook or nurse the sick or run a boardinghouse. Who could tell? "Without joking," Megquier assured her daughter on May 12, 1849, "gold is very plenty." There was no need to worry. "In about one year, you will see your Mother come trudging home with an apron full."

CHAPTER EIGHT

A ROPE OF SAND

OR SHIPBOARD TRAVELERS LIKE the Megquiers, the frustration was that treasure sat waiting for them, if only they could get under way. For overland travelers, the end of the trail had come to seem elusive and fanciful. Months before, they had set off at a sprint, eager and carefree. Now it took all the energy and will-power they could muster to picture the golden reward at the end of their wandering.

Even the strongest spirits reeled under the strain of "our incessant journeying," as Alonzo Delano put it. They had come a long way, but that was little consolation. All they had achieved, the emigrants realized with sinking hearts, was to put themselves in limbo, with the finish line still nowhere in sight but home now so far behind that to turn around would be pointless.

"Day after day, week after week," Luzena Wilson recalled, "we went through the same weary routine of breaking camp at daybreak, yoking the oxen, cooking our meagre rations over a fire of sage-brush and scrub-oak; packing up again, coffee-pot and camp kettle; washing our scanty wardrobe in the little streams we crossed; striking camp again at sunset, or later if wood and water were scarce. Tired, dusty, tried in temper, worn out in patience, we had to go over the weary experience tomorrow." Sisyphus in a bonnet.

Wilson's lot was even harder than she made out, because women on the trail had it worse than men. The year 1848 marked the first women's rights convention, in Seneca Falls, New York, but American culture as a whole scarcely took notice of such odd gatherings.* The natural order was plain. "Home is the palace of the husband and the father," one 1852 book of inspirational essays decreed, spelling out the all-but-universal view. "He is the monarch of that little empire, wearing a crown that is the gift of Heaven, swaying a scepter put into his hands by the father of all, acknowledging no superior, fearing no rival, and dreading no usurper."

A cramped and lurching wagon on the Great Plains was no palace, but the rules from home held on the road, too. "The Victorian structure of domestic power was carried westward along with bedsteads and porcelain teacups," the trail historian Elliot West observed, and the division of labor was strict. Men took charge of driving the animals by day and guarding them by night. Women's province was "home" or what passed for home, and all the tasks that came with it.

In life as in the adage, that work was never done. Making matters worse, women on the trail seldom had anyone to commiserate with. ("My health at present is rather feeble & I find it difficult to keep up a usual amount of cheerfulness," one Oregon-bound mis-

---

*The few responses to the convention fell on a spectrum that ran from mockery to outrage. Philadelphia's *Public Ledger and Daily Transcript* declared, for example, "A woman is nobody. A wife is everything. The ladies of Philadelphia...are resolved to maintain their rights as Wives, Belles, Virgins and Mothers."

sionary's wife wrote in her diary in 1838. "If I were to yield to inclination, I should cry half the time without knowing what for.")*

Rarely but memorably, a put-upon woman would protest. In 1847, after laboring hundreds of miles across the plains, one exhausted emigrant declared that she'd had enough. The trip was folly, she told her husband. They would never reach the Pacific; they should return home; she would not proceed another step. When he refused to listen, she set their wagon on fire.

Good-natured Alonzo Delano was not one to challenge society's rules, but it dawned on him eventually that either he would do his own household chores or no one would. After several weeks on the trail, he and a few companions tried washing their own shirts "for the first time in our lives." They struggled for an hour or two, bent over their scrub-boards. By the time they gave up, their backs were sore, their hands red, and their clothes as grimy as ever. "We thought of our wives and sweethearts at home... [and resolved that] we should heartily have asked their pardon."

Onward they marched. Bone-tired and no longer quite so sure they had been wise to throw away their old lives, men squabbled and companies broke apart. Men who had left home swearing vows of lifelong friendship now stood toe to toe screaming over whose turn it was to collect buffalo dung for the fire or to fetch water for coffee. Fights started with insults and shoves and quickly escalated. Alonzo Delano gaped with horror at a "cruel and fiendish murder"

---

*Mary Walker was no softie. Her diary entry from March 16, 1842, read: "Rose about five o'clock, had an early breakfast, got my housework done up about 9. Baked six more loaves of bread. Made a kettle of mush & have now a suet pudding and some beef boiling.... Nine o'clock P.M. was delivered of a son."

fought over a bar of soap. (The victim had been building a fire, to cook dinner. A man named Brown asked the cook to fetch him a bar of soap. *Get it yourself; I'm busy.* Without another word, Brown plunged his knife into the cook's back and fled. A search party set out in a fury but came back stymied; presumably Brown had melted into another wagon train.)

Murder was rare, but fights and threats were an everyday affair. "The Devil seems to take full possession of three-fourths of all that come on to the 'route,'" Israel Lord complained. Lord, who spewed adjectives like confetti at a parade, detailed his companions' shortcomings. They were "cross, peevish, sullen, boisterous, giddy, profane, dirty, vulgar, ragged, mustachioed, bewhiskered, idle, petulant, quarrelsome, unfaithful, disobedient, refractory, careless, contrary, stubborn, hungry, and without the fear of God and hardly of man before their eyes."

Two days after his diatribe, Lord watched one man flail at another with a knife. When he missed, both men grabbed their rifles. "It all ended as it began, in nothing," Lord noted wearily. "This quarreling is almost universal."

On those occasions when it did end in something, the emigrants improvised a response. With no laws in place and no sheriffs or judges or other authorities on hand, justice was slapdash and often brutal. The men in one wagon train saw that a member of their group was hurrying off alone. Where was the companion he had been traveling with? After a short hunt, they found the missing man shot to death, partly hidden under a few shovelfuls of dirt. A search party chased down the escapee. The trial took almost no time: Charge—murder. Verdict—guilty. Sentence—death.

A more troubling problem on the treeless plains was finding a gallows. The solution, which was the only time-consuming aspect of the whole affair, was to bring three wagons together, raise the tongues into a tripod, and attach a noose. One eyewitness described the story's final scene. The condemned man was forced atop a horse, someone jabbed a knife into the horse's rump, and "the wretch was swung into eternity."

Company after company fell apart, one emigrant noted sadly, like "a rope of sand." Joseph Bruff had vowed from the start that *his* men would not split up, no matter the obstacles in their way. Charismatic and capable, Bruff was a natural leader, but the Washington City and California Mining Association did not share his belief that they were enlisted men and he was their commander.

On the night of July 9, 1849, one Washington City man punched another in the face. Bruff raced into action. "I immediately convened the Company into a drum-head court, tried the offender, broke him of his office, and inflicted 4 extra-guards on him."

In Bruff's mind, a sentence of four extra rounds of guard duty was a fitting punishment. The men went along this time, but they had already begun to mutter and snarl. Only two weeks later, on July 24, Bruff noted "great dissension in the company....All the bad traits of the men are now well-developed. Their true character is shown untrammeled, unvarnished. Selfishness, hypocricy, &c. Some, whom at home were thought gentlemen, are now totally unprincipled." And home was far, far away.

So was California. For weeks the weary travelers had looked forward to reaching South Pass, in the Rockies in present-day Wyoming, which marked the halfway point in their long journey. Many of the emigrants had pictured the spot as an impossible-to-miss feature of the landscape. Crossing the Continental Divide, they had imagined, would be roughly akin to clambering up one side of a steep roof and starting down the other.

It proved far less dramatic. "No one would ever suspect this to be the summit," one emigrant wrote, "the country is so level, and the aspect of the whole distance is so gradual." But better a smooth rise than a vicious crest. An easy passage through formidable mountains—South Pass sits 7,550 feet above sea level—was a welcome and unlikely gift, and western boosters cited it as yet more evidence that God meant for Americans to move west across the continent. (John C. Frémont had told an eager audience in Congress a few years before that the climb across the Rockies was no more strenuous than the "ascent of the Capitol hill.")

Joseph Bruff had been sick and grumpy for a few days—"some of my men seem to be perfectly stupid and childish, and it is with difficulty I can make them attend to certain duties for their own welfare"—but he cheered up a bit at this milestone. On August 1 his company took its midday break at South Pass and hung a flag in the breeze, to honor "this elevated and noble back-bone of Uncle Sam's."

Alonzo Delano found himself more inclined to mope than celebrate. South Pass marked not only a division in the landscape but a division in his life. "In a musing mood," he wrote, "I climbed a high hill to take a parting look at the Atlantic waters, which flowed towards all I held most dear on earth....As I turned my eye eastward, home, wife, and children rushed to my mind with uncontrolled feelings, and in the full yearnings of my heart, I involuntarily stretched out my arms as if I would clasp them to my bosom."

No embrace came in response. "In its place," Delano continued, "there lay extended before me barren reaches of table land," and bare hills, and desert plains, and long trains of covered wagons creeping across the empty landscape.

The emigrants funneled through South Pass in enormous numbers. "The road, from morning til night, is crowded like Pearl Street or Broadway," one man wrote, in amazement, and the swarm of travelers briefly turned the vast Wyoming emptiness into a sprawling city. By now they had traveled a thousand miles, with another thousand to go.

One imperative took precedence over all the others—as they moved west, the gold-seekers had to stay close to water. So far nature had cooperated with that scheme. No longer. From here on, all the way to the goldfields, rivers tended to run north–south rather than east–west. For the emigrants, that meant that the days of following smooth, grassy river valleys had ended. Now they would be crawling across deserts or scrambling up and down a seemingly endless series of sharp-sided canyons and ravines, staggering their way from one unsatisfactory river to the next.

The main goal, five hundred miles ahead, was the Humboldt River, which meandered some 350 miles across the Nevada desert. The Humboldt was a sluggish, narrow, soapy stream, more a vile canal than a proper river but essential nonetheless. It would carry them to the final obstacle, the Sierra Nevada. If they made it as far as the Humboldt, the emigrants knew from their guidebooks, they would cling to it and curse it with equal fervor.

Until a decade or two before the gold rush, maps of the West had depicted a mighty river called the Buenaventura that ran all the way from the Rockies to the Pacific Ocean. As renowned an authority on the West as Frémont fully believed in its existence. In the winter of 1843–44 the Pathfinder set out to map this westward-flowing river. Confident at first, then bewildered, then horrified, he finally gave up his search in January, 1844.*

No Buenaventura meant that there was no highway west, no river like the Platte for the emigrants to follow. As they'd headed toward the Rockies, nearly all the gold-seekers had followed essentially the same route. From here on, they would divide up, some opting for supposed shortcuts and others sticking with familiar routes, before coming back together again in Nevada.

By 1849 guidebooks had at least deleted fictional rivers from their maps. But the result was a landscape dotted with blank spaces and dubious shortcuts. The gold-seekers took on the gaps with hope and guesswork, and some who guessed wrong paid with their lives.

First came a sprawling, featureless wasteland called the Green River Basin, in Wyoming. Israel Lord found himself unable to muster the strength for a full-fledged denunciation of the landscape. "The whole country is one vast sand bed," he noted dismissively, "poorly covered with sage and bunch grass." But it had to be crossed. Worse still, the trek featured a forty-five-mile stretch of desert. There would be no water for humans or animals, except what they could carry, until they reached the Green River. The journey was best made at night, when it was comparatively cool. Alonzo Delano's company started at four in the afternoon, hoping they could reach the Green in a single, twenty-four-hour marathon.

Night fell and they plodded ahead in the darkness, through the sand and gravel, everyone on foot to spare the cattle. Dozens of dead oxen marked the trail. As the night wore on, conversation

---

*He had planned to spend the winter nestled along the river's banks, safe and sheltered, but instead Frémont and his men ended up nearly out of supplies, desperately fighting their way across the Sierra Nevada through snow so deep it swallowed up the horses.

died away. Occasionally someone cursed, but after a time there were no human sounds at all, and finally no noises of any sort, hour upon hour, except the creaking of wheels and the howling of wolves.

By daybreak, Delano's company had made it halfway. They stopped to give the animals water and then took to the road again. At the start Delano had tried to fill a rubber bag with water for himself, but it had burst when he poured in one last bucket. He did without. The dust was ankle-deep. A gale began to blow. The men shuffled along like convicts in chains and tried to wipe their eyes and nostrils clean. "Our faces, hair, and clothes looked as if we had been rolling in a heap of dry ashes."

The date was July 2, 1849. Delano noted later that it was his forty-third birthday, "the hardest one of all my life." He had walked fifty-five miles in a day, without sleeping, and he had made it to the Green River.

Green River was a milestone, but hardly one to make the heart soar. After an all-night march of his own, Israel Lord did his best to dismiss the whole trek with a brief, bitter joke. "All is dry, dry, dry. Let those who are troubled with water in their cellars move their houses up here." Such restraint in the face of genuine hardship was typical of Lord, whose fury was stirred only by trifles. The sight of an unshaven jaw or a garish shirt could move him to red-faced outrage; a desert crossing inspired only quiet fortitude.

Generally, though, when the gold-seekers looked around at Green River they felt more inclined to slump in despair than to grit their teeth and carry on. "This whole region is a miserable, dreary waste," wrote John Banks, a member of Ohio's Buckeye Rover company. "You seldom see a bird and he can scarcely warble for sadness."

But even here, the rush showed its variety. Few of the gold-seekers felt much like warbling, but some in the giant crowds did find an entrancing picture where most saw only an empty frame. "Our road led in sight of the snow mantled peaks of the Rocky Mountains," wrote Eleazer Ingalls, and as he trudged through the desert night he marveled at how the moonlight transformed the snow and ice into "mountains of molten silver."

A lawyer with a lyrical streak, Ingalls delighted in the stone-clad vistas. "Green River presents the most romantic scenery in the world; it is deep set in the midst of bluffs that take the shapes of towers, castles, cities, and of every imaginable work of art." From the bluffs, the river "looks like a silver thread winding through a green landscape.... It would be a paradise for a landscape painter."

Joseph Bruff, too, found that the rushing river seen from above "appeared like a curved silver thread." Then he turned his gaze to the "perilous descent" the wagons would have to take down the steep bluffs, and that put an end to the poetry. On both sides of the trail down to the river, the way was lined with "fragments of disasters in the shape of upset wagons, wheels, axles." Earlier that morning, the path had been so steep that the mules had sat on their haunches and inched their way downhill. Now Bruff's men had come to an even sharper drop, one-third of a mile long, over sand, loose stones, and chunks of slate. Slowly they descended—*very* slowly.

All safe at the water's edge, finally, with no one hurt and no runaway wagons to join the roadside junkyard. "One of the hardest tramps I ever took," Bruff wrote, "and extremely hard on the mules."

Now came an unexpected break. The Bear River Valley, in what is today Idaho's southeast corner, charmed even Israel Lord. The river wandered through the mountains "until it opens into the most romantic and beautiful valley we have yet passed, or that I ever saw," wrote Lord, who tended to find more solace in landscape than in his fellow human beings. The valley was perhaps sixty miles long and twenty across, Lord reckoned, and "covered with timber" and "dotted with patches of snow." A large lake gleamed a dark blue so enticing that for a moment Lord let down his guard.

In roughly the same area, Alonzo Delano gazed about in delight, briefly disoriented by the first grove of trees he had seen since crossing the Missouri. "For more than two months we had been traveling, exposed to the fervid heat of the sun or the cold and stormy blasts along the Platte, without a leaf to offer protection." But now they had come to "deep green foliage" and shade and quiet and birds. These familiar sights offered a bittersweet solace, a short-lived diversion from the endless labor of walking mile upon mile, day upon day. Delano dissolved into a fit of homesickness, consumed with memories of the "happy and favored land" he had left behind.

Such wistfulness was only one strand in a complex braid of emotions. Delano and all those who had thrown away their old lives yearned for home, but at the same time they took pride in knowing that they had left home far behind, in every sense. They had seen sights—mountain panoramas, especially—that surpassed anything that anyone back east had ever seen. "When we commenced the journey, trifling hills were considered great obstacles," wrote Eleazer Ingalls, "but now we lock our hind wheels and slide down a thousand feet, over rocks and through gullies, with as much sang froid as a school boy would slide down a snowbank."

But all such boasting came with a queasy undernote. Pride and trepidation rubbed uneasily together. "You may think you have seen mountains and gone over them," one gold-seeker wrote to his family back in Missouri, from Idaho, "but you never saw anything but a small hill compared to what I have crossed over, and it is said the worst is yet to come." In the next sentence, he reminded himself (and his family) not to lose heart: "But never mind. Gold lies ahead."

Throughout his journey west, the indomitable Joseph Bruff had kept up with his sketches, his notebooks, and his counting and collecting and recording. (Even during the gruesome, waterless, all-night desert crossing to the Green River, he had paused, when it was still light enough to see, to gather fossils.) Almost regardless of his company's plight, Bruff found something to engage his curiosity or distract his mind. He might take note of dire news in one sentence—"Men & oxen suffering much from dust, heat, and sandy trail"—and, in the next, bounce cheerily to a description of his newfound fossils.

At one campsite, Bruff was delighted to discover "innumerable large black mice," all of them temptingly "fat and very soft & silky." He roasted one and "found it very tender and sweet." Two days later he found an abandoned wagon and near it, on the ground, a small piece of apple pie. *Delicious!* Near Soda Springs, Idaho, the "character of the country very interesting and picturesque to me." Water sprayed into the air in natural fountains and "only needed lemon syrup to render it perfect soda water."

If no other distractions presented themselves, Bruff could always revive his spirits by communing with whatever dog the company had recently adopted. A large yellow mutt named Bull was the latest favorite. Bull's routine was to beg his breakfast in the morning and then, when the men began the tedious process of hitching up the mules, to start ahead on his own. He would find a shady spot, doze off, and then amble on again when the train drew near. Bruff came to look to Bull for help in choosing a spot for the company's midday rest. "Bull would come up and whining look towards a stream, and bark at the train," Bruff noted proudly, "as much as to say, 'Halt here, it is time.'"

But few emigrants could match Bruff's stamina. Many of the gold-seekers now passed over their sufferings in a few exhausted words. Alonzo Delano sagged almost visibly. "Weary, weary, weary," he wrote on July 17, not far from Soda Springs. The next day, "with nothing in the view to cheer the traveler," he sunk even lower, his disappointment all the keener "after having passed through the fine valley of Bear River." They had reached Fort Hall, a trading post run by the Hudson's Bay Company and, in the glory years of the fur trade, an always-bustling bazaar. Now the fort saw more emigrants than trappers, but Delano came up empty—earlier arrivals had cleared the shelves.

He settled for information instead. *How much farther?* Seven hundred miles, his informants at Fort Hall told him. This made sense, but it was disheartening news even so. The landscape, which only weeks before had startled the emigrants with its new forms, had lost its power to distract and console. "Through burning sand, and in dense clouds of dust, we pursued our way," Delano wrote, "with the scenery of the plain but little varied."

They met other travelers who were worse off still. "We began to see many traveling on foot, begging their way—having broken down their animals and having no way forward but to walk." Those few in Delano's company who had anything to spare offered up meager handouts. Eight days later Delano met an especially sorry wanderer, whose story was biblical in its torments. His oxen had died, and he had bought a horse. His horse had died, and now he was on foot, alone, limping his way along, his only possession a bag of flour tied around his neck.

The gold-seekers dragged themselves past the towering, mysterious stone monoliths of what is now City of Rocks National Reserve, Idaho, and across the blisteringly hot and misleadingly named Thousand Springs Valley, where the few springs were boiling hot or icy cold.

Ahead lay Nevada and Nevada's own River Styx, the Humboldt.

———————

Jennie and Thomas Megquier sat in Panama City, stranded, waiting for a ship. "Here we are yet in this miserable old town with about 2,000 Americans all anxiously waiting for a passage to the gold regions," Jennie wrote her daughter on May 12, 1849. Occasionally a ship did turn up and take away a few fortunate passengers, but the flood of new arrivals more than made up for them. The Megquiers had tickets for the steamer *California*, which seemed to have vanished.

Two weeks before, a whaler had turned up, lured by rumors of crowds of desperate passengers willing to pay virtually any price to reach San Francisco. (The captain had unloaded his oil in Peru and sped to Panama.) The Megquiers decided to sell their tickets for the *California* and take their chances on the whaler, but its departure was delayed, and then someone spotted the *California* on the horizon. The Megquiers changed plans again. The steamship drew near. Wrong ship. The Megquiers waited.

As they sat fretting, the steamer *Oregon* arrived from San Francisco. Homeward-bound argonauts spilled ashore, and the waiting crowds pummeled them with questions about life in the diggings. Jennie passed along the "great news" to her daughter in a breathless word geyser worthy of Molly Bloom. "The passengers that come in here are all loaded with gold, but they have to endure many hardships, and it is almost impossible to get a shelter for your head, but womens help is so very scarce that I am in hopes to get a chance by hook or crook to pay my way, but some women that have gone there are coming home because they can get no servants to wait on them, but a woman that can work will make more money than a man."

In the meantime, with the *California* lost, the Megquiers did their best to distract themselves with sightseeing. Jennie, a glutton for all things new, finally spotted her whales, and schools of porpoises, too. She and Thomas and some companions visited an island nine miles off the coast, Jennie exulting at the sight of unfamiliar trees, lush flowers, and pelicans "in flocks so large they look like a cloud, when rising from the ground." Everyone slept on the floor or in hammocks, with lizards scurrying by "in every direction."

From the moment she left Maine behind, Jennie had wallowed in new experiences; the unknown was not a threat but a glorious opportunity. In her letters home, she gleefully passed along offhand descriptions of sights that she knew would induce squeals and shivers. "We killed two scorpions in our sleeping room," she wrote. "The Doctor was stung by one." *Not a crisis.* "Another insect which is rather troublesome, gets into your feet and lays its eggs. The Dr. and I have them in our toes—did not find it out until they had deposited their eggs in large quantities; the natives dug them out and put on the ashes of tobacco—nothing unpleasant in it, only the idea of having jiggers in your toes."

At a picnic one day, in the shade of a mango tree, someone spotted an enormous snake climbing on a branch just overhead. "One of the party shot him," Jennie wrote. "He measured nine feet, about as large as my arm a little above the wrist." Later in the day, a second giant snake slunk down a nearby tree. It, too, was killed. "The gentlemen took them to the village," Jennie teased, "to show what big things they had done."

Megquier liked to confound expectations, but her toughness was real. While traveling, especially, she shrugged off hardships with proud disdain. (One hotel room had "scarce light enough to see the rats and spiders," she noted offhandedly, and grim meals with "bristles on the pork and weavels in the rice" did not faze her. "My stomach is not lined with pink satin," she boasted.) In an age when men ruled and women curtsied, the New England lady in the long dress had more strength and spark than nearly all the gun-toting adventurers she would meet on her way.

When the Megquiers returned from their stint fending off snakes and scorpions, they found that the crowd waiting with them for passage to the goldfields had grown even larger. Where was the *California*? The Megquiers would have wept at the answer. The *California had* sailed from New York in October, 1848, bound for San Francisco. The plan called for the ship to ply a Pacific circuit, back and forth on a monthly Panama City–San Francisco–Oregon route. But that scheme had fallen apart.

When the *California* had first set out to sea, no one in the East believed that California's gold was real. The two-hundred-foot paddle wheeler left New York carrying a grand total of six passengers. Even those six had no interest in California; each planned to depart at an intermediate stop along the way. Then, in December, President Polk gave his State of the Union speech touting California's gold.*

---

*Just four days before Polk's speech, another steamer, the Panama-bound *Falcon,* had slipped out of New York empty and unnoticed. Then came the speech, and men chased after the *Falcon* in desperation, as if they had seen a winning lottery ticket swept away by a gust of wind. Hundreds galloped on horseback to New Orleans, the *Falcon*'s first port of

On the day of Polk's announcement, December 5, the *California* was fighting its way through storms in the Strait of Magellan, at South America's southern tip. By the time the *California* steamed into port at Valparaiso, Chile, that city was in a gold frenzy. Captain Cleaveland Forbes, who had been warned that hordes of ticket-holding passengers were awaiting him farther north, in Panama, passed the Chileans by. But when he reached Callao, Peru (now called Lima), Forbes gave in to the throng and took seventy Peruvians aboard.

In the meantime, in Panama City 1,500 angry, impatient men spent their days scanning the horizon for the *California*. (The Megquiers, who had yet to reach Panama City, were not among them.) The ship's capacity was 250. On January 17, 1849, the *California* arrived; the crowd learned there was room for only a few of them. Disaster was averted when the captain assured the furious Americans that they would not be left to sulk in Panama while foreigners got rich on American gold. The Peruvians would not be thrown overboard or locked up — these had been popular suggestions — but they would give up their cabins and sleep on deck instead. The *California* would carry as many Americans to the goldfields as could squeeze aboard.

In the end, some 250 Americans clambered onto the *California*, where they joined the 150 passengers already on board and filled the ship far beyond its safe capacity. The price for a single ticket had risen as high as $1,000. The *California* reached San Francisco

---

call, hoping to catch her. Even if they made it aboard, they would have to slog their way across Panama to catch another ship on the Pacific side. *Fine, we'll take that chance.* For years to come, no ship bound for California, or even its general vicinity, would sail empty again.

on February 28. All the passengers raced off to make their fortune. So did all the crew except a single engineer.

Which left the *California* in need of a new crew before she could return to Panama for another batch of argonauts. And left the Megquiers, and everyone else with tickets to San Francisco on the *California*, in limbo.

For Jennie and Thomas Megquier, rescue came in the form of the steamer *Oregon*. Like the *California*, the *Oregon* had left New York in the autumn of 1848 and sailed around Cape Horn to San Francisco. The *Oregon*, too, planned to sail a Pacific circuit. But the *Oregon* trailed a month behind the *California*. Her captain had heard all about how the crew of the *California* had bee-lined their way to the diggings. When *he* reached San Francisco, he put his men in chains.

On May 22, the Megquiers squeezed their way onto the *Oregon*, taking their place among (by Jennie's tally) "four hundred passengers, five ladies, and two servants." Jennie had written to her nine-year-old son, Arthur, the day before. "I am now writing the last letter to my little boy that I shall write in Panama," she assured him. "I am going aboard the steamboat *Oregon* in the morning to go to California in the morning.... I shall pick up the lumps and come home as quick as possible."

CHAPTER NINE

GONE!

FOR SEA VOYAGERS LIKE the Megquiers, the summer of 1849 marked the end of their long journey. Safe in California, they could turn their thoughts to cashing in. For emigrants on the overland route, on the other hand, summer meant that they had reached the worst deserts on their crossing at the worst time of year.

Nevada in summer baked under a relentless sun. Squinting against the light, tiny figures inched across a vast landscape empty of nearly everything but sage, sand, and distant mountains. Even today, in a car on a highway, the isolation can make you feel trapped in an end-of-the-world movie. Not only are there no towns or motels or billboards, but there are not even other cars. When the gas gauge hits the halfway mark, you start to worry about whether you'll find a station before you reach empty.

Nature dictated the emigrants' route — they needed to follow a river, and the foul-tasting, algae-covered Humboldt was the only possibility. So many animals had died in the Humboldt and along its banks, one traveler wrote, that the river was "nothing but horse broth, seasoned with alkali and salt." And it was not only that the river was filthy. Just as bad, the Humboldt meandered in the slowest, most maddening way, nearly doubling back on itself over and over and over again. Where it curved, it pooled up, and scum and mosquitoes flourished.

This was water, but barely. "The reader should not imagine the Humboldt to be a rapid mountain stream, with its cool and limpid waters rushing down the rocks of steep inclines," wrote one dismayed emigrant. "There is not a fish nor any other living thing to be found in its waters, and there is not timber enough in three hundred miles of its desolate valley to make a snuff-box, or sufficient vegetation along its banks to shade a rabbit."

In the blasting desert heat — one emigrant recorded a temperature of 140 degrees — water was a constant preoccupation, and even the most putrid drink was better than none at all. Doctors and lawyers who five months before had sent waiters scurrying for another glass of wine now filled a tin mug in the warm, rancid river and gulped it down. "In the creek we found great numbers of the carcasses of dead horses and cattle," wrote Franklin Langworthy, a minister from Illinois. "It requires some little practice to relish a beverage in which putrescent flesh has been for months steeping. But here we have no choice."

Newspaper accounts beckoning travelers to the Golden West had never featured scenes like these. "I have seen a man eating his lunch and gravely sitting upon the carcass of a dead horse," Langworthy went on, "and we frequently take our meals amidst the effluvia of a hundred putrescent carcasses."

One traveler detailed the process of collecting drinking water from the Humboldt. "For about ten days the only water we had was obtained from the pools by which we would camp. These pools were stagnant and their edges invariably lined with dead cattle that had died while trying to get a drink. Selecting a carcass that was solid enough to hold us up, we would walk out into the pool on it, taking a blanket with us, which we would wash around and get as full of water as it would hold, then carrying it ashore, two men, one holding each end, would twist the filthy water out into a pan, which in turn would be emptied into our canteens, to last until the next camping-place."

The emigrants choked down the tepid, salty liquid, gagging on the rotten-egg smell. "Our great want now is: water! water!! water!!!" one traveler moaned, as he stumbled along the Humboldt and fantasized about cool, soothing, satisfying drinks. "Good spring water, good well water, good snow water, good river water. Our dreams are of water."

Thirst killed animals and drove men mad. Even the most mundane diarists, whose entries virtually never ranged beyond notations of the number of miles covered, lavished a few words on these horrifying scenes. "One of the men had got crazy and took most of the cover off the wagon," one emigrant wrote. "They had to hold him & pour water in his mouth twice before he knew enough to drink."

Alonzo Delano pushed along gamely, but ankle-deep ash and dust made each step an ordeal. Hoping for firmer ground, Delano ventured off the trail, only to find that "the parched and dry alkaline crust broke under our feet like frozen snow."

Breathing proved as hard as walking. Gusts of wind swept ash and alkaline grit into the air and hurled it in the emigrants' faces. Dust stung their eyes, filled their nostrils, choked their throats, coated their food. "Suppose dry ashes and fine sand were thoroughly mixed together," Bernard Reid wrote to his brother back home in Pennsylvania, "and I should take a shovel and toss a large pile of the mixture against your face, head, and whole body — suppose then you should run up and down a steep hill in a hot August sun till the perspiration oozed from every pore almost in streams. Let me then give you another coating of dust and ashes; and your appearance would then be a pretty good sample of that of every one of us, at every noon and night halt."

Even the staunchly religious seemed shaken by the bleak vistas. They wrote with a bit of extra fervor, in whistling-past-the-graveyard fashion. "It is a dreary barren spot," wrote a young gold-seeker from Ohio, "but the Lord Jehovah is here. The universe is his great Temple — and the devout worshipper can everywhere look up to his Father in Heaven and be in fellowship with him."

Bernard Reid felt no such inspiration. "Towards sundown," he wrote, "the air becalms and the dust after rising a few feet high overspreads the plain like a lake of smooth muddy water. Along our line of wagons some are completely submerged in it. Others show only their tops, which seem to go floating along like little boats in the water. Here and there the heads of the men on foot stick up and glide along in rows and groups like ducks on a pond."

Deprivation and miles had toughened and transformed everyone. Greenhorns they had been, but that seemed long ago. ("On leaving home it looked like a hardship to sleep upon the ground," Alonzo Delano recalled, "but habit had changed us so completely that I could sleep as well and sweetly on a bare rock as upon a bed of down.") The gold-seekers had gained skills and confidence, but they had come almost to the end of their strength. "The appearance of emigrants has sadly changed since we started," wrote an Illinois man. "Then they were full of life and animation, and the road was enlivened with the song of *'I am going to California with my tin pan on my knee / Oh, California, that's the land for me.'* But now they crawl along hungry and spiritless, and if a song is raised at all, it is, *'Oh carry me back to Old Virginia, to Old Virginia's shore.'*"

Men took to walking at night, in the hope that it would be cooler. Wolves howled in the distance and sometimes crept close when the exhausted travelers fell to the ground to sleep. Starving men were a daily sight now, working their way from company to company pleading for a bite of food or a sip of water. Famished mules, ribs poking through their skin, ate ropes, bags, bits of leather, sweat-soaked hats. Horses collapsed onto the ground and struggled, futilely, to regain their feet.

Then the river disappeared.

As they'd staggered along, the emigrants had seen the Humboldt narrowing, but they had not quite understood. Proper rivers grew bigger as they went along, as tributaries fed in. This river got ever smaller and muddier and saltier and soapier tasting (because it *had* virtually no tributaries). Eventually there was nothing to do but acknowledge the miserable truth they had been warned of— the Humboldt did not go to the sea or anyplace else inviting but simply grew narrower and shallower until it finally vanished altogether, sucked down by the desert sand and cooked away by the sun. "We have absolutely used up a good-sized river!" one shocked emigrant wrote. "Have run it into the ground! It is gone!"

The Humboldt Sink, this final resting spot was called, and it was a dispiriting sight. One emigrant had imagined "a great rent in the earth, into which the waters of the river plunged with a terrible roar." Instead, he found "a mud lake ten miles long and four or five miles wide, a veritable sea of slime, a 'slough of despond,' an ocean of ooze, a bottomless bed of alkaline poison, which emitted a nauseous odor and presented the appearance of utter desolation."

Now their suffering would grow worse. One stunned, exhausted diarist tried to make his punctuation convey an agony his words could not. "Sand!!! Hot!!! Grass parched and dry." When the Humboldt's silty pools dried up at last and the river vanished completely, the diarist wailed his despair in the cadences of an ancient prophet. "From slew to Sink (O barrenness)."

*   *   *

It had taken some four months of hard walking, from early spring
to late summer, to reach this point. The desert stretched ahead.
Forty miles, scarcely any water, the animals dying, the emigrants
themselves nearly out of strength and food, and all this on the heels
of a grueling 350-mile crawl across Nevada. Worse yet, a trap triggered months before was about to snap shut.

At the start of their journey, the emigrants had been forced to
wait for the spring grass to come up. Condemned by that late start,
they had reached the desert at the hottest time of year. The best
plan now, they decided, was to load their barrels with carcass water
and take their chances. Trying to coax a few more miles out of the
half-starved mules and oxen, they set off late in the day and planned
to walk far into the night, to avoid the brutal sun. By the next day,
they hoped, they'd have made it across.

"It was a forced march over the alkali plain," wrote Luzena Wilson, and this was simple fact, for Wilson was temperamentally
incapable of complaining or dramatizing hardship. The gold-
seekers had entered a tableau from a medieval painting; embellish-
ment was unnecessary. "The road was lined with the skeletons of
the poor beasts who had died in the struggle. Sometimes we found
the bones of men bleaching beside their broken-down and abandoned wagons. The buzzards and coyotes, driven away by our presence from their horrible feasting, hovered just out of reach."

In camp that night Mason Wilson came to Luzena with a
strange story. Did she remember the Independence Company, back
in Missouri? She did. When she and Mason had barely begun their
journey, she had pleaded to join the Independence men. Their
company was so large, hers so small. Could the Wilsons' party

This is one of the original bits of gold from Sutter's mill that set the world racing to California. (Division of Work and Industry, National Museum of American History, Smithsonian Institution)

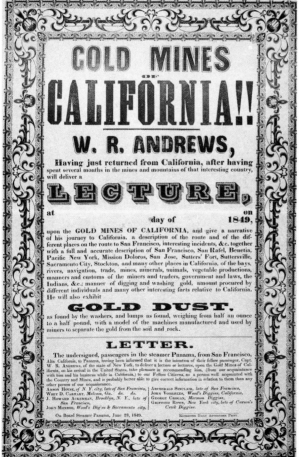

Audiences around the world clamored for news of the goldfields. No one had ever imagined that an ordinary person could get rich overnight. (Library of Congress, Rare Book and Special Collections Division)

HO! FOR CALIFORNIA.

When the president of the United States himself proclaimed that all the rumors were true, adventurers scrambled to find a way west. This cartoon from 1849 depicted the variety among the gold-seekers, who included muscular toughs in work clothes, young swells in tailored coats, pudgy parsons, and men of affairs in top hats. (The New York *Atlas,* January 14, 1849. American Antiquarian Society, Worcester, Massachusetts)

THE WAY THEY GO TO CALIFORNIA.

In the year 1849 alone, some ninety thousand young men joined the stampede west. Cartoonists mocked their eagerness and their naïveté. (Currier & Ives, Library of Congress, Prints and Photographs Division)

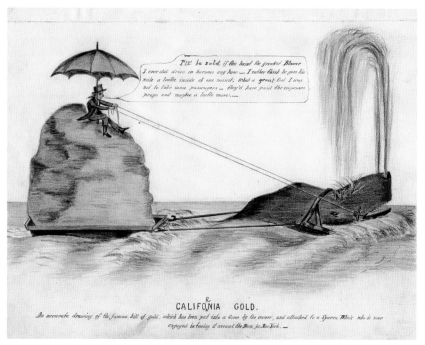

CALIFORNIA GOLD.

An accurate drawing of the famous hill of gold, which has been put into a scow by the owner, and attached to a Sperm Whale who is now engaged in towing it around the Horn, for New York.

A newly rich emigrant heads back home in this cartoon, riding in a scow atop a golden boulder so huge that it requires a whale to pull it. (California History Room, California State Library, Sacramento)

Newspapers of the day were notoriously unreliable, and at first no one believed the astonishing tales of California's riches. In 1835 the New York *Sun* had reported straight-faced, on page one, that astronomers had discovered humanlike creatures living on the moon, complete with wings. (New York Public Library)

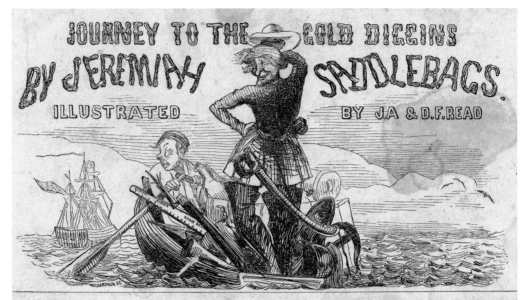

Many of the emigrants were city slickers who had never spent a night outdoors or dug a hole, except perhaps to plant flowers in the garden. Utterly unprepared, they set out on a cross-country journey, on foot, or a months-long ocean voyage. (*Top:* J. A. Read, *Journey to the Gold Diggins.* Yale Collection of Western Americana, Beinecke Rare Book and Manuscript Library. *Bottom:* California History Room, California State Library, Sacramento)

The emigrants relied on guidebooks and newspaper accounts, like this one from the *Detroit Free Press* in 1849. (*Detroit Free Press,* January 19, 1849)

Calculation for six persons' outfit to California.			Weights.	
8 Mules	$50 00	$400 00		
Wagons and Harness for do		100 00		
6 Saddles for do		60 00		
1 Extra wagon and harness		150 00		
6 pairs Mackinaw blankets	4 00	24 00	lbs	35
6 Buffalo skins	2 00	12 00		30
12 pairs Boots	1 50	18 00		
6 doz. Woolen Socks	2 50	15 00		
30 yards Osnaburg for 2 tents	12½	3 75		
20 " Drillins		2 00		
Rope for 2 tents		25		
Sewing tents		1 50		
6 Rifles	20 00	120 00		120
6 Revolvers with moulds	10 00	60 00		50
2 kegs Gunpowder	5 00	10 00		100
100 lbs Lead		3 50		
6 good Bowie Knives		1 50		
2 Camp Kettles		2 00		10
6 Tin cups and plates		60		
900 lbs Side Bacon		36 00		900
600 " Crackers	4 00	24 00		600
100 " Coffee		16 00		160
200 " Sugar		20 00		200
10 " Tea		7 50		10
Tea and coffee pot		1 00		
100 lbs Salt		1 00		100
5 " Pepper		62		5
2 Cheese		7 00		100
10 gallons Brandy	2 00	20 00		100
Medicine		5 00		5
Our share of a guide		30 00		
6 Axes	1 00	6 00		30
6 India rubber cloaks	5 00	30 00		
6 Passages to Inkependence	10 00	60 00		
		$1,218 22		2550

John C. Frémont, "the Pathfinder," had explored the West and written rapturously about it. Seduced by such reports, many of the gold-seekers quit their jobs, left their families, and spent their savings on the trip west. (National Portrait Gallery, Smithsonian Institution / Art Resource, New York)

One of the ablest emigrants was Joseph Goldsborough Bruff, an architectural draftsman and amateur artist from Washington, D.C. Bruff, shown here in a self-portrait, kept perhaps the best and most complete of all the gold rush diaries.

Below is his drawing of Nebraska's Chimney Rock, one of the landmarks on the overland journey (with a tiny figure on horseback, at bottom right, for scale). (Joseph Goldsborough Bruff, *Diaries, Journals, and Notebooks*. Western Americana Collection, Beinecke Rare Book and Manuscript Library, Yale University)

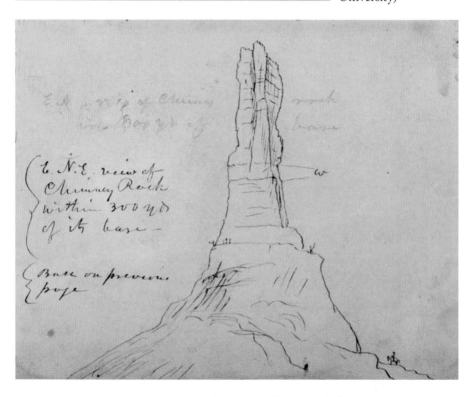

The emigrants crammed their wagons with clothing, food, furniture, pots, pans, silverware, and books. They would throw so much away, to save weight, that parts of the trail west came to resemble a colossal yard sale. (National Archives and Records Administration)

River crossings were especially hazardous. Wagons capsized, animals foundered, and men drowned. (Nebraska State Historical Society)

The Magnificent, Fast Sailing and favorite packet Ship,

JOSEPHINE.

BURTHEN 400 TONS, CAPT.

Built in the most *superb* manner of Live Oak, White Oak and Locust, for a New York and Liverpool Packet; thoroughly Copper-fastened and Coppered. She is a very fast sailer, having crossed the Atlantic from Liverpool to New-York in 14 days, the shortest passage ever made by a *Sailing Ship*. Has superior accommodations for Passengers, can take Gentlemen with their Ladies and families. Will probably reach ☞ SAN FRANCISCO THIRTY DAYS ahead of any Ship sailing at the same time. Will sail about the

10th November Next.

For Freight or Passage apply to the subscriber,

RODNEY FRENCH.

New Bedford, October 15th. **No. 103 North Water Street, Rodman's Wharf.**

Many American gold-seekers who lived near the coast opted to travel by ship. The journey took some five months; the choice was to sail around the tip of South America or else to Panama, then travel overland, and finally up the Pacific coast by way of a second ship. (The Bancroft Library, University of California, Berkeley)

Jennie Megquier chose the Panama route. (She may have been the first American woman to make the crossing.) Feisty and funny, she described her adventures in letters to her family back in Maine. (Uncatalogued daguerreotype, Mary Jane Megquier Papers, the Huntington Library, San Marino, California)

Ships no sooner arrived in San Francisco than their crews ran off to the gold-fields. This photograph shows abandoned ships in San Francisco Bay in 1853. (Daguerreotype by William Shew, National Museum of American History, Smithsonian Institution)

The goldfields were known as "the diggings," and in the early years, tools were primitive. Men worked with picks, shovels, pans, and "cradles," which were akin to colanders intended to sift gold from dirt. (The Bancroft Library, University of California, Berkeley)

Panning was the simplest technique, though it was hard, wet work. The recipe was utterly basic—shovel gravel into the pan; add water; swirl carefully, letting the water carry away the lighter-weight grit; throw away any big rocks; swirl again; scan the last remaining bits of grit for a glint of gold. (The California History Room, California State Library, Sacramento)

Daguerreotype studios appeared almost at once, and miners posed proudly. (Unknown photographer, Untitled [Miner with Shovel], circa 1850. Quarter plate daguerreotype, 5 x 4 in. Collection of the Oakland Museum of California, Oakland Museum Purchase)

Women were rarities in California's early days, outnumbered by men thirty to one. Some blacks came west on their own, as free men; some hoped to earn the money to buy family members out of slavery. Some slave owners brought their slaves with them, to dig them a fortune. (The California History Room, California State Library, Sacramento)

Driven from home by famine and poverty, Chinese miners came to the diggings by the tens of thousands. Whites marveled at these exotic strangers, with their odd language and unfamiliar clothes, but the Chinese endured harsh mistreatment and prejudice. (*Top:* Isaac W. Baker, Untitled [Portrait of a Chinese Man], circa 1853. Sixth plate daguerreotype, 3.75 × 3.25 in. Collection of the Oakland Museum of California, gift of an anonymous donor. *Bottom:* The California History Room, California State Library, Sacramento)

The gold-seekers had traveled thousands of miles from home, and they eagerly posed for pictures to show their families how they had changed. (*Top:* Unknown photographer, Untitled [Two Miners with Gold Nugget Stick Pins], circa 1853. Quarter plate daguerreotype, 4.15 x 5.063 in. Collection of the Oakland Museum of California, Prints and Photographs Fund. *Left:* The Bancroft Library, University of California, Berkeley. *Bottom:* The California History Room, California State Library, Sacramento)

Entertainers raced to California, which was rich, restless, and starved for entertainment. Lola Montez, a singer and dancer known more for her love affairs than for her talent, was one of the great draws. (The Bancroft Library, University of California, Berkeley)

In 1853 a Connecticut miner devised the "water cannon," which could blast away hillsides to reveal the gold hidden under tons of dirt. The day of the free spirit laboring on his own was done. As corporations moved in, the chance for a single man to strike it rich disappeared. "It takes a mine," a newly coined proverb declared, "to run a mine." (Lawrence & Houseworth, California, Yale Collection of Western Americana, Beinecke Rare Book and Manuscript Library)

travel with theirs, for protection? Haughty and in a hurry, the men of the Independence had turned their backs and ridden off.

Now here they were, "their mules gone, many of their number dead, the party broken up, some gone back to Missouri... [and the survivors] not distant forty yards, dying of thirst and hunger." Luzena took pity on them. "Who could leave a human creature to perish in this desolation? I took food and water and found them bootless, hatless, ragged and tattered, moaning in the starlight for death to relieve them from torture. They called me an angel; they showered blessings on me; and when they recollected that they had refused me their protection that day on the Missouri, they dropped on their knees there in the sand and begged my forgiveness."

Sunrise the next day opened a curtain on a nightmare, unveiling "a scene more horrid than the rout of a defeated army," in the words of the Illinois lawyer Eleazer Ingalls. "Dead stock line the roads, wagons, rifles, tents, clothes, everything but food may be found scattered along the road; here an ox, who standing famished against a wagon bed until nature could do no more, settles back into it and dies; and there a horse kicking out his last gasp in the burning sand, men scattered along the plain and stretched out among the dead stock like corpses, fill out the picture."

Ingalls concluded with a heartfelt prayer. "The desert! You must see it and feel it in an August day, when legions have crossed it before you, to realize it in all its horrors. But heaven save you from the experience."

Before the emigrants dared hope that their ordeal might be near its end, the animals sensed it. For miles now, the exhausted travelers had sustained themselves with the knowledge that somewhere ahead were the cold, clear rivers—and water!—that came down from the Sierra Nevada.

"While we were yet five miles from the Carson River," Luzena Wilson wrote, "the miserable beasts seemed to scent the freshness in the air." Heads raised, nostrils distended, the weary oxen did their best to speed up. Half a mile from the river, "they broke into a run, a perfect stampede, and refused to be stopped until they had plunged neck deep in the refreshing flood; and when they were unyoked, they snorted, tossed their heads, and rolled over and over in the water in their dumb delight."

Wilson had a soft spot for the faithful cattle that had carried her so far. "It would have been pathetic had it not been so funny," she wrote happily, "to see those poor, patient, overworked, hard-driven beasts, after a journey of two thousand miles, raise heads and tails and gallop at full speed, an emigrant wagon with flapping sides jolting at their heels."

Exhausted, ecstatic men and women celebrated just as fervently. After the endless, empty desert, all sand and scrub, here were trees, and water, and life! "Men were seen to rush up, half crazed with thirst and hunger," one emigrant wrote, "and embrace those noble old trees and weep as children, and bless God for their deliverance."

Many of the travelers couldn't talk, because their tongues were black and swollen, and when they plunged their faces in the water they found that at first they couldn't drink, either. "We buried our faces in the clear bright water, guzeled it up as best we could," wrote an emigrant named James Carpenter, "then waited a few minutes and guzel again." While Carpenter and his companions sprawled in the shallows, gulping down water, a team of desperately thirsty oxen charged into the river nearly on top of them. *Fine.* "We wanted a drink as bad as they did and laid there and drank with a cow on each side of us."

*   *   *

Looming overhead were some of the steepest mountains in North America. The mountains in children's drawings take the shape of an upside down V, with the peak neatly placed in the middle. Not so the Sierra, which rise abruptly on their eastern face and slope gradually on the western, Pacific-facing side. The emigrants would be climbing nearly straight up and making their way along narrow passes flanked by vertiginous drops.

The climb was brutal, "as steep as the roof of a house," in one emigrant's judgment. In places you could touch the ground without bending over. A trick of perspective made matters appear even worse—the mountains rose so sharply that, to the emigrants' bewilderment, the wagons high above them seemed to be floating in midair, atop the trees. On some routes, the emigrants ran into sheer ledges that soared into the sky and hemmed them in, like dungeon walls cutting off a prisoner's escape. "Just ahead," wrote one dismayed traveler, "was a wall several thousand feet high which had to be climbed to get out of this valley."

With no choice but to carry on, the emigrants took their wagons apart and dragged them up over the ledges with ropes (and then had to find a longer way around that the oxen or mules could negotiate). Or they wrapped ropes around the trees, block and tackle style, and dragged the wagons uphill inch by inch. In many places, barrel-sized rocks blocked the way. The emigrants pried and levered their wagons over the obstacles, all the time keeping an uneasy eye on the fractured boulders overhead. "It made one's flesh creep to look up and see huge crags suspended," one emigrant wrote, "wanting only the vibration of an echo to break the frail ligatures, and grind you into eternity."

Franklin Langworthy, the Illinois minister, described the climb with pride and horror. The trail along a pass called Devil's Ladder was so steep that at times the oxen had to "creep upwards upon their knees." On either side of the road were giant drops, and for the last two miles "it was necessary for several men to brace themselves against a wagon to prevent its upsetting and rolling down the side of the mountain."

Langworthy struggled his way to the summit. At 9,300 feet, he and his company were 2,000 feet higher than South Pass, in the Rockies. "I do not think it possible to drive teams over heights more difficult than those we have ascended," Langworthy wrote proudly, "being twice the height of the Alleghenies, and as high as the White and Green Mountains piled upon each other, and I think higher than any of the passes of the Alps into Italy."

Hannibal and Napoleon had "gained deathless renown by crossing the Alps," Langworthy added, and now he and thousands of other anonymous emigrants had outdone them.

High in the mountains, mission nearly accomplished, the goldseekers paused for breath. Langworthy was drunk on scenery and accomplishment. "Bewildered and lost amidst the boundless expanse," he gazed in awe at mountains that receded into infinity and trees that soared out of view. Trees a dozen feet in diameter and too tall to measure loomed over his campsite. "By the side of such a grove, the stateliest pine forests in the eastern States would appear like humble shrubbery."

Eleazer Ingalls waxed philosophical. "It does not take much to make man happy after all," he mused. He and his companions had managed to shoot three woodchucks, and life had taken a definite upturn. "Here we have been starving along for the last month, crossing deserts, drinking rotten, alkali or salt water, or deprived entirely, and now we've got to the top of the Nevadas, around our campfire amid snow drifts, with plenty of good water and three woodchucks for three of us, and we are the happiest mortals alive."

Luzena Wilson, as brisk and practical as ever, had no inclination to sing hymns to the trees or to ponder human nature. The climb up and over the mountains, almost from the moment she completed it, had begun fading into history. And Wilson, an American to the marrow of her bones, viewed "history" in the American sense: it meant not the essential background needed to understand a story but excess baggage that only bogged a person down. "Already we began to forget the trials and hardships of the past," Wilson wrote, "and to look forward with renewed hope to the future."

CHAPTER TEN

MAROONED

JOSEPH BRUFF HAD GOT off to a late start back in Missouri, and he had never made up the time. Now the bill came due. On September 14, 1849, in Nevada, he made an innocuous-sounding entry in his journal. "I had determined to take a northern route if practicable," he wrote, "to avoid the long deserts" and the lurking hazards of the Humboldt Sink, the Forty Mile Desert, "and last, tho' not least, a very elevated, rugged, and dangerous Pass" across the central Sierra. Bruff had decided to take a shortcut.

Five days later, he came to the fork in the road where his preferred northern route veered away from the Humboldt River. In high spirits, he wrote a proud note and jabbed it into the ground on a stick, near other notices. "The Washington City Company, Capt Bruff, pass'd on the right-hand trail, September 19th, 2 p.m. 1849."

Bruff had opted for a supposedly quick and easy route called the Lassen Cutoff, after a Danish-born rancher and entrepreneur named Peter Lassen who owned an immense tract of land about one hundred miles north of Sutter's Fort. Lassen had "found" the new path, more or less, in 1848 when he tried to lead a ten-wagon company to his land. (In previous years he had traveled back and forth to his ranch on established routes.) His plan was to sell the easterners land near his own, but he had misplaced his ranch. After a series of desperate misadventures—Lassen's company nearly lynched him—he managed to stumble home. Unchastened by the near disaster, Lassen sent agents to intercept other California-bound emigrants and direct them to his new route, and he had signs posted at a bend in the Humboldt announcing that the goldfields were only 110 miles ahead.

This was a hideously dangerous lie. Lassen's shortcut was two hundred miles *longer* than the better-known routes through the Sierra Nevada. Moreover, the route led directly across Nevada's Black Rock Desert, one of the harshest landscapes on the American continent, and then veered north, nearly to the California-Oregon border, precisely the wrong direction for the goldfields. When the trail swung back in the proper direction at last, it left the worn-out emigrants one last climb over the mountains just when they were hungriest, and the animals weakest, and the winter snows nearest.

But in 1849, almost no one knew any of that. The Lassen Cutoff lured emigrants with the promise of a short haul and a low mountain pass, with plenty of grass and water along the way. Thousands of emigrants—Joseph Bruff, Alonzo Delano, and Israel Lord among them—took the bait. By 1850, nearly everyone had heard of their travails. From then on, almost no one opted for what had come to be known as the Death Route.

The first milestone on the shortcut hinted—heavily—at trouble to come. Rabbit Hole Springs had no springs, it turned out, but only wells that earlier travelers had dug. On September 20 Joseph

Bruff picked his way toward the wells, navigating between animal corpses. In one well, he wrote, was "a dead ox, swelled up so as to fill the hole closely, his hind legs and tail only above ground." Bruff hurried off to fetch his water elsewhere. Another well, another ox.

Dead oxen littered the ground as if some bizarre battle of the animals had just ended. Bruff made a careful, horrifying drawing. "I counted 82 dead oxen, 2 dead horses, and 1 mule in an area of 1/10 of a mile." He noted, too, a fresh grave, with an inscription written on a headboard from an abandoned wagon. As always, he copied it down. "M. De Morst, of Col. Ohio, died Sep. 16th, 1849, Aged 50 Years, Of Camp Fever."

The desert came next, and it made the springs seem like an oasis. Black Rock Desert was the dried-mud bed of a prehistoric lake. Barren and waterless, without a blade of grass or the puniest shrub, "it seemed to be the River of Death dried up," one early emigrant wrote, "its muddy bottom jetted into cones by the fires of perdition."

Israel Lord came this route, too, staggering through the unrelenting heat with the sun a "monstrous, unmeaning, vacant, lustreless eye staring at you from every point of the compass." By now

THE RABBIT-HOLE SPRINGS.

the mules and oxen were nearly too weak to pull. So many had died that the road was strewn with carcasses, bodies bloated and rotting and legs extended stiff. Some of the fallen animals lay next to abandoned wagons, their yokes still around their necks, their tongues hanging from their mouths. The stink hung so heavy in the air, Israel Lord wrote, that he could *hear* it. (Travelers in the next few years would shuffle past dozens of mummified animals, their leathery bodies looking eerily alive because flecks of sand on their open eyes glistened in the light.)

He had not seen a tree in two hundred miles, Lord lamented, and had drunk water only twice in the past twenty-four hours. "Nothing but rock and sand and clay and ashes and dead animals," he wrote, stunned by the emptiness, and he took to conferring his own names on landmarks on the way: Point Misery, Mud Lake, Golgotha, Point Distress, Valley of the Shadow of Death, Gate of Desolation.

Desert gave way to canyon and cliffs. Lord preferred these surroundings. In one chasm he shouted with all his might and found he could hear "eight distinct echoes, the first six very loud." He scrambled to the top of a precipice, sat down on the edge, and lowered a weight tied to a string. "By actual measurement 428 feet high."

Bruff, far more of a Boy Scout at heart than the moody Lord, would have loved to climb rocks and sing at the top of his lungs. He had little opportunity. His company had taken to squabbling. "The selfishness of my men was exhibited to such a degree" — apparently there had been a kerfuffle to do with divvying up supplies — "that I had to interfere in a peremptory manner."

Three days later, more trouble. "Held a meeting to inflict

penalties for guard and other delinquencies, and to consider an application from . . . 2 of the most obnoxious men in the company, who prayed that we would grant them . . . a full discharge." The two wanted to head off on their own, with mules and six days' food. "It was unanimously passed with 3 cheers. Such was the company's opinion of the men, and such their joy at the riddance." But Bruff may have misread the general mood. "At night the disaffected gang, or 5 of them, stole the wine, reserved for medical purposes." They swore they hadn't taken anything — *the wine must have leaked from its keg* — but Bruff "noticed great laughter & hilarity in their wagons at night."

Now the trail moved into the mountains. The highest pass on the route was at 6,100 feet, considerably lower than those farther south, but more than high enough. The ascent was "pretty steep," Bruff acknowledged, and several wagons set out with twelve yoke of oxen rather than the customary two or three. Bruff instructed his lead wagon to fly the Stars and Stripes when it reached the top, as they'd done at South Pass, to encourage the others.

A wagon in another company had nearly reached the summit when a harness snapped. Bruff saw the wagon careen backward down the mountain while the women and children inside screamed, and the men outside chased after. Finally the wagon ran into a dead ox in the road, caromed into a team of oxen pulling a heavy wagon, and slowed enough that it could be wrestled to a halt. Everyone survived.

Over the course of the next several days, Bruff took occasional breaks to gaze around him. "What a scene from here! The Snow Butte [Mount Lassen] and his blue neighbors, deep vales, silver-thread like streams . . . & in every tint of one of natures most extensive landscapes!" He caught himself. "Pshaw! Enraptured with a landscape! How ridiculous!" Especially for a man with responsibilities. "I must look out for the train, or there will be some accidental capsizements, maybe a broken neck or leg! No time now for the Fine arts, we must patronize the rough ones."

Israel Lord, at about the same spot, found himself not enraptured by the scenery but utterly sick of it. He had worked hard to get this far, and where was he? "To admire is a long way behind me," he grumped. "I am heartily tired of being shut up among hills and mountains, with loose blocks of granite or basalt hanging over my head." Let others rhapsodize. Lord polished off the climb in four impatient words. "Ascended the Sierra Nevada."

Irritable and frustrated, Lord found himself pondering just what mountains were *for*. What was the point? The experience of struggling up one mountain valley and down the next, he decided as he mulled it over, was the gold rush in a nutshell. The whole trip west amounted to nothing but "a mere game of seesaw. Go up to go down...take from one pocket to put not as much into the other." At the end of your travails, Lord felt with a shudder of premonition, you would be no wiser, no richer, just the same old fool with a few new bruises.

While in this melancholic mood, Lord saw a man lying dead on the ground. Half an hour before, the man's friends said, this hapless emigrant had raced ahead "to look on the promised land from the summit." He had stopped to make a snack of wild parsnips, and poisoned himself. Lord, who could not watch a cloud pass overhead without drawing a moral, clucked in dismay. Within yards of his goal, "as full of life and vigor as any of us," John A. Dawson of Saint Louis now lay "like a dog, in a hole, without a coffin, a board, or even a blanket, unshaved, unshrived, and unannealed." Lord took a scrap of wood from a wagon and engraved the dead man's name, so that he would have, at least, a tiny memorial.

"The dead know nothing," Lord wrote in his diary that night, "and the living care for nothing." The only thought in the minds of the men who had buried Dawson, wrote Lord, was "that there would be one less to dig gold in California." One more death, one fewer rival.

By fall, on the Lassen Cutoff especially, many of the emigrants still on the trail were in a bad way. On October 14, 1849, Joseph Bruff encountered a rescue party that had been sent out by California's military governor to find stragglers in the mountains and bring them safely home. Bruff approved of the mission—he had copied down inscriptions from four graves that very day—but he explained to Major D. H. Rucker that he and his company didn't need help.

Bruff's men disagreed. "The company very anxious for me to make application to Major Rucker for supplies." Bruff maintained that the food was expressly for "starving families—women and children," but he was shouted down. Some of his men, Bruff told Rucker shamefacedly, "would take a biscuit out of a woman's mouth." Reluctantly, Bruff accepted thirty-one pounds of bacon and fourteen pounds of crackers on the company's behalf. While Bruff sorted things out with the major, his men hurried off with the crackers, "not reserving me an ounce."

One week later, on October 21, Bruff's company had made it to within thirty-two miles of Lassen's Ranch. They were down to six wagons (and had only enough mules to pull four) and had nearly run out of food. Around the campfire that night, Bruff proposed a plan. The company would not split up—Bruff was immensely proud that he had "brought them to this point, together, and more prosperous than any company of men in this vast emigration"— and they would proceed, together, to the ranch. The only catch was that they would have to leave two of the wagons and their contents behind, to fetch later.

That meant that someone would have to stay behind, briefly, to guard the wagons. Bruff volunteered; a captain does not abandon his ship. Until his men returned for him in a few days, he would settle in. He lent one man his horse. Another, named Willis, said he would stay with Bruff. The others marched off. Bruff and Willis totted up their supplies—a couple of handfuls of rice, two biscuits, two pounds of beef, a few ounces of coffee. But they had rifles and ammunition, and this was deer country. "We pitched our tent and made ourselves contented."

As the two men waited, emigrants streamed by, all of them tattered and hungry. On October 26, Bruff counted sixty travelers, looking more like wartime refugees than adventurers out to claim a fortune. "Thin with hunger, as well as anxiety," in Bruff's words, they struggled along to his fire and tried to gather their strength. Bruff noted down their stories. One had met an old man on the roadside, nearly dead of scurvy and abandoned by his companions. Another had encountered a man breaking his saws and other tools over a tree stump. They had cost plenty back in Saint Louis, he snarled, and if *he* couldn't use them, he'd make sure that nobody could. A group of emigrants had purposely set fire to a meadow so that those trailing after them would have nowhere to let their livestock graze. The modern counterpart would be filling up at the last gas station on the edge of a wilderness and then burning down the station.

On October 29, a group of men from Bruff's company returned to camp, back from Lassen's. The visit proved to be anything but a reunion. They'd brought no food, no supplies, and hadn't even returned Bruff's horse. Bruff shouted abuse; the men shouted back. *We return for you, and this is the thanks we get!* Bruff erupted (and, in his journal, he underlined his words indignantly). "<u>You came for</u> <u>me!... No sir! You came for those wagons and their contents, that's</u> <u>what you came for! Take the plunder and roll on. I'll not disgrace</u> <u>myself by further companionship with you! I shall go in when it</u> <u>suits me.</u>"

Bold words but foolish ones. With winter coming on and food running low, this was not a time to dawdle. Bruff's health had been precarious for months. He needed to get out of the mountains as quickly as possible, before bad fortune or bad weather made it impossible.

Two days later, as if to drive home that message, Bruff woke to the sound of a man screaming for help. It was one o'clock in the morning in a driving storm. A huge oak tree had crashed to the ground, smashing a tent with four men inside. Bruff ran to see what he could do. "An aged, grey headed man and his grown son, with their hips buried in the ground and their ghastly eyes turned up in death! Next another son, and beside him, a young man, his comrade, slowly dying in agony, with broken legs and mutilated bodies." Bruff covered the dead bodies with a coat and started digging graves. Snow and rain pelted down.

By the next morning, November 1, the two younger men had died. Bruff borrowed a prayer book and read the burial service. One of the widows wanted to look at the faces a last time. Bruff climbed down into the grave, found his footing between the bodies, and peeled back a bedsheet. Later he wrote a poem for the grave marker. *"They here sleep together, in one grave entombed, / Side by side as they slept on the night they were doom'd!"*

Another storm hit on November 2. Bruff, the least jumpy person alive, began to wonder whether soon it would be time to worry. "Alas for the sick & helpless, in these hills tonight!" Lassen's Ranch was only a few days' journey, but the road was bad "and rheumatism and hermarhoyd forbid my attempting it on foot, and I have failed, in several applications to emigrants, to take me in, they are generally too selfish."

Bruff did his best to convince himself that he was not stranded but merely biding his time. Just think of his precious drawings and journals, not to mention his mineral collection; to abandon camp would be to leave it all behind. Looked at in the right way, this brief delay was a fortunate break. "I have the opportunity here, which I could not have below, of correcting my notes and drawings." He was bound to regain his strength in a few days. He could travel then.

Emigrants continued to pass by, and Bruff played host as if presiding at a mountain lodge. "2 ox wagons passed; 2 women and a little girl, on foot, called to warm their feet at my campfire. I had just prepared my dinner, of roast venison & coffee (no bread) and invited them to partake, which they did."

On November 4, in a snowstorm, Bruff made the acquaintance of a companion destined to prove a loyal friend. This was a bull terrier puppy, soon dubbed Nevada. Bruff tucked her under his poncho and brought her home. Tagging along in the storm, too, were a young woman clutching at Bruff's coat "to assist her in walking over the wet & slippery trail," followed by her two "poor little girls, hand & hand, slipping & tottering and crying with cold and wet."

Bruff's plan, such as it was, was to wait for a break in the weather and hope that he and Willis could find mules or oxen to bring them to Lassen's. In the meantime, he collected abandoned clothes and boots, dried them by the fire, and handed them over to "many a poor, wet, tired, and ragged hombre" to replace their torn and sodden gear. "Hundreds I have had the pleasure of thus assisting," he wrote. "I keep up a large fire.... I have no food for them but plenty of coffee, and a good strong pot full is ever at their service."

This was a good plan for the emigrants, not so good for Bruff himself. His journal entry for November 11 ended with a worrying observation. "Unsuccessful hunt today, meat getting low. The sick men are improving, except myself." Somehow the deer never seemed to venture within range of a rifle shot. Bruff returned to the same theme a few days later. "I have a very severe headache today," he wrote on November 14, and, on the same day, "Hunters returned unlucky. Quite ill tonight, with headache & fever." Newly arriving emigrants began to report ominous news. "For about four miles the snow was above the hubs of the wheels, and up to the oxen's bellys, and the wheels became immense circular blocks of snow."

Bruff had pictured that any day now he would wake up sound and strong and ready to travel; instead, he'd grown steadily weaker. And he'd expected a lull in the weather, but no sooner did the sky clear than another storm swept in. The one consolation was that he'd found a new ally. This was an old friend, William Poyle, who had not seen Bruff since the Platte. Now he'd turned up in the Sierra and had vowed not to part from his companion again. (Bruff's Washington Company acquaintance, Willis, had gone off, supposedly to hunt, and had not returned.)

Bruff would need his friend's help. By mid-November he could scarcely fight through the pain to venture out in search of food. As if that weren't enough, he had taken on a new responsibility, a sick little boy with a neglectful father. On November 16, Bruff learned the story of "an inhuman wretch camped here, by the name of Lambkin." The improbably named Lambkin had brought his four-year-old son across the country with him, and one day Bruff happened to hear the half-starved child crying, alone, shivering next to a burned-out campfire. Bruff tracked down Lambkin and told him his son was crying. "'Yes, d—n him,' says he, 'let him cry!'"

It was a thundering shame to treat a poor little child so, Bruff shouted. If he could manage it, he would protect the child himself. Lambkin stormed off. Later that day he turned up in Bruff's camp, young William in tow. He was headed off to round up supplies. He would return in a few days. If Bruff wanted William so badly, *he* could take care of him.

By November 25, Bruff admitted he was in trouble. He was now too sick to hunt or even to walk any distance, and he was nearly out of food. "Home" was a crude, three-part lodge. In the center was a tall tepee, open at the top, with a fire. Bruff's tent joined the tepee at one side, Poyle's at the other. Poyle continued to hunt but with little success. Stuck in his tent, Bruff could only hope that someone would bring help. "Unless succor is sent me from the valley, I am corner'd, for a spell."

The weather grew worse. December 3 saw "strong gales and snow all night, causing our cotton castle to oscillate much." On December 13, Bruff and Poyle ate their last piece of venison. They gave William the biggest share. Now they were down to two meals a day, of soup made from boiled ox bones or deer bones. Poyle could have made it safely out of the mountains but he refused to abandon Bruff, who was now too weak to travel. Young William was feverish and malnourished, his eyes sunken, his skin pale. Bruff and Poyle cut back further on their rations, to leave more for William.

Bruff thought he knew the whereabouts of an ox that had died not far away. If they could find it in the deep snow, its meat would be "as safe as in a refrigerator, if the wolves and bears have not found it." But help was bound to come soon. Otherwise, "I & the child are doomed, perhaps." Poyle was strong and should survive.

The snow grew deeper. It was hard to find enough dry wood to keep a fire going, and hard to chop it up, harder still to find carcasses in the snow to butcher, nearly futile to hunt. The poles that held up the tents and tepee (cut from tree branches) buckled and cracked under the snow's weight. In the collapsed tents, Bruff and Poyle did their best to regroup. "All wet, and confusion."

By December 19 they had cut back to one meal a day. Bruff looked ravenously at Nevada. "An extremity has come," he wrote, "and we are considering about killing & cooking her." But Bruff was a soft touch and the gruff words a sham. The poor pup was so skinny, Bruff observed. What kind of meal would she make? And without their loyal dog, who would guard the camp at night?

In the end, Bruff indignantly rejected his own suggestion. "Must I then eat my faithful watch? My poor little Nevada, who has shared my sufferings? For one meal and then die regretting it? I will not."

They could eat their candles, if it came to it. These were ordinary, cheap candles made of animal fat, not expensive ones made of beeswax. A few bites of melted fat hardly made a meal, but *something* in your belly was better than nothing. Nevada could share a candle or they might try soap again. She'd eaten it, the first time. On December 21 Bruff shot a raven. On December 22, he found a few bones from a deer's leg that had been stashed away eight weeks before. (The idea had been to use the bones as a source of oil, for their rifles.) Roasted, the bones provided a tiny bit of meat, along with a considerable quantity of burnt hair.

Bruff and Poyle struggled through the days, not quite cheerily, perhaps, but far from downcast. The menu on December 23 was rotten ox—they had found a carcass under the snow and dragged it home—washed down with coffee. After the meal, "we enjoyed our pipes and a long chat and consoling ourselves with the argument that there are thousands in the world worse off than we are. We hear small birds singing quite merrily."

Bruff, who had counted so many things on his journey, now

tallied his blessings. "We are exceedingly fortunate in having plenty of good coffee, condiments &c., bedding and clothing in abundance, arms and ammunition, matches, some spermacetti and tallow candles, a couple of good lanterns, 2 iron candlesticks. In fact we only needed provisions, a more secure protection from the weather, and fuel more convenient to get in severe weather, and we would have laughed at the elements." All they were missing, in other words, was food, fuel, and shelter.

On December 24, Bruff managed to shoot a squirrel. As usual, he was exuberant rather than embittered. "So we have a Christmas dinner." First, they would have a Christmas breakfast. The resourceful Poyle set to work early on Christmas day. He chopped up a few shards of neck and shoulder from an old ox, added the squirrel, threw some deer bones into the pot, sprinkled in plenty of salt and pepper, and stewed it all for an hour or two. Bruff beamed with pleasure. "Are there not persons, surrounded by plenty and every comfort, who do not enjoy their breakfast as we do?"

Later in the day Poyle recalled the whereabouts of yet another ox carcass under the snow. More food for dinner! Bruff and Poyle fed young William and then tucked into their feast. Poyle proposed that they improvise some after-dinner entertainment. "We can each sing a song and tell a story," Poyle suggested, "and then take a pot of coffee and call it ale, egg-nogg, or what you please." And so they did. The world looked brighter. "The child is doing well," Bruff remarked, "and we can probably keep our pup."

But the respite was brief. Rotten meat and imaginary ale could not sustain a man. Even Bruff conceded that things looked bleak. "Poyle and myself are too weak to walk far," he wrote, "and the absence of one would seriously jeopardize the life of the others." The weather was cool and drizzly, not snowy, "but if another violent and long storm comes over us soon, we are doomed."

The next few days brought no relief. On December 29, dinner was a bit of ox meat fried in a melted candle. "We are rapidly failing," Bruff admitted. On the first day of the new year, he copied down the inscription from one more grave marker. Bruff had written this one himself. "WILLIAM, Infant son of LAMBKIN, an Unnatural Father, Died Jan. 1, 1850."

By now Bruff had accumulated so many afflictions that he could scarcely list them all. "Pain in my face very severe," "my mind much depressed, anxiety, weakness, and forebodings of evil," "swelling of body," "severe toothache," "pain and extreme weakness of the spinal column." New ailments joined the list almost every day—"pain in back very bad," "legs and loins very weak," "pain in kidnies very annoying"—and no old ones ever dropped off.

Bruff could rarely muster the strength to hunt, but he and Poyle had gained a companion. Their new ally, Warren Clough, was himself an emigrant to the goldfields and a self-described "old hunter, and used to a rough life." Clough "expressed a desire to join me," Bruff wrote happily, "from motives of humanity alone." He would prove as loyal a friend as a man could have.

The men had set up a new camp, Bruff staggering and almost fainting on the way. It was only a mile from where he'd passed the previous two months, but perhaps a move would bring a change in fortune. It didn't. On February 5, Bruff sent Poyle to get help. No desperate man ever shouted for rescue in so formal a way. Poyle carried a letter from Bruff explaining his predicament in carefully composed polysyllables. "A series of circumstances & misfortunes have detained me here, and for upwards of two months, I have been too feeble to travel any distance." Bruff requested aid in "extricating me from a very disagreeable exigency." He would of course repay any pecuniary outlay involved in coming to his rescue, and he would forever cherish the feeling that "such an act of friendship must indelibly make on a grateful heart."

With Poyle gone, Bruff and Clough settled into a routine. Every morning Clough took up his rifle and ventured off for a day's hunting. February 24 was typical. "About 7 p.m. my comrade returned wet, cold, and fatigued, and luckless," Bruff wrote. "His hair was full of snow and froze to his cap. Shirt sleeves froze stiff. He shot 2 deer but they escaped in the brush; the storm & lateness of the hour prevented him from searching for them." Bruff's role was more domestic. "I always have a good hot meal ready when he returns from a hunt." That hot meal, many nights, was mashed acorns and coffee.

At ten in the morning on March 25, Clough set out once again. In the rain and fog, deer might be hard to find. Clough thought he might have to spend the night out. Two days later, he still had not returned. Lame and sick, Bruff was alone. "I am now in a snap truly," he wrote on March 27, "without food, helpless, and subject to spells of prostration."

On March 28 Bruff managed to shoot "a very small blue woodpecker. I took a small saucepan of water, put an inch of tallow-candle, the bird, pepper & salt, in; and boiled it; and made a pot of coffee. This is the first meal I have had in 48 hours." Nonetheless, the sky was clear and the wind mild. "What a delightful day!" Bruff exclaimed. If only he weren't starving to death.

On March 30 Bruff found some scraps of deerskin with a bit of dried-out flesh still clinging to the hide. He scraped off the worms with a butcher knife. "This boiled with 2 old cracked leg-bones, and another inch of tallow candle, made me broth, which with coffee, had to serve for breakfast." Then he went out hunting, stumbling through the woods. He collapsed on the ground in a faint and dreamed that he was at home and his little boy was patting him on the head. A wolf's howl roused him, and he limped home. "I made coffee and eat the grounds, with salt, for supper."

The next morning Bruff forced himself out into the rain, to try hunting once more. He followed the tracks of a grizzly bear to an ancient, mangled ox carcass and cut off a few ribs for Nevada. For his own dinner, Bruff made broth from deer hooves, water, and candle wax, with a side dish of coffee grounds and salt.

Around midnight a grizzly bear—was it the same one?—began snuffling around. Nevada barked furiously. Bruff muzzled her with a handkerchief. The bear approached within ten feet, contemplated Bruff contemptuously over the course of three long minutes, and ambled off.

Bruff now began each day with a grim reckoning. April 1 marked "the 8th day of Clough's mysterious absence!...and the 56th of Poyle's." Bruff threw some ancient bones into a kettle with water and put his coffee on the fire. Then, tragedy! "Attending to the coffee, my kettle of broth fell over, and I thus lost my *last meal!* I picked up the pieces of bone & gnawed them, drank my coffee, and eat a spoonful of the grounds."

He shouldered his rifle and tottered into the woods. After two miles he gave up. Back in camp, Bruff found a half-decayed deer's head. He chopped it up with his hatchet, gave half the tongue to Nevada, and cooked the other half for himself. The sound of a far-off wolf—but was it a wolf or his own labored breathing?—echoed incessantly in his ears. Bruff began to fear that he was losing his mind.

Over and over again, he contemplated his options. He was too weak to travel. If he set out, he would collapse, and bears and wolves would devour him. Or he could stay put and heal. Perhaps he could finally shoot a deer or another bird. He still had a few candles to eat.

On April 3, Bruff did shoot a little bird, about the size of a sparrow. He cut off the wings and gave them to Nevada, and made the rest into soup for himself. That night two wolves ventured within thirty yards, snarling and snapping their teeth. Bruff changed his mind. He could die in his tent or he could die on the trail. He would give it a go.

He set out on April 4, headed for the nearest camp or cabin, so weak that he had to stop and sit every thirty or forty paces. As the day wore on, he grew weaker still. Now he fell after every few steps. Nevada would run several feet ahead and whine, as if to implore Bruff to try to get up. By day's end he could not walk twice his body length. He collapsed one last time. Several deer came in view, but he didn't have the strength to find his rifle and take aim. Dinner was coffee grounds. "Made a fire, rolled up in my thin quilt, and laid down for the night, may be for ever."

On April 6, still tumbling his way along, stopping occasionally for a bite of candle, Bruff saw a group of men in the distance. "I saluted them, staggered, fell, and asked in the name of God, for something to eat, that I was starving!" These were prospectors, it turned out, and one handed Bruff a piece of bread smeared with a little pork fat. When he had revived a bit, he happened to see a gravestone by the roadside. Dutiful as ever, he copied down the inscription.

The next morning the prospectors shared their breakfast of biscuits, pork, and coffee, and then rode off, leaving Bruff empty-handed. He fumed. "They hearty and robust, with 8 or 10 days full rations, and I an emaciated starveling! Such is human nature! Oh selfishness, thou makest wolves of mankind!" Then he scolded himself. "I will not, however, be ungrateful. They fed me, and saved my life. For this, I am very thankful."

On April 8 Bruff spotted a fresh footprint, made by someone barefoot. Aha! *That's* what Nevada had been barking at the other night. An unchivalrous thought popped into his head. "My mouth fairly watered, for a piece of an Indian to broil." Bruff ate his last piece of candle and gave the wick to Nevada. He came to a creek and bent a pin into a hook, with a beetle for bait. Nothing doing. But Bruff managed to kill a lizard with a stick and roasted it for dinner.

Staggering on the next day, he met a small, nearly naked Indian holding a bow and arrow. Bruff tried a few words in Spanish. Nothing. Bruff signaled that he was hungry. The man indicated that he had no food and was on his way to shoot birds. The two men parted, but Nevada ran after the Indian's dog. Bruff shouted for the stranger to shoo Nevada away, which he did. Could this be the very Indian Bruff had dreamed of eating only the day before? But he couldn't shoot a man in the back. "Besides, he had done me a favor."

Bruff trudged on. *Only a few miles more…* He kept himself going by murmuring, "I will soon have plenty to eat! Bread and meat, coffee and milk! A house to sleep in! And an end of my sufferings!" Eventually he fell to the ground and sank into a sleep. Nevada's barking roused him, but Bruff was too weak to stand. He lifted his head. Poyle!

His loyal friend had found him. There was a cabin only three hundred yards off. It took fifteen minutes to stumble the distance. Breakfast was "pancakes & molasses, rolls and fresh butter, stewed and boiled beef, coffee & milk!"

PART III

REALITY

CHAPTER ELEVEN

FIRST PEEKS AT THE GOLDEN LAND

HAPPY BUT EXHAUSTED, LUZENA and Mason Wilson crept toward the finish line. They had climbed over the Sierra Nevada. Sacramento was nearly in reach. Now they spotted a man riding toward them. This was thrilling. A visit from an earlier arrival meant firsthand news of what to expect in California. But almost at once, excitement gave way to mortification.

Since they had left Missouri, the Wilsons had seen hardly anyone but their fellow emigrants, all of them as worn and shabby as they were themselves. Now, imagining this outsider's gaze, Luzena cringed. "The sight of his white shirt, the first I had seen for four long months, revived in me the languishing spark of womanly vanity." Her achievement forgotten, all Luzena could think of was that her "skirts were worn off in rags above my ankles. . . . My sleeves hung in tatters above my elbows; my hands, brown and hard, were gloveless." Pulling her ragged bonnet low over her suntanned face, she retreated behind the wagon.

The newcomer explained that he had only recently arrived in

California himself, but it was clear to Luzena that his transformation had already begun. "A day or two before, this man was one of us," she marveled. "Today he was a messenger from another world, and a stranger."

The next-to-last day of Luzena's journey, September 29, 1849, offered her a peek at the promise of that new world. She had cooked dinner over the campfire, as usual. A miner who happened to be nearby spotted her. Hungry, and drawn by the sight of a woman besides, he inched closer and announced, "I'll give you five dollars, ma'am, for them biscuits."

Luzena hesitated. Five dollars was a week's pay. For a plate of biscuits? Luzena looked quizzically at him. The miner misread her look. "He repeated his offer to purchase, and said he would give ten dollars for bread made by a woman, and laid the shining gold piece in my hand."

Luzena took the coin and handed over the biscuits. She ran to tell Mason of their good fortune. The couple gazed at their gleaming prize and hid the precious coin away "as a nest-egg for the wealth we were to gain." Who doubted California now?

When she fell asleep that night, Wilson dreamed of bearded, wealthy miners at work in the diggings. Every swing of a pick turned up gold, and much of that gold tumbled her way. Morning brought less cheery news: tipped over on its side on the wagon floor was the little wooden box where Wilson had put her ten dollars. The box was empty, the coin presumably lost somewhere on the trail. "So we came, young, strong, healthy, hopeful, but penniless, into the new world." No matter. They would start again.

Before them lay Sacramento. "All around us twinkled the camp fires of the new arrivals. A wilderness of canvas tents glimmered in the firelight; the men cooked and ate, played cards, drank whisky, slept rolled in their blankets, fed their teams, talked, and swore." A few glanced up at the new arrivals and saw a woman. "They stared at me as at a strange creature," Wilson wrote, "and roused my sleeping babies, and passed them from arm to arm to have a look at such a novelty as a child."

In time the young, lonely men handed Wilson's children back to her. "We halted in an open space, and lighting our fire in their midst made us one with the inhabitants of Sacramento."

Since she'd left home, Wilson had imagined that she would eventually find work cooking or running a boardinghouse. Her encounter with the biscuit-buying miner emboldened her. Within three days of arriving in Sacramento, the Wilsons sold their oxen, for $600, and used the money to buy part ownership of a hotel.* It was hardly a grand structure, but it was made of wood, not canvas, and in the circumstances that counted as high-toned. ("The present of this city is under canvas and the future on paper," wrote a New Yorker who had arrived in Sacramento just before the Wilsons. "Everything is new except the ground and trees and the stars, beneath a canopy of which we slept.")

The kitchen in Luzena Wilson's hotel took up one room. The rest of the space had a less familiar look. Decades later she could still conjure up her first peek inside. "Imagine a long room, dimly lighted by dripping tallow candles stuck into whisky bottles, with bunks built from floor to ceiling on either side," she wrote.

This single room, jammed with miners, was virtually the entire

---

*Wilson did not tell us how much the oxen had cost back in Missouri, but presumably she made a handsome profit. Another newly arrived emigrant, who had reached California at about the same time as Wilson, wrote home that "all kinds of animals have risen from 500 to 5000 percent. I have this day sold a mule which I purchased last July for $8, for $360."

hotel. The bar stood in one corner. Two or three miners clutched their drinks. An elegantly dressed barman, resplendent in blue shirt and flaming red sash, presided over the rows of bottles and the collection of glassware. A barkeep was an important figure, and his loud voice and imperious manner conveyed that message to the greenest newcomer.

In the opposite corner several men sat around a table, playing cards. A clumsy fiddler wrestled with a tune called "Money Musk" *("Whirls Mary Martin all in blue / Calico gown and stockings new"),* while half a dozen men did their best to dance. A homesick young man, not yet old enough to shave, sat by a candle reading a letter and crying.

Around the edge of the room, stuffed in their bunks like letters in the pigeonholes of a post office, were the hotel's residents. "Some of the men lay sick in their bunks," Wilson wrote, "some lay asleep, and out from another bunk, upon this curious mingling of merriment and sadness stared the white face of a corpse."

No one had bothered even to pull a blanket over the dead man's face. "Nobody missed him. They would bury him tomorrow to make room for a new applicant for his bunk. The music and the dancing, the card-playing, drinking, and swearing went on unchecked by the hideous presence of Death. His face grew too familiar in those days to be a terror."

From here on, this would be Luzena's world.

Luzena Wilson's moment of jaw-dropping astonishment at California's wealth passed quickly. Most new arrivals stumbled around a while longer, happy and befuddled, content to gawk at the riches on display around them.

"Every new-comer in San Francisco is overtaken with a sense of complete bewilderment," wrote Bayard Taylor, only twenty-four years old but already a star at the *New York Tribune*, which had sent him to cover the biggest story of the age. Taylor was a cosmopolitan figure and a quick study—he had published a book of poetry at nineteen, and roamed Europe on foot for two years in his early twenties and written a much-admired book on his wanderings—and he took pride in thriving wherever life took him. A hut in Panama, with pigs snuffling around a dirt floor, made for a fine excursion; so did a palace in Vienna. But San Francisco sent him reeling. "One knows not whether he is awake or in some wonderful dream. Never have I had so much difficulty in establishing, satisfactorily to my own senses, the reality of what I saw and heard."

The sights confronting him at every turn, Taylor wrote, would strike his readers as make-believe. Out of fear for his credibility, he went on, he hesitated to report what he'd seen. He had met a soldier, a Mexican War veteran, who was reputedly a millionaire with an income of $50,000 a month. Another man had died in debt to the tune of $41,000; by the time his affairs were settled, his real estate holdings had gained so much in value that, after his heirs had settled his bills, they still had $40,000 a year left over.

Taylor had come from New York, but the pace he now encountered was like nothing he'd ever seen. San Francisco began bustling at sunrise, and everyone raced at top speed through the day. "You speak to an acquaintance—a merchant, perhaps," Taylor wrote. "He utters a few hurried words of greeting, while his eyes send keen glances on all sides of you; suddenly he catches sight of somebody in the crowd; he is off, and in the next five minutes has bought up half a cargo, sold a town lot at treble the sum he gave, and taken a share in some new and imposing speculation."

Entrepreneurs with big dreams cast about for backers, but everyone, regardless of station, joined the golden scramble. In the street in front of the grandly named United States Hotel, Taylor watched a dozen men on their hands and knees gouge up clumps of ground with knives and then crumble the dirt to powder in their hands. They blew the dust away and scanned their palms for specks of gold. The gold had leaked from miners' bags or been swept out the door by someone wielding a broom. In a single day these urban miners could earn five dollars. If the streets weren't actually *paved* with gold, they were at least littered with it.*

Everything was "hurry and skurry," as one newcomer put it, and all the commotion centered on money. Every conversation turned on how one could make a fortune; every dream turned on how one could spend it. "It is impossible to witness this excess and dissipation of business, without feeling something of its influence," Taylor wrote. "The very air is pregnant with the magnetism of bold, spirited, unwearied action, and he who but ventures into the outer circle of the whirlpool is spinning, ere he has time for thought, in its dizzy vortex."

Jennie Megquier felt a bit dizzy herself. She had opened a small boardinghouse in San Francisco, and she scarcely had time to catch her breath. "People seem to be very near crazy. God only knows where it will end, some days we have made fifty dollars but I have to work mighty hard."

She thrived on the speed and the commotion. San Francisco had materialized almost instantly, like a stage set of a city wheeled into place between the acts. Where two days ago a lot had stood vacant, a visitor might find a store packed with merchandise and jammed

---

*Con men knew these stories, too. In front of the Parker House, in San Francisco, one man sneaked out at night and spilled a few ounces of gold dust into the muddy street at a spot he could locate again. The next day, he "found" the gold, while a gawking crowd of forty or fifty gathered. The crook's partner happened to have on hand a stock of tin pans for the crowd to buy, at two dollars each rather than the usual ten cents.

with customers. Over the course of those two days, a total of forty new buildings might have risen up. Anyone trying to take a census would have been trampled by newcomers—between 1849 and 1851, San Francisco's population would grow some thirtyfold.

"The most busy streets in New York will not compare with the business here," Megquier wrote excitedly in September, 1849. "Goods of all kinds nearly fill the streets & yards." Six weeks later, the pace had only picked up. "There never was a place where money is spent so lavishly as here." Megquier had seen a single pair of boots sell for ninety-six dollars. "Gold is so very plenty," she wrote, "it makes but very little difference what they have to pay."

By now, the Megquiers had been in California five months. "We have made more money since we have been here than we should make in Winthrop in twenty years," Jennie crowed. Even somber Thomas Megquier, knocked happily off-balance by fifty-dollar paydays, could not resist a bit of boasting. Go ahead and buy his son some new winter clothes, Thomas wrote to a friend back in Maine who was helping to look after the children, "and you shall be paid in California gold."

In the city named in honor of that mild saint, Francis of Assisi, quiet and contemplation had no place. "People lived more in a week than they would in a year in most other places," one emigrant remarked. "More money was made and lost, there was more buying and selling, more sudden changes of fortune, more eating and drinking, more smoking, swearing, gambling, and tobacco-chewing" than anywhere else in the world.

The gold-seekers reveled in the anything-goes openness, at least at first. "A man, on coming to California, could no more expect to retain his old nature unchanged," Bayard Taylor observed, "than he could retain in his lungs the air he had inhaled on the Atlantic shore." The first change was a fit of exhilaration akin to the bucking and snorting of a horse that slips its rider and bounds away unconstrained. A "reckless and daring spirit" marked the new Californians, wrote Taylor, no matter how placid they had been at home. "It was curious to see how men hitherto noted for their prudence and caution took sudden leave of those qualities."

For many of the gold-seekers, this social freedom proved fully as important as the economic freedom that had lured them in the first place. Gold might prove hard to find; freedom was impossible to miss. Life in California was different from life elsewhere, hugely different and different in a huge number of ways.

"You are right in thinking that we live here just as we please," a miner named Franklin Buck wrote to his sister back home in Maine. "If we want a hot whisky toddy we have it. If we choose to lay abed late, we do so. We come and go and nobody wonders, and no Mrs. Grundy"— the nagging, censorious voice of conventional morality— "talks about it. We are free from all fashions and conventionalities of Society, so called with you. I like this."

So did many others. And even those who feared the unaccustomed freedom recognized that there was no point in denying its existence. In new, wide-open California, warned one San Francisco minister, "gigantic temptations" lurked. Fretful mothers and nosey neighbors were two thousand miles away. A young man could trample the hometown rules and no one would notice or care. Nearly everyone was young, single, male, rolling in money and eager to spend it or dead broke and eager to forget it.

San Francisco was a city packed with lottery winners, and they lorded it over everyone else. Newly flush miners pushed their way into gambling halls, sauntered over to the tables, and bet a bag of gold on the turn of a single card.* They sent off their tobacco-stained shirts and grimy underwear by clipper ship—to be laundered in Honolulu or Canton. No one quite lit a cigar with a hundred-dollar bill, but the fashionable way to pour a drink was to spill an entire bottle of liquor into a wineglass, so that the excess splashed out in exuberant bounty. Drinkers who were even more flamboyant opted for the boldest flourish of all—they strode up to the bar, took a glass, filled it partway with gold dust, and handed it to the barman. His task was to exchange that gleaming glass for one filled with wine or whiskey to the same level. (Like barbers who found gold in their patrons' trimmed whiskers, barmen quickly learned to sift for gold after they swept the floor at the end of the night.)

In this raw, money-mad culture, conspicuous display was the norm from the start. At Sutter's Fort, in the Christmas season of 1848, one observer noted "great numbers of young men…with at least a thousand dollars worth of finery upon them. They were almost loaded down with trinkets." The dandies strolled up and down, basking in the stares of passersby. One young man, all in black, wore a large cloak, also black. Though the night was cold, he kept his cloak unfurled so that it would flap and billow and draw the eye. Another well-dressed man marched back and forth in front of a busy tavern. "In his right hand he held a large bell, and at short

---

*A miner named Vicente Pérez Rosales told of watching a stranger, completely silent and expressionless, placing such all-or-nothing bets. The gambler put his sack of gold down next to one of the two face-up cards on the table. (You won if a match for your card—a ten to match your ten, say—came up before a match for the other.) The gold weighed about a pound. The stranger lost. Still silently, still intently, he took another sack the same size and bet again. And lost again. Without changing expression or uttering a word, he unwrapped a long, thin bag of gold from around his waist—this one weighed about six pounds—and placed it beside the card he wanted. Then he took out his pistol, cocked it, pointed it at the dealer, and gestured for him to deal. This time he won.

intervals he would stop and tingle his bell, as much as to say 'Look here, this is me.'"

To witness such scenes was to burn with hope and envy. One new arrival described his torment. Everywhere he looked "the returned gold-diggers were there with their 'piles,' exhibiting the glittering 'lumps' and bags of 'scales' and 'dust'; elated with their acquisitions; in some instances, giddy with their suddenly acquired wealth." It was almost impossible not to wonder if you, too, could live so splendidly.

Miners who had made a strike took special delight in parading through town and teasing and tantalizing brand-new arrivals. A group of Chileans ran into a friend from home and thrust their wealth under his nose. "Wrapped in rags were nuggets as big as walnuts," the newcomer gaped, "and gold dust like lentils." Another group banded together, adorned themselves with knives and pistols, and staggered conspicuously through the streets carrying heavy sacks (laden with sand) labeled "MUCHA ORA" and supposedly full of gold. "The immigrants would stop in amazement...and ask all sorts of questions," one of the pranksters exulted. Some of the greenhorns panicked that there would be no gold left, and others thrilled at the prospect of infinite riches soon to come their way.

In Sacramento, where Israel Lord had temporarily landed, life was just as outsized and unfathomable. Lord was "struck all aback" by the casual way the local shopkeepers handled gold. When a miner brought in his dust, "it is poured out and weighed almost as carelessly as rice or pepper in the States, and very few ever pick up any scattering flake, unless larger than a pin-head, and some pay no attention whatever to so small matters." The bigger the shop, the less finicky the shopkeeper. "In the large establishments, the dust is dipped about in pint tin cups. In a word, it is an article of produce, as easily got as wheat or corn in the States, and handled with much the same feeling, and comparatively with the same waste."

*   *   *

Not only miners but land speculators, merchants, farmers, and entrepreneurs of every stripe prospered. Streams of money poured everywhere, and countless newcomers splashed happily in the current. "Everyone must do something, it matters but very little what it is," Jennie Megquier observed. "If they stick to it, they are bound to make money."

California needed everything and had nothing—no picks or shovels or beds or blankets or nails or bricks, and few men willing to do any labor except dig for gold. (In 1850 there were 624 miners for every 1,000 people in California.) With nearly everyone off to the mines, wages for carpenters, blacksmiths, and masons tripled and quadrupled, sometimes reaching $15 or $20 a day. Anyone who could drive a nail, stitch a boot, plow a field, bake a pie could rake in money. Deliverymen could earn $6,000 a year ($120,000 in today's money).

After a brief, exhausting stint in the mines, a sign painter named Lyman Bradley retreated to the city and made the happy discovery that he could make more money with a paintbrush than with a shovel. Speed was everything, skill nearly irrelevant. "All were in a hurry," Bradley recalled. "If you could get a job done quick enough to suit, you could have almost any price your conscience allowed you to ask." Gold from gold.

The big names—like Sam Brannan, the entrepreneur and con man who had roused San Francisco by waving a bottle of gold in the streets and shouting "Gold! Gold!"—had already begun accumulating their fortunes. The surprise was that this was a mass frenzy, not a game for high rollers only. Brannan's wife, Ann, was one of countless small fry who joined in the fun. "Now is the time for making money," she wrote to her sister-in-law in New York, in

September, 1848. "You will hardly believe me when I tell you that this summer in little more than three months I have cleared five hundred dollars by making and getting made cheap clothing."

It was *so* easy. Pants and shirts that would bring twenty-five cents in New York sold for six times as much in San Francisco, "and they have only one pocket in them," Ann Brannan exclaimed, so that it was no challenge at all to make five or six in a day. *Come out here!*

A month after his arrival in San Francisco, in December, 1849, a New York artist named William Jewett could hardly count his money. Jewett specialized in painting the newly rich, and they lined up for the honor. "I charge from one hundred and fifty to eight hundred dollars—shall paint two or three per week if they come fast enough." Amidst such plenty, Jewett reported, he was "as jolly as a clam at high water."

He branched into real estate and prospered there, too. At one point he bought an empty lot in San Francisco for $200; three days later, he sold half of it for $250. (In real estate especially, prices rose seemingly without limit; a lawyer who was looking for office space found that "a cellar in the earth, about twelve feet square and six feet deep," commanded $250 a month in rent.) One man cornered the market in candlewicks, of all things, and made a killing. Another bought up $10,000 worth of barley and resold it in a week, for $20,000. A musician could earn two ounces of gold in two hours ($600 in today's money), a French miner observed, "by scraping on a squeaky fiddle...or by puffing into an asthmatic flute." A group of new arrivals in San Francisco sold a flock of chickens for $25 each (in today's money $500 apiece).*

---

*Perhaps the entrepreneurs deserved their windfall. The chickens had arrived with them on shipboard, the descendants of three hens who had flown the coop ten days out from Salem, Massachusetts. The passengers of the *Lagrange* had insisted on sending out a lifeboat to retrieve the escapees, and the rescue was a success.

*   *   *

The career of a farmer named John Horner highlighted just how extravagant California's reality could be. Horner, originally from New Jersey, had arrived in San Francisco in July, 1846. (A Mormon, Horner was one of the passengers who had traveled to California on the *Brooklyn* with Sam Brannan.) He planted wheat, barley, peas, and potatoes but earned no money at all that first year, and when gold was discovered, he took off for the diggings. This turned out to be a miscalculation. "We did not get much gold," Horner recalled, "but we got the ague without much exertion, and did considerable shaking."

Cured of gold fever, Horner returned to farming. When the hordes of gold-seekers poured in, he was ready. "Nothing seemed to be craved by the appetites of these people so much as vegetables; many of them had, or were rapidly approaching, scurvy. They would eat a raw onion or potato with as great and apparent relish as though it were a nice flavored apple." Horner was the only farmer around. In 1849 he cleared $8,000 (in today's money, $160,000).

In January, 1850, Horner's brother arrived in California and joined him on the farm. "We worked and flourished together the next four years," John Horner wrote, "perhaps as no other farmers ever flourished before in America, in so short a time." He may well have been right. "Fortune is said to knock at least once at every man's door," Horner would recall in his old age. "She found us at home; we opened the door and bid her welcome, and thankfully accepted her offer."

This was an innovation — farming on an industrial scale, farming to make a fortune rather than feed a family. As much as mining, it would become a hallmark of California life. In 1850 alone, the Horner brothers' vegetables brought in $150,000 (in today's money, $3 million).

———————

While everyone had dreamt of fortune, few new arrivals knew just what you would need in order to thrive in the diggings. The overland travelers had been too busy and too tired to spend much time planning. Those who came by sea, on the other hand, had spent months with little to do but buff and hone their fantasies. On countless ships converging on California, passengers whiled away the days tinkering with gold-finding machines and cobbling together containers to carry home the gold they would dig. Aboard the clipper ship *America,* for instance, one eager young man had fashioned leather pouches from the legs of old boots; another preferred bags sewn from canvas; still another favored empty pork barrels, which could be rolled rather than lugged.

Yet another passenger spent his time polishing a scheme to fish for gold without the nuisance of getting his feet wet in a river. He devised a sheet-iron scoop that he planned to attach to a long pole. Safe on shore, he would perch in the shade of a tree and gather up bite after bite of rich, golden sand.

Other men had brought elaborate, gold-extracting machines equipped with a crank, or two cranks, or a treadle. One especially large mechanism, admired and envied by all, required three attendants—one to turn an enormous handle, another to pour gold-bearing dirt and water in the top, and one more to take the sieved gold from the bottom, stow it in pork barrels, and then fasten the barrels shut. The proprietor of this giant mill, a Mr. Allen from Cambridge, Massachusetts, had brought his servant with him to turn the crank.

On arrival in San Francisco, the men of the *America* found the shoreline littered with hundreds of similar contraptions. Even Mr. Allen recognized the message. He abandoned his prize machine in the crowded junkyard.

With machines or without, the point was to get to the diggings and join the carnival. After their long journey, the new arrivals could scarcely wait. On his first day ashore in California, an Ohio man named Samuel McNeil fielded a question from a stranger — would he help with some carpentry, hammering up the support beams for a canvas-sided building? The job paid eight dollars a day, with meals thrown in free.

"I had never earned over one dollar a day before," McNeil recalled, "in twenty years as a shoemaker." But he waved the offer aside without hesitating a moment. For twenty dollars he found a place on a schooner and headed for Sacramento, on the way to the goldfields.

McNeil and countless others raced off to dig without even pausing to buy provisions. Once at the goldfields they would find someplace to sleep, something to eat. "As for the prospects of mining," Alonzo Delano wrote his wife, just before heading out to make his fortune, "all agree that it ranges from eight to a thousand dollars per day. If you get a good place, a few hours will yield hundreds, perhaps thousands, but after getting the hang of the barn you are sure of eight dollars. This is the lowest that I have heard."

At a time like this, who could take the time to run from store to store? As soon as they reached the diggings, the emigrants knew, they would reshape their lives. Almost as exciting, they would reshape themselves. A young gold-seeker from Cincinnati, twenty-two-year-old William Perkins, nearly burst with excitement when he sighted his first miners. "Here were real, live miners, men who had actually dug out the shining metal and who had it in huge buckskin pouches in the pockets of their pantaloons. Men who spoke jestingly, lightly of chunks of gold weighing one, five or ten pounds!

"These men were the awful objects of our curiosity," Perkins went on, "the demi-gods of the dominion.... Their long rough boots, red shirts, Mexican hats; their huge, uncombed beards covering half the face; the Colt's revolver attached to its belt behind; the cuchillo [knife] stuck into the leg of the boot—all these things were attributes belonging to another race of men than ourselves, and we looked upon them with a certain degree of respect and with a determination soon to be ourselves as little human-like in appearance as they were." Clerks no more.

A first peek at the work itself (as opposed to a glimpse of off-duty miners) proved less enticing. One novice on his way to the diggings witnessed the reality almost as soon as he left town. "Four or five men were working in a ravine by the roadside," wrote John Borthwick, a Scottish gold-seeker, "digging holes like so many gravediggers." Undiscouraged by his own analogy, Borthwick worried only that he might be hurrying by huge masses of gold just inches beneath the ground.

The diggings themselves did not prove entirely reassuring. Before he arrived at the Feather River, Alonzo Delano had harbored vague thoughts of hardy men, vigorous work, and grand views. "You hear of men picking out lumps of gold from the crevices of the rocks as if all they had to do was to stoop down and dig it out," he wrote. He knew the work would be harder than that, but he had not anticipated just how harsh conditions would be. "On my arrival at the mines there was a heavy rain of twelve hours," he continued, "and I know of four men who lay out in it, all of whom were too sick with chills and flux to sit up. I let my own blanket and buffalo skin go to cover one man from the storm within two hours after my arrival. His bones now lay on the mountain's side where the cold storm will trouble him no more."

This was indisputable reality. But so was this, in a letter written at almost the same time and place, by two brothers newly arrived in the mines: "Now I will tell you what we have done since we got here; we have worked eight days and have made $16,000." In one week, in other words, the Springer brothers had made five years' pay. "There are a great many in the gold diggings at work," they continued, "some are making fortunes and some are spending fortunes. A man that will half work can make a great fortune in three years."

In truth, a miner could count on nothing except that he would work not at half his capacity but to the extreme limit of his strength and stamina. The diggings were aptly named. "The labor of gold-digging is unequalled by any other in the world in severity," wrote one dismayed soldier-turned-miner. "It combines, within itself, the various arts of canal-digging, ditching, laying stone-walls, plough-ing, and hoeing potatoes."

To pass from the city to the diggings was to fall through a trap-door. Life in the city was rowdy and easy, for those who had money; life in the diggings was brutal and harsh, for almost everyone. Miners hefted a shovel or swung a pick while sweating in the sun or freezing in a stream, hour upon hour. Often they were sick; nearly always they were malnourished. And these were men, one of them acknowledged, whose "hardest work at home" had been pushing a pen or dancing a polka.

Each miner worked in a strange kind of isolation, only a few feet from his companions but cut off from them by the sound of tumbling water and clanging tools, and by exhaustion. Within these noisy cocoons, each man labored on, searching for a rhythm that would ease his task. It was hard to find. One minute a pick would bite into soft gravel, which made a moment's break. But the next swing might smack a hidden rock and send a shock like an electric charge up the arms and into the shoulders. Swing again and you might crash against a thick layer of stone as hard and unforgiving as pavement.

Spurred by gold, men worked with a zeal that no boss or overseer could ever have commanded. Life was reduced to grunts, curses, clatter, mud and water, rock and sweat. "It was altogether a scene which conveyed the idea of hard work in the fullest sense of the words," wrote John Borthwick, the Scottish miner, "and in comparison with which a gang of railway navvies would have seemed to be merely a party of gentleman amateurs playing at working *pour passer le temps.*"

Often men turned down jobs with a guaranteed wage double what they were likely to earn in the mines. What was the choice, really? The moment a man took a job with a salary, no matter how high, the possibility of an unbounded future vanished and an impenetrable ceiling crashed into place. Security was not the stuff of dreams; opulence and independence were. *Treasure, not wages!*

The gold-seeker Prentice Mulford described a day in the life. First, you dragged yourself awake. Young as they were, the miners rose slow and creaky, like aged warriors. "Working all the day previous, possibly in the water, or with it splashing all about, tugging at heavy boulders, shouldering wet sluices, to say nothing of the regular pick-and-shovel exercise," wore down the strongest men. Miners who had the luxury of cabins, rather than tents or lean-tos, usually slept on the floor. A few of the more fastidious preferred a table or a bench to the ground, but no one had a mattress, so it made little difference. Men slept in their boots or shoved them beneath their head, as a pillow.

If a cabin did happen to boast chairs or a table (rather than tree stumps or flour barrels), one observer noted, the floor was sure to be so uneven that the furniture stood on three legs rather than four, "reminding you constantly of a dog with a sore foot." Boarding-houses were seldom much better. Each morning the first task that faced one hard-pressed proprietor, in Negro Bar, was "scaring the Hogs out of my kitchen and Driving the mules out of my Dining room."

Getting dressed took no time. Mulford described the routine: "A pair of damp overalls, a pair of socks, a pair of shoes, or possibly the heavy rubber mining boots. Flannel shirts we slept in." Then a splash of cold water from a tin basin and a swipe with a comb, which took care of the sprucing up. "Who was there to dress for? Woman? The nearest was half a mile, fifty years of age, and married."

You gulped down some flapjacks or fried potatoes while half registering the dreary view through the open door. "There lies the bank of red earth as you left it yesterday," Mulford recalled. "There is the reservoir full of coffee-colored ditch water which had run in during the night after being used for washing in a dozen claims 'up country.' Then you draw on those damp, clammy rubber boots, either to the knee or hip high, the outside splashed with the dried reddish mud, and smelling disagreeably of rubber as you pulled them on and smelling worse as you became heated and perspiring. In these you waddle to the claim."

The makeshift towns carried ugly, aggressive names — Red Dog, Gouge Eye, Hangtown, Lady's Crevice, Jackass Gulch — as if in warning. There was truth in this advertising. Camps were filthy, with bottles and bones and old clothes flung into mud streets dotted with knee-deep bogs. Empty cans of preserved meat, sardines, and oysters heaped up at every doorway.

Everything was improvised, and most of it was shoddy. In a camp called Indian Bar, a woman died and was laid out on a board that rested atop two butter tubs. Her coffin was made of unstained pine planks. No screws could be found, so the lid was nailed shut while onlookers cringed at the sound of the hammer. Before the march to the graveyard, someone thought to borrow a piece of green cloth from a gambling table, and draped it across the coffin.

CHAPTER TWELVE

HARD TIMES

IN THE EARLY DAYS in the mines, technology was nearly beside the point and muscle power almost the only tool. But with treasure as the prize, even the most punishing work was worth a try. One of California's great virtues was that it abounded in placer gold — the word is pronounced with a short *a*, like *plaster* — which was to say, gold sitting on the surface or hidden by only a shallow layer of rock, clay, and gravel, as opposed to gold encased in stone and nearly inaccessible. In ages past, placer gold *had* been trapped inside rock, like gold elsewhere in the world. The miracle of California was that in countless places time and water had broken the gold free, and rivers and seasonal floods had washed it into streambeds where a man could pick his way to opulence.

So the miner's challenge was not to chop gold out of solid rock but to separate the lucrative bits and chunks from vast heaps of debris composed of dirt, gravel, sand, clay, and chunks of rock. It was as if, eons before, careless gods had crisscrossed an immense, stony beach while carrying sacks filled with gold dust fine as flour, and golden flakes like butterfly wings, and pea-sized golden pebbles, and coal-shaped golden lumps. All that gold had spilled, and through the ages nature had hidden it away. It *might* lie on the ground, but often it lay buried six feet deep or more, under what the miners called "top dirt." Below the worthless "top dirt" and above the impenetrable bedrock was "pay dirt," so named because *this* layer of rock and gravel might contain enough gold to repay the labor of sifting it.*

Time had gathered these riches into discrete heaps, a treasure trove over here, perhaps, and then a vast, barren expanse and then, possibly, more treasure over there, and on and on. The miner's task was to keep digging until his labor paid off. This was simple in concept, backbreaking in practice. All you had to do was gather a mound of muck and pour water on it. The water would carry away the light bits and leave behind the gold. The earliest tool, quickly superseded, was a pan with a solid bottom and sloping sides.† The recipe was utterly basic—shovel gravel into the pan; add water; swirl carefully, letting the water carry away the light-weight grit; throw away any big rocks; swirl again; scan the last remaining bits of grit for a glint of gold.

The first advance in technique was, in essence, to poke holes in the bottom of the pan and to catch the heavy grit that fell through. This was the idea behind the cradle, or rocker, which did in fact resemble a baby's cradle. A cradle was a wooden trough about four feet long, sitting on rockers and open at one end. Mounted in the cradle, like a drawer in a bureau, was a removable box with a perforated screen as its bottom side. A miner shoveled gravel into the box

---

*Hence the term "prospector," for a miner who tested the prospects of a new site by digging down to paydirt and washing a pan of gravel to see how rich it was.

†Plain as they were, pans were valuable. At the end of a working day, miners flung their picks and shovels to the ground and left them to mark their claims, but they carried their pans home. "It is no uncommon thing," one miner noted, "to see the same pan used for washing gold, washing clothes, mixing flour cakes, and feeding the mule."

and then poured water on top of the heap with a dipper, to make a thin, gritty porridge. Sandy, gravelly water—perhaps containing bits of gold—spilled through the holes in the screen. Rocks and bigger chunks of gravel were held back. Then the miner rocked the cradle, which sent the slurry sloshing back and forth and tumbling out the cradle's open end. The gold remained in the bottom of the cradle, where wooden cleats trapped it in place.

A further refinement, called a long tom, soon made the cradle obsolete. (In some mining camps, abandoned cradles by the hundreds dotted the riverbanks.) Little more than a trough fifteen or twenty feet long and mounted so that it sat at a tilt, a long tom was effectively a stretched-out cradle. Scale made all the difference. A hose (rather than a dipper) directed a steady stream of water into the tom's upper end. A team of miners shoveled dirt into the tom as fast as they could manage. A man standing farther along the tom stirred the stony gruel and threw out bits of rock. As in a cradle, an iron screen pocked with holes held back the large bits of debris. Water and grit fell to the tom's bottom. The crucial task was to gather that grit and wash it again, carefully. Even in a good location, a ton of dirt might yield only an ounce of gold.

From the start, all miners knew that to find gold you needed water. You searched in rivers, because that was where gold landed as streams and floods sent it on its rolling, tumbling way downhill. And you searched *with* rivers, because you relied on water to separate ounces of gold from the tons of mud and dirt that usually hid it. In the earliest days, when technology was at its simplest, miners used the river directly, crouching along the bank or standing knee-deep in the current, dipping their gravel-laden pans into the water and washing, sifting, and repeating, hour upon hour. The whole apparatus of rockers and toms and the linked-together troughs called sluice boxes represented nothing but a series of better responses to the same challenge—how could you harness more and more water so that you could wash more and more gold-bearing gravel?

Within a very few years, miners would find solutions that made outsiders gasp, sometimes in admiration and, more rarely, in horror. In free and independent California, the bold and the ruthless thrived. Gold was the only consideration; nature was a bank whose riches were meant for use, not a museum with exhibits in glass cases. If you wanted to divert a river out of its course (the better to scour the now-exposed channel for gold), go to it! If you chose to chop down all the trees in a valley to get wood for a flume to carry the diverted river, start to work! If the dam you built flooded out your neighbors' claims, let them build their own dam!

It was progress, nearly everyone agreed, but no one claimed it was pretty. "A mighty river taken up in a wooden trough," wrote Louise Clappe, a sharp-eyed Massachusetts woman living in Indian Bar, "strikes me as almost a blasphemy against nature." And this was far from the only blasphemy. In every camp, holes gouged deep into the ground pocked the landscape and posed a mortal danger to the drunk and the careless. Amputated trees stood as silent sentries on scarred hillsides. Mercury by the ton oozed into pristine rivers.* Canvas hoses slithered along the ground, carrying water to countless long toms; they looked, one miner wrote, "like immensely long slimy sea-serpents."

With thousands of miners laboring along every river in gold country, the days when you might stumble upon a nugget of gold

---

*Mercury binds to gold, but it is poisonous and its fumes are especially dangerous. Californians quickly grew to recognize the "pale, cadaverous faces" of those who worked with it. Miners poured mercury into the sluices where they rinsed their gold, and used it as a kind of gold-seeking magnet. Water passing down the sluice carried away mud and gravel but the gold/mercury amalgam was so heavy that it got caught by the wooden ridges along the sluice's bottom side. The mercury could be boiled away, leaving the gold.

ended quickly. Miners scraping futilely in the dirt along the Yuba and the American and the Feather and a score of other rivers soon had no choice but to move farther upstream or higher into the foothills. Early on, they had dug only a few feet down to paydirt. Then they dug holes as deep as wells. Now they dug shafts hundreds of feet down into the blackness—"coyote holes," they called them—or they dug horizontally a thousand feet, if that seemed the most direct route to a buried mine.

Coyote digging was work for a lone man who spent his days in near darkness, filling and refilling a bucket that his colleagues in the daylight would hoist up and empty. Horizontal shafts were team efforts. Bent over in the gloom (because they had too little room to stand upright), hoping that their candles would not flicker out for lack of air, the miners burrowed their way along with pick and shovel, or crammed wads of gunpowder into chiseled crevices in the wall, lit slow fuses, and retreated to what they hoped was a safe distance.

At the surface, battalions of men dug long, snaking ditches and canals or built wooden aqueducts to carry water to wash the hard-won buckets of dirt. Clumsily built at first but soon better engineered, these ditches and flumes stretched for miles, meandering across the hills like stitches on the torso of a stabbing victim.

Some gold-seekers found, after a brief try, that they simply could not meet the physical demands. "Prying up and breaking huge rocks and shoveling dirt from deep pits" was not what he had imagined back at home, one soft-muscled newcomer lamented, as he conjured up the innocent days when he had decided to make "the exchange of the pen for the crowbar." Another miner, Lucius

Fairchild—the young man who'd spent time in his father's store "selling rags to the ladies of Madison"—came to a similar melancholy insight. "We work from five in the morning until Eleven and then lay by until three when we work until Seven," he wrote home, "making ten hours a day which is work enough for a counter Hopper like me."

William Perkins, the Cincinnati greenhorn who had stared goggle-eyed at real, live miners, found himself amazed that *anyone* could summon the strength to persist. Then he recalled the adrenaline-fueled poker marathons he knew from back in the States. He had often watched "a party of gentlemen sit playing poker for three days and three nights without sleep or rest." Jazzed by cash-drenched fantasies, they'd played hand after hand, eagerly and alertly, "when not one of them but would have been half dead with fatigue by the end of the first night, had he been called upon to sit up with a sick friend." In the mines as at the poker table, Perkins concluded, a chance at a golden jackpot could energize a corpse.

For the same reason, no one in California paid much heed to grim accounts of how rare it was to strike it rich. The odds didn't matter nearly as much as the size of the treasure. A miner grubbing in the dirt might be exhausted, filthy, and poor today, but so what?—he could be rich tomorrow.

So on they dug.

Every miner learned quickly that caprice was the first law of the diggings, and caprice could drive men mad. "The fever and uncertainty of mining made the people grow old and haggard," Luzena Wilson recalled. "They might dig, dig, dig, fruitlessly for days, making scarcely enough to keep body and soul together, and then disheartened, sell the worthless claim for enough provisions to last till they struck another camp. Perhaps the first day's work on the old claim by the new owner would yield hundreds of dollars."

Faith in tomorrow's big strike could sustain a man through many a wet, miserable, fruitless day. But to live in the gutter while dreaming of the stars was a hard fate. The very psychology that sustained one man—*If you keep at it, you could still win!*—might break the heart of his neighbor. "I have seen a thousand dollars washed out of a single panful of dirt," wrote William Perkins, and his exclamation rang with hope and frustration both, for it seemed equally difficult to quit and to persist.

The problem was not merely that nature paid out her prizes willy-nilly. Everyone knew that mining was a lottery. The problem was that *this* lottery ran by especially devilish rules. First, the price of a ticket was so high. "It was strength, absolute brute force, which was required to win the gold of the placers," Alonzo Delano remarked, and there were no shortcuts. And every day required a new ticket, purchased in sweat. As the bitter lyrics of one gold rush song put it, *"They told about the heaps of dust and lumps so mighty big, / But they never said a single word how hard they were to dig."*

Second, the prizes were distributed in plain view, so that downcast losers could not avoid the sight of exultant, shouting, back-pounding winners hoisting bottles of champagne and springing for drinks all around. It was the fate of every embittered, empty-pocketed miner to retreat to the bar, night after night, and toast other men's good fortune. "There seems to be but one way to work in the mines," Alonzo Delano wrote, "and that is to stick to it till your turn and time comes, and be not discouraged because you are getting nothing and the man within three feet of you is taking out $100 per day." The catch—and Delano, a thoughtful man, knew it—was that his advice was virtually impossible to follow. None but a saint could look on even-tempered at a neighbor's triumph while he himself was trapped deep in a useless ditch.

In tandem, the two rules made mining both a physical and a psychological ordeal. To mine was to work to the limits of one's strength, tormented by exhaustion but afraid to stop for fear that the next turn of the shovel might unearth a bonanza. "The miseries of a miner might fill a chapter of woes," wrote Hubert Bancroft. "Digging and delving with eager anxiety day after day, up to the waist in water, exposed now to the rays of the burning sun, and now to cold, pitiless rains...heart and brain throbbing and bounding with success, or prostrate under accumulated disappointments.

"It was," Bancroft concluded simply, "more than a man with even an iron frame could endure."

The whole point of the gold rush, everyone had proclaimed from the beginning, was to make a pile and then run home with it. In practice, gold-seekers no sooner found a fortune than they threw it away. To strike it rich and to go home rich, it turned out, were vastly different things. "I have myself seen dozens who have worked for a week, made one, two or three thousand dollars and have then thrown up work until the whole of the amount was spent," wrote William Perkins. "I have seen men invent the most extravagant means to get rid of their dust."

Let a man heft a handful of gold, and he forgot in an instant every maxim about putting away today what could be used tomorrow. Euphoria fogged the mind. Yesterday a man moaned, "If I ever make my pile, I'll never let it go." Today he proclaimed, "Plenty more where that came from." Perkins witnessed such scenes again and again, but never quite figured out what lay behind them.

"Gold became a drug, and the class of people then in California did not value it," he wrote. "In those days almost every miner made what is called a 'strike' every week or so that gave him a small fortune, and he then seemed to be on thorns until it was spent."

The journalist Bayard Taylor, by training and temperament an observer rather than a participant, looked on and marveled. "Weather-beaten tars, wiry, delving Irishmen, and stalwart foresters from the wilds of Missouri became a race of sybarites and epicureans," he wrote. "Secure in possessing the 'Open Sesame' to the exhaustless treasury under their feet, they gave free rein to every whim or impulse which could possibly be gratified."

Many of those impulses took the shape of food and drink. "It was no unusual thing," Taylor went on, "to see a company of these men, who had never before had a thought of luxury beyond a good beef-steak and a glass of whiskey, drinking their champagne at ten dollars a bottle, and eating their tongue and sardines, or warming in the smoky camp-kettle their tin canisters of turtle-soup and lobster-salad."

Partly this was the exuberance to be expected of men who had never had money to spare and suddenly had more than they could fathom. Many of the miners "only knew the difference between having money and having none," one of them wrote. "A hundred dollars was to them as good as a thousand, and a thousand was in their ideas about the same as a hundred." When it came time for a spree, "they made a clean sweep of everything and spent their last dollar as readily as the first."

Without a second thought, miners paid any price a hotelkeeper or bartender asked. In Coloma, two miners gulped down a not-especially-grand breakfast of sardines, bread, cheese, and two bottles of ale, and handed over $43 (in today's money, $860) without a qualm. One grizzled loner, who claimed to have dug up between

$30,000 and $40,000 (in today's money, $600,000 to $800,000), spent all of it on the most luxurious meals he could find—cans of oysters or corn or peas at $6 a throw and champagne at every meal. In Indian Bar, a drunken bash began at nine in the evening on Christmas Day 1851 and roared on for *three weeks*. The festivities began with an oyster and champagne supper in the Humboldt, the hotel and gambling hall in town, and moved on to toasts, songs, speeches, and dancing. "They were dancing when I went to sleep," wrote Louise Clappe, "and they were dancing when I woke the next morning." Three days later they were still dancing. "On the fourth day," Clappe wrote, "they got past dancing" and moved on to "howling." Some "barked like dogs, some roared like bulls, and others hissed like serpents and geese." Come New Year's the party spun to a newer, rowdier level.

High spirits and inexperience fueled much of the spending, but a touch of the perverse figured in, as well. Take a reckless chance and you were flirting with self-destruction, but at the same time you were demonstrating that you were a free man who dared to thumb a nose at fate. Precisely because it made no sense, the man who flung his hard-won gold onto the gambling table was a swash-buckling buccaneer, to be admired and envied, and not a rule-bound bookkeeper, to be pitied.

Israel Lord—an antidrinking, antismoking, scripture-quoting Baptist—was the last man in the world to feel the temptation, when standing at the edge of a cliff, to step off. But Lord was a real-ist who saw that, though recklessness and indulgence repelled *him*, they exhilarated many others. Gambling was "a perfect mania" across California, he wrote, and in Sacramento, in December, 1849, he saw dozens of gambling halls jammed with "insane" min-ers who placed bets from breakfast to midnight. "Common laborers, mechanics, etc. will risk a whole day's earnings on the turn of a card"—and they did it *eagerly,* Lord noted, and you can hear the disdain in his voice change to astonishment—"as if it was a pleasure to get rid of the stuff."

Seldom have extravagance and deprivation been so entwined as in gold rush California. Ten years before Dickens wrote that "It was the best of times, it was the worst of times," one gold rush diarist after another wrestled with the paradox of living in a golden slum. Men fed on cold beans and slept on dirt floors and woke hoping that the day's work would see them transformed into millionaires—and sometimes it did.

It was not simply a matter of wealth and poverty bumping heads. "The character of the pioneers was a paradox," wrote Luzena Wilson. "They were generous to a degree which we can scarcely realize, yet selfish beyond parallel." Despite the crowds and the brand-new cities, men talked often of isolation and seldom of common bonds. "There were few close ties and few friendships," Wilson noted, "and when a familiar face dropped out, no one knew whether the man was dead or gone away, nobody inquired, nobody cared."

This indifference had partly to do with how transient the mining camps were, with new arrivals perpetually showing up and older hands daily heading off to look for richer grounds. Fatigue made for a kind of isolation, too, for at the end of the day, men had enough energy to take a drink or place a bet or collapse in a heap, but seldom much more.

The longer they spent in the diggings, the weaker the miners grew, their vigor sapped by sickness and their miserable diet. Meals were an endless succession of grease and starch unrelieved by even an occasional bit of greenery. Food was "stewed beans and flapjacks," one miner recalled, "and they were generally served twenty-one times a week." Cooking techniques were primitive. Men learned, by sad experience, that rice could not simply be flung into a pot and put on the fire, but required water. So did beans.

A well-equipped cabin had a frying pan and a cooking pot, both permanently grimy. The "table" might well be a shelf built out from the wall. Plates sat out all day, seldom washed (but, on the bright side, always in place for the next meal). A potful of pork and beans would last several days. Between meals it would sit out, to be dipped into as required. Flapjacks, made of flour and water, usually took the place of bread, which required more skill.

Israel Lord, who had ventured into the mines along the Feather River, could almost see his strength ebbing. "Cramp is so common that a person can hardly hold his hand tightly closed for a moment and open it again, without a violent effort to overcome the spasm which is almost sure to follow a strong contraction of a muscle. Rheumatic pains are rife; scurvy as common as damaged flour, and diarrhea haunts the dwellers of this famous land."*

The men lamented their predicament in song:

I've lived on swine 'till I grunt and squeal,
No one can tell how my bowels feel,
With slapjacks swimming round in bacon grease.
I'm a lousy miner,
I'm a lousy miner; when will my troubles cease?†

The tone was light, but such songs were laments in jaunty dress. The carefree life of a gold-miner too often took on the aspect of a

---

*It is significant that the image that popped into Lord's mind, when he wanted to convey that a sight was completely routine, was of flour gone bad.

†"Lousy" had long since come to mean "contemptible and miserable" as well as "filthy and lice-ridden." Both definitions applied.

prison sentence at hard labor, with sickness only adding to the misery. Miners talked of "bloody flux" and "chill-fever" and other vague, untreatable afflictions. Medical care was little more than quackery, and nursing unavailable. With hundreds or thousands of miners crammed into primitive camps upstream and downstream from one another, with nutrition abysmal and sanitary standards low or nonexistent, dysentery and intestinal woes were all but universal.

Those too weak to stagger to work lay in fetid rags, shivering convulsively with fever, clutching their bellies as dysentery emptied their guts, watching helplessly as scurvy turned their flesh black and loosened their teeth. "Each squalid death," wrote the historian Kevin Starr, "and there were thousands, turned California's golden fleece into a vomit-stained shroud."

Of all the miners' afflictions, scurvy was perhaps the most dreaded. Men with scurvy "rotted to death by inches," one miner wrote, and he described one sick man so bent in pain that he was "drawn up into a kind of ball, and could have been rolled over and over like a bale of carpet."

Scurvy had been known since ancient times, but it had always been an affliction of sailors on long voyages on the open ocean.* To their sorrow, the gold-seekers had learned firsthand that the disease could fell landbound travelers, too. Now it had taken hold in the California foothills, where countless men dug in the soil but few had time to plant a row of potatoes or tomatoes. Miners spoke of "land scurvy" and "bachelor's scurvy." In desperation, they choked

---

*An explorer on one of the first Spanish expeditions to California, in 1602, wrote a shocked description of his shipmates' agony when scurvy struck. "The sensitiveness of the bodies of these sick people is so great that the best aid which can be rendered them is not even to touch the bedclothes.... The teeth become so loose and without support that they move while moving the head."

down fistfuls of grass or tried such folk remedies as burying themselves in the ground, up to the neck. (The idea was that the soil had healing powers.) "Whole camps were sometimes buried at once," wrote one surprised observer, "except a few who remained out to keep off the grizzlys and coyotes."

When the rainy season began, in October in a typical year, the picture grew darker still. Rivers burst their banks and made work in the diggings nearly impossible. Cold, wet, hungry miners escaped to town or retreated to their crude cabins, or tents, or simply shelters beneath a tree, and tried to wait it out. They called these months the "sickly season."

Mining was a race against the coming of the rain. In the hot, dry days of spring and summer, when rivers ran low, miners worked ferociously. Even Israel Lord found himself caught up in the excitement. "The bottom of the river is covered with gold," he wrote his brother from Long's Bar on the Feather River, "& a company strong enough to dam it frequently will take out several 1000 dollars in a day."

The challenge was to take advantage of low water, by forcing the river out of its accustomed course. Only starstruck men could have conceived the notion of lifting up entire rivers and setting them down to one side. The territory was rugged and remote, the tools rudimentary, the entire scheme unprecedented and madly ambitious. Trained engineers would have blanched, and these were farmers and lawyers making it up as they went along.

The danger was a match for the difficulty. Miners wrestled boulders and packed tons of dirt to make dams and then hammered together long wooden flumes to carry the diverted river away from its now-exposed bed. Then they dug with all their might, hunting for gold the river had left behind, while the clock ticked. "The whole current of the river is turned into the flume," one miner wrote. "The descent being rapid, the water moves with such velocity that men have been drowned in a flume in which the water was less than two feet in depth."

The remote Sierra foothills swarmed with crowds of men whipsawing planks for the flumes, hammering together supports to hoist the waterways into the air, and, everywhere, digging, shoveling, tunneling. Hundreds of miles of flumes zigzagged their way downhill. Countless waterwheels powered pumps that drained water from spots where the river had escaped the flume and pooled up. Innumerable heaps of dirt and gravel rose next to deep pits, as if a race of gigantic terriers had been set free in the night.

"I have often been in a position upon some projecting point of a mountain," one gold-seeker wrote, "where at a single view I could see a river thus flumed for several miles. The river seems to be all alive and in motion. Hundreds of wheels are rolling, each with its accompanying pumps working, and through the entire distance, throngs of men of various colors, with blue or red woolen shirts, broad brimmed hats and long Jew beards, digging with picks and shovels on each side, or immediately under the rushing torrent coursing its way over their heads."

When the floods came, the game was up. On November 7, 1849, Israel Lord made a worried entry in his journal. "Rained all night long, more deliberately—more maliciously, more unmercifully than ever." The rain smacked against the roof with a sharp, unrelenting clatter. "This journey is through extremes," Lord wrote. "In the desert we had no water. Dying of thirst. We are now in danger of drowning."

On November 10, Lord noted that there had been no letup. "Rained all night, steady, deliberate pouring and the river has raised in that time seven feet and is rising fast." Swollen, rushing rivers pounded through dams and broke flumes and sawmills into matchsticks. When the Feather River careened through one camp, wrote a startled miner, "the Methodist church turned around on its foundation like a dancing master on his heel."

Foam-capped waves swept downhill. Barrels, pans, and splintered boards spun and bobbed in the surging waters. "The river seemed as if it had suddenly arisen to assert its independence and take vengeance for all the restraints which had been placed upon it," one awed miner wrote, as he looked out on a hillside suddenly stripped of everything man-made. A mine could vanish as if it had never been.

So could the miners who worked it, as Luzena Wilson had noted. In California you risked dying unnoticed and unmourned. You might die broke, besides, despite the money all around. But you would not die without ever having lived, trudging your life away only to collapse at last like a beast in harness. Instead, you would die, if it came to that, like a man who took a valiant leap across a mountain chasm and fell short. That was California's dark bargain, but only now did the miners read the fine print.

This two-edged freedom — the freedom to be left alone (to do as you pleased) and to be left on your own (regardless of need) — marked California from the outset. Here was a society that was cosmopolitan, rowdy, violent, brand-new, thrilled with itself when it was not horrified, exploding in size, knee-deep in wealth, with no entrenched leadership class but instead a churning, changing hierarchy based on fortunes newly made and newly lost. Some gold rush boosters insist that this heritage continues to shape California today — that California remains the land of the fresh start, the new idea, that Silicon Valley's visionaries and entrepreneurs are direct descendants of the dreamers who took to the Sierra foothills armed with little more than nerve, ambition, and a shovel.

Certainly the new emigrants believed they had walked into a place like no other, where a man could shed his past like a snake sloughing off its skin. The freedom to grow rich was only part of it. Gold rush California was the land of the self-invented man and the second chance. "If he could blow a fife on training days, he will be a professor of music here," wrote one early arrival. "If he have built a pigsty or kennel at home, he will be a master-builder in California." One Englishman found himself addressed as "Captain," for no good reason. "If I was a real Captain," he noted wryly, "I should of course be a General there."

A popular song captured the mood. *"Oh, what was your name in the States?"* it began, *"Was it Thompson, or Johnson or Bates? / Did you murder your wife / And fly for your life? / Say, what was your name in the States?"*

Jennie Megquier was one of many who exulted in her newfound freedom. "It is all the same whether you go to church or play monte," she wrote a friend. "That is why I like [California]; you very well know that I am a worshipper at the shrine of liberty."

Worshippers at that shrine tended not to spend much time in silent prayer or even quiet deliberation. California was loud, rambunctious, and dangerous, its brand of liberty smacking more of the fraternity house than of the Greek public square or the New England town meeting. The new arrivals set the tone from the get-go. On Independence Day 1849, in San Francisco, oratory and top hats played little role. "The glorious Fourth was ushered in by drinking to the constitution in bumpers, until the celebrants were half-seas over," wrote one miner who had arrived in California only the week before. "Then began the fun. Instead of firecrackers, pistols were used. Instead of sending up rockets, men would show their adroitness with the gun by shooting through windowpanes, hitting lighted lamps or candles and offering to shoot off buttons from their friends' garments."

Parlors, chaperones, and church socials belonged to another world. Gambling dens, saloons, and bordellos took their place. Professional gamblers — "knights of the green table" — were the most admired men in town. "There, sin is stealthy, and cunning, and still, and goes in the dark," the Reverend Charles Farley declared in a Thanksgiving sermon in 1850, in San Francisco's First Unitarian Church. "Here it is open, unmasked, makes no apologies and asks none. It unfurls its flag in the most public and conspicuous places."

But fear not, Farley went on. The gold-seekers had the fortitude to resist all temptation, and they had better things to do besides. "Time here is money, and they are a great deal too busy to spend much time at Vanity Fair, or to make common cause with the devil."

Well, maybe. The reverend had a good heart but a dull eye. An excited miner from North Carolina did a better job of capturing the glee of the hordes of young men who found themselves running free. "I have seen purer liquors, better segars, finer tobacco, truer guns and pistols, larger dirks and bowie knives, and prettier courtesans here, than in any other place I have ever visited," twenty-six-year-old Hinton Helper exclaimed, "and it is my unbiased opinion that California can and does furnish the best bad things that are obtainable in America."

Dizzy at the opportunities on offer, the new residents of California did their best to sample those bad things. Lucius Fairchild spoke for many in the boisterous throng. Fairchild would go on to a distinguished career, first as a brigadier general in the Civil War (he lost an arm at Gettysburg) and then as a three-term governor of

Wisconsin. In time, he would pose for John Singer Sargent in formal dress and bedecked with medals. (The portrait looked to him, Fairchild told his wife, like "a lot of badges running off with a bald-headed man.") But in 1850 Fairchild was not a grand and imposing figure but a randy young man on the loose. "Gambling, drinking and houses of ill fame are the chief amusements of this country," he wrote a friend back home. "Therefore you see that we have nothing but work, reading and writing to amuse us," he teased, "as we are all nice young men and do not frequent such places."

Gambling halls and saloons conjured up countless ways to separate lonely young miners from their money. For an ounce of gold, a young woman would sit next to you while you nursed a drink or played a hand of cards. Some gambling dens found more creative ways to lure miners inside. They featured "artists' models" who posed in see-through silk or gauze or even, for those miners whose taste ran to the classics, "clothed in nature's robes."

In eastern cities, brothels and saloons were hidden in the bad part of town. California was different. San Francisco and Sacramento and the rowdy mining camps had sprung up overnight and helter-skelter, and bordellos and gambling dens sat on main street, next to hotels, restaurants, and stores. Even a man of sedate tastes was bound to bump up against gamblers, brawlers, and painted ladies. A man *seeking* diversion did not have far to look.

Teetotaling Israel Lord stepped inside a gambling den in Sacramento and gazed about in mingled horror and fascination. "It is fitted up like a palace," he wrote. "On one side is a counter, 30 feet long, behind which stand three fine looking young men dealing out death in the most inviting vehicles—sweet and sour and bitter and hot and cold and cool and raw and mixed." Nearby, "more like a dream than reality," stood tables lined with "oyster and lobster and salad and sauce and fruit and flesh and fish and pies and cakes," and, astonishing even to tell, "this department is served by females." Even across a gap of 150 years, we can see Lord flinch.

His every sense assaulted, Lord reeled in dismay. On a balcony high above the crowd, musicians bleated out tunes in random keys and shaky tempos. Drinkers sang in loud, cracked voices. Laughter and curses rang out. Tobacco smoke rose in thick clouds. Accommodating women smiled and flirted. "The walls are covered with pictures, many of them men and women almost or quite in a nude state," Lord squawked. "Everything is got up, arranged and conducted with a view to add to the mad excitement of gambling."

Gambling halls all employed good-looking female dealers, as if gambling itself was not enough of a temptation. One young miner witnessed a shooting at a card table, which started as an argument and ended with a man slumped dead with a bullet through his heart. Through it all the beautiful "Mademoiselle Virginie" carried on unperturbed. "She greeted me with a fascinating smile," wrote William Perkins. "'Ah Monsieur, quel horreur!' turning up her brilliant eyes towards the roof, and dealing slowly the cards at the same time."

With women in California so rare, men reveled in the most cursory encounters. Any woman anywhere, including those who had nothing whatever to do with gambling or any other shady behavior, drew a crowd. "Every man thought every woman in that day a beauty," Luzena Wilson recalled. "Even I have had men come forty miles over the mountains, just to look at me, and I never was called a handsome woman, in my best days, even by my most ardent admirers."

Nineteenth-century etiquette forbade anyone to speak openly of prostitutes or sex. Prostitutes were "soiled doves" or "fallen angels" or, in the sympathetic words of one woman in the diggings, "unfortunates who make a trade—a thing of barter—of the holiest passion, when sanctified by love, that ever thrills the wayward heart of poor humanity."

Language was coy, the doves themselves less so. Some were "quite shameless," one miner observed, "often scrawling their names and reception-hours in big letters on their doors." For many prostitutes, exploited by pimps and abused by customers, life in California was as ugly and dangerous as elsewhere. But those who managed to fight their way to a bit of independence found that, like other entrepreneurs, they could boost their prices sky-high and nobody in gold-mad California would blink. In Sonora, one shocked Philadelphia native wrote to her family at home, several brazen women had not only set up a bordello but kept "a man servant to clean their house, and they eat in a restaurant." When the women had first arrived, they'd sent someone "out with a drum to excite notice," literally drumming up business.

A young miner named Henry Packer took the bold step of writing to his fiancée about the exotic women all around him. "Look— a back door stands ajar. Take a peep in—papered walls, a table on which a fire globe lamp stands... by heaven, a woman stands at the door. She is richly dressed. In her ears and on her fingers are massive gold rings, displayed around her neck a chain of the same. Glossy curls play over her full neck and shoulders." In an age when an ankle was an erogenous zone, these were sights to make a man gasp.

"On her countenance," Packer went on, "plays a smile that would bewitch if not beguile a minister."* Finally, the woman spoke. "'Come in, you fellow with mud on your hat. I like a miner.'" The miner hurried in. "Do you blame him?" Packer asked. He himself "did go in just once," he wrote, "only once, and then but for a few minutes."

---

*Somehow Packer anticipated Raymond Chandler's famous line about "a blonde to make a bishop kick a hole in a stained glass window."

CHAPTER THIRTEEN

AT EASE IN A BARBAROUS LAND

FOR JENNIE MEGQUIER AND countless others who would follow in her footsteps, freedom meant far more than an excuse to pick a fight or place a bet. Gambling halls and saloons were not the draw; the thrill, after a hemmed-in and cloistered life, was in flinging open the windows and breathing fresh air. When her children passed along news of old friends in Maine, Megquier stifled a yawn. "I am right glad to hear they are enjoying themselves so much," she wrote back, "but I have seen so much of things a little more exciting I fear I shall never feel perfectly satisfied with their quiet ways again."

Ministers back east had warned against California for precisely this reason. "Will you not bring back with you a restless, morbid desire for change, excitement, and wild adventure?" the Reverend Elisha Cleaveland had challenged his congregation in Connecticut in 1849.

Yes, it turned out, yes, you would, if you ever came back at all. *Just try to imagine the contrast between stodgy New England and dazzling San Francisco,* Jennie Megquier asked her children. "In San Francisco," she wrote excitedly, "you can step out of your house and see the whole world spread out before you in every shape and form. Your ears are filled with the most delightful music, your eyes are dazzled with everything that is beautiful, the streets are crowded. The whole city are in the street."

Within steps of her house, she went on, was "a splendid ice cream saloon which surpasses anything I have seen in the states." This temple of indulgence boasted large windows, silk curtains, marble floors and tables, and was "as light as day at all hours of the night." *What fun!* "The homeliest man in the city treated me to an ice cream there a few nights since at one dollar a glass."

Megquier looked past California's squalor and violence and reveled in the tumult and the new sights all around. "I suppose you will think it very strange when I tell you I have not attended church for one year, not even heard a prayer," she wrote to her mother, in April, 1850. *What of it?* she asked, as if she could see her mother's glare across a continent. "The churches are very well attended without any of my help."

This would become a familiar theme. "I suppose she thinks I am very wicked," Megquier griped a few weeks later, taking on her mother again, this time in a letter to her daughter, and still bristling. "That which says 'I am more holy than thou' has no resting place in my bosom." And besides, her new neighbors, rough as they were, had virtues of their own. "There is no such thing as slander known in the country, no back biting, every ones neighbor is as good as himself."

Megquier liked corresponding with her daughter. Angie was nearly twenty, and Jennie dished to her as if they were peers. "You would be astonished could you peep in at one of our parties. The gaiety of dress, the lots of belles, beautiful dancers, splendid music, bouquets of the richest kind, sumptuous tables, last & not least so many fine looking men." Jennie wrote happily of dancing until two or three in the morning.

If only Angie could come to San Francisco herself. But Jennie hadn't made much headway there. "Your Father thinks it is no place for you. I suppose he is afraid you will be led astray. He has his hands full to keep me straight."

Megquier loved concerts and theater as well as dancing, and San Francisco offered every kind of spectacle. Not all were to her taste, but she liked the bustle. Performers high and low swarmed to California, which everyone knew was rich, restless, fast growing, and starved for entertainment. Crowds flocked to see prizefights, minstrel shows, magic acts, Shakespearean plays, juggling exhibitions, "bullfights" that featured not a matador but a grizzly bear pitted against a bull. Lonely men gawked enthralled at such visiting stars as Kate Hayes, "the Swan of Erin," and Elisa Biscaccianti, "the American thrush." Megquier was especially eager to see Lola Montez, a notorious singer and dancer who was distinguished more for her biography than for her talent. Beautiful, exotic, and racy, Montez was the one-time mistress of the king of Bavaria and supposedly the ex-lover of, among many others, Franz Liszt.

People said that "it is not proper for respectable ladies to attend," Megquier complained, "but I do want to see her very much." Montez's prize number was her "Tarantula Dance," which featured a vigorous search for a spider that had supposedly hidden itself under her clothes. Megquier enjoyed it, though she conceded that "some thought she was obliged to look rather higher than was proper in so public a place."

Megquier's enthusiasm calls to mind the most talented of all gold rush writers, Louise Clappe, who came to California in 1849 and soon headed off to Rich Bar, on the North Fork of the Feather

River. A "shrinking, timid, frail thing," as she put it, Clappe was originally from Amherst, Massachusetts (she was a near contemporary of Emily Dickinson). To her astonishment, she flourished in conditions that should have left a proper New England lady clutching her hankie and wincing. "I have slept on tables, on doors, and on trunks," she wrote her sister, who had stayed home. "I have reclined on couches, on chairs and on the floor." In former times she had been guided by other people's opinions, but "now I generally act, think and speak as best pleases myself."

In the diggings Louise Clappe lived without churches, lectures, gossip, or ladies' lunches, among rough, hairy miners who often found themselves "in that transcendental state of intoxication, when a man is compelled to hold on to the earth for fear of falling off." Not to worry, she reassured her sister. "I *like* this wild and barbarous life. . . . I look kindly to this existence, which to you seems so sordid and mean. Here, at least, I have been contented."

Jennie Megquier was often happy, too, though perhaps only occasionally content (her style ran more to bursts of glee punctuated by fits of restlessness than to tranquil nights by the fireplace). But eager as she was to embrace new experience, her new life was not all concerts and ice cream. In every letter home, she begged for letters in return ("I will give a dollar a word for one long letter"); she had nightmares about her children dying while she was thousands of miles away; though she and Thomas had more money than ever before, they never had quite enough to declare victory and return home in triumph. And her work was endless.

At the boardinghouse she ran in San Francisco, Jennie's workday started at seven o'clock. "I get up and make the coffee," she wrote, "then I make the biscuits, then I fry the potatoes, then broil three pounds of steak and as much liver." Guests ate breakfast from eight o'clock to nine, and then Jennie started in on lunch. "I bake six loaves of bread (not very big), then four pies or a pudding," and she prepared lamb, beef, pork, turnips, beets, potatoes, radishes, salad, soup. After lunch came tea, with some kind of cold meat and a sauce, and more bread, and cake.

"I have cooked every mouthful that has been eaten," Megquier moaned, and that was only part of the story. "I make six beds every day and do the washing and ironing...and if I had not the constitution of six horses I should have been dead long ago." Miners weren't the only ones who worked like demons.

The work itself was nothing new; women in California did not suddenly become doctors and lawyers. What was new was the opportunity to do so well, so quickly, doing work that had traditionally been relegated to women and taken for granted. This was hard-earned money—Megquier had long since lost patience with dreamers who thought they could wander into the diggings and make their pile in a carefree day or two—but it was real, and it was substantial.

Luzena Wilson saw the same opportunity that Jennie had, and she grabbed on just as fiercely. She and her husband had lost everything in an enormous flood in Sacramento in 1849. Battered but not defeated, they dragged themselves to Nevada City, at the time little more than a canvas campground but destined to become one of the busiest, best-known mining towns.

"I cast my thoughts about me for some plan to assist in the recuperation of the family finances," Wilson recalled. "As always occurs to the mind of a woman, I thought of taking boarders." But where would she find a boardinghouse?

"I bought two boards from a precious pile belonging to a man who was building the second wooden house in town," Wilson went on. "With my own hands I chopped stakes, drove them into the ground, and set up my table. I bought provisions at a neighboring store, and when my husband came back at night he found, mid the weird light of the pine torches, twenty miners eating at my table. Each man as he rose put a dollar in my hand and said I might count him as a permanent customer." She named her not-quite-hotel the El Dorado.

"From the first day it was well patronized," Wilson recalled proudly, "and I shortly after took my husband into partnership."* (Mason Wilson was the head of the household. Luzena, who would not say so outright, was the brains and the muscle.) In six weeks Wilson earned $700 — about two years' pay for a workman back east and enough to cover all the family debts. Soon after, with her makeshift hotel now a rambling, wooden structure with a roof, "we had from seventy-five to two hundred boarders at twenty-five dollars a week. I became luxurious and hired a cook and waiters. Maintaining only my position as managing housekeeper, I retired from active business in the kitchen."

These were flush times. "Everybody had money," Wilson wrote, "and everybody spent it. Money ran through one's fingers like water through a sieve." It didn't *all* run through. Within six months of opening her hotel, Wilson added a store (with $10,000 worth of goods on the shelves) to her fledgling empire.

Guests at the El Dorado sometimes paid their bills in gold. Wilson stored bags of gold dust in her oven overnight and stuffed the overflow under her mattress: "At one time I must have had more than two hundred thousand dollars lying unprotected in my

---

*This was a remarkable assertion. Married women in the first half of the 1800s had scarcely any economic rights — "The husband and the wife are one, and the husband is that one," the law declared — though change was coming. Around midcentury many states passed laws declaring that husbands did not have the right to dispose of their wives' property as if it were their own. The notion that a wife could be an equal partner was new and bold; the notion that, like Luzena Wilson, she might be the *lead* partner was almost out of the question.

bedroom." Wilson seized this opportunity, too, entering the banking business and lending money at 10 percent a month.

Wilson had been a farmwife in an out-of-the-way corner of the country, struggling to get by. Now, in topsy-turvy California, she was prosperous and admired and in charge. Her husband had wanted to go west and leave her behind. She had gone with, and now she had gone ahead.

For men, California's opportunities were even more disorienting. When the job demanded that a man shovel tons of dirt or wrestle rocks and sandbags while standing half submerged in a mountain stream, what use was a law degree or a rich daddy?

Alonzo Delano delighted in the "perfect equality" that reigned in the diggings. "Sparta could not hold a candle to it. The judge, the ex-member of Congress, the lawyer, the merchant, the farmer, the mechanic, the sailor, the soldier, the scholar, all grades, shades and classes, 'mingle, mingle, mingle,' and you would as often take the dunce for the judge, as the judge for himself."

A common sight, Delano went on, was a judge or a college professor "bending over the wash-tub . . . or sitting on the ground with a needle, awkwardly enough repairing the huge rents in his pantaloons." Few pleasures compared with seeing a great man engaged in so humble a task and teasing him, " 'Well, Judge, what is on the docket today?' "

Once set in motion, the push for equality was hard to slow. Delano himself watched with dismay when his two indentured servants ran off. "Smith and Brown, whom I had brought across the plains, and with whom I had a written agreement to continue in my employ, taking advantage of circumstances where there was no law to enforce the fulfillment of their contract, immediately left me, and I never received one farthing by way of remuneration."

Even skeptical Israel Lord found it hard to resist the notion that in California a man could break his shackles. He jotted down the cheery lyrics of a song he heard one night in the diggings. A group of Ohio miners contrasted a farmer's life of drudgery with a miner's independence. Verse after verse proclaimed the same glad message: No bosses in the Golden West!

Oh, doom me not to slave and toil,
Beneath a master's eye,
Stripp'd of my title to the soil,
And robb'd of Liberty;
But let me dig the mountain land,
No tax, no tariff for the free,
With beef and bread and golden sand;
Oh, that's the work for me,
Oh, that's the work for me.

In this shifting culture, respect went not to the man who could hire others to work on his behalf but to the man who could fend for himself. (One newcomer who asked for help with his bags in a San Francisco hotel was proudly informed that the hotel had no porters. "Every man is his own porter here.") For ages past, hard labor and low pay had gone together. California snapped that link. In a land seeded with gold, a ditchdigger might be more likely than anyone else to find a treasure.

With the prospect of wealth went respect. In California, one artist-turned-miner wrote with surprise, the common notion was that "*not* to labor was degrading—that those who did not live by

actual physical toil were men who did not come up to the scratch."
Labor, for once, had dignity.

This was astounding—Bayard Taylor described the marvel he
had seen in astonished capitals: "LABOR IS RESPECTABLE"—
but it did not truly mean that the world had turned on its head.
Labor had merit not because it was honest, useful work but because
it could make a man rich. "It was one intense scramble for dollars,"
one miner wrote. "The man who got the most was the best man.
How he got them had nothing to do with it."

What looked at first like a revolution was in fact an embrace of
the old notion that money trumped all other considerations. *Money
Above All* remained the credo of the age. Surprisingly, this grab-it-now
doctrine bound men together more than it drew them apart. Everyone sought the same prize—gold—with the same tools—
muscles, diligence, luck. While they dug endless day after endless
day, they all baked under the same sun and shivered in the same
streams. That experience of shared hope and shared misery seemed
to unite men separated by deep gulfs of language and culture, in
one of the most multinational societies the world had ever seen.

At least it did for a short time.

CHAPTER FOURTEEN

TAKING THE BREAD FROM AMERICAN MINERS

IN THE EARLY DAYS, when it seemed there would be enough gold for everyone, American miners regarded the peculiar ways of strangers with more curiosity than hostility. In almost the same breath, one newcomer described the wonders he had seen in California — "grisly bears" (1,600-pound animals with huge paws and "hair resembling that of a Newfoundland dog"), and "trees completely changed to the hardest kinds of flint or quartz," and "the Chinese [who] use neither knives, forks or spoons, but take their food by the aid of two straight sticks (chop-sticks) about six inches long, which they handle with wonderful dexterity."

Despite the jumble of nationalities and ethnic groups, California was no melting pot. Racism was not a shameful prejudice but an assertion of a fact too obvious to debate — the world was run by

English-speaking white people, as it should be. (The word "racism" did not exist in the nineteenth century, presumably for the same reason that talking fish would not have a word for water.)* Nearly every gold rush journal abounds with descriptions of "lazy Mexicans" and "money-loving Jews" and the clannish Chinese, who jabbered like geese and ate rat pies. Typically the tone is casual, the insults treated as descriptions akin to remarks on the height of the trees or the intensity of the rains. *Nothing personal...*

Letters and diaries described sightings of "copper-hued Kanakas" (from Hawaii) or "Mexicans rolled in their sarapes and Peruvians thrust through their ponchos," as if the writers were bird-watchers in a new locale. As the most unfamiliar strangers of all, the Chinese drew especially close and puzzled notice. Americans called them "Celestials" (because China was the "Celestial Empire") and stared in open wonder. "Their hats are made of stiff splints of bamboo, and are as unpliable as a basket made of oak....Their pantaloons are extremely wide, resembling petticoats, and a short garment, something like a loose gown, completes their external costume."

Everyone knew the ethnic stereotypes (though they would not have used this word, either), and nearly everyone took them for granted. Mexicans were violent and treacherous, Jews cunning and unwilling to tackle physical labor, the Irish sullen and dangerous. The Germans — dull and plodding — and the French — licentious and harboring peculiar tastes in food — got away comparatively lightly. (A daily chore for one boardinghouse cook was "making

---

*According to the *Oxford English Dictionary*, the word "racism" was first used in the 1930s.

coffee for the French people strong enough for any man to walk on that has Faith as Peter had.")*

As more and more foreign-born gold-seekers poured in, the tone in the Americans' letters and diaries changed from bemusement or irritation to anger and resentment. Strangers were seen not as exotic features of the landscape but as intruders. Israel Lord kept his cool, but he was unusual. "I, for one, contend that they have the same right to dig for gold here as in the older States for iron, or wheat, or potatoes." Digging was digging, after all, the same backbreaking work for everyone.

Far more typical was the outraged yowl of Lucius Fairchild, the governor-to-be of Wisconsin. Now he railed against "foreigners." All they wanted was to snatch some gold and carry it home. "It's a shame," Fairchild complained, "that our government will allow themselves to be run over by the off scourings of all Gods creation who are taking the bread out of the American miners mouths, or the Gold which is the same."

In April, 1850, California's fledgling state legislature passed a Foreign Miners' Tax, which called for foreigners in the diggings to pay twenty dollars a month for the "privilege of taking from our country the vast treasure to which they have no right." More an angry gesture than a prudent policy, the tax pulled in two directions at once. Its backers insisted that the tax would drive foreigners out of California and would, at the same time, fill the state's coffers with the foreigners' fees.

---

*Israel Lord, though less inclined than most to pigeonhole whole groups, disliked the French for their indulgent ways. "This evening, some Frenchmen, a few doors off, are drinking champagne and rowdying largely," he complained a few days after Christmas 1850. Next day, a Saturday, "The Frenchmen are at it again." Not only did they sing—"and make enough noise for a nail factory"—but they made matters worse by insisting on singing in French.

By then it already seemed a long time—though it was only a year or two—since Bayard Taylor had noted, with happy surprise, that the miners showed no signs of "a grasping and avaricious spirit." On the contrary, he had written on first arriving in California in 1849, "the co-mingling of so many races and the primitive way of life gave a character of good fellowship to all its members."

The camaraderie of the early days, it quickly grew clear, had been artificial. It was not so much that men of all sorts got along as that, in some places, men had only begun to bump up against strangers. As early as July, 1849, Chilean and Peruvian miners found themselves pushed off their claims on the American River. Near the site of the original gold discovery, tacked-up notices spelled out the bad news. Spoken threats sharpened the written warnings. Word came down that "all those who were not American citizens had to leave the area within 24 hours," one Mexican-born miner recalled, "and that force would be used against those who failed to obey. This was supported by a meeting of armed men, ready to make good this announcement."*

"The weak are meat the strong do eat," the proverb has it, and so it proved in California. In 1850, on Weaver's Creek, a miner and ex-soldier named Edward Buffum watched a mob of about two hundred men shouting "Hang them!" in the direction of two Frenchmen and a Chilean. The three had been accused of attempted robbery and murder, and found guilty by the mob. Buffum climbed on a tree stump and pleaded for the men's lives "in the name of God, humanity, and law." None of the accused men understood English. The three were placed upon a wagon. Nooses went around

---

*The miner was Antonio Coronel, a one-time schoolteacher who had lived in California since 1834. In his first three days in the diggings, Coronel and two companions found 12½ pounds of gold. Suddenly wealthy, Coronel would go on to become mayor of Los Angeles and one of California's most prominent citizens.

their necks, and black handkerchiefs over their eyes. At a signal, the wagon lurched out from under them.

The tens of thousands of Chinese in California came in for some of the harshest abuse. Chinese miners "generally work in diggings that white men have condemned and abandoned," a gold-seeker wrote matter-of-factly, as if this were yet another quirk of the unfathomable strangers in stiff hats and broad pants, "but should these places happen to prove better than was anticipated, they are commonly soon expelled by the more unscrupulous whites."

Shoving "interlopers" aside was, in the American view, if not exactly admirable, then close to inevitable. It was simple fact that Americans were strong and willful, and the Chinese timid and docile. "A dozen armed white men will drive a thousand of these Celestials, as easily as they would a flock of timorous sheep."

It was the miners' inflated self-regard that made such bullying seem natural. Disdain for the rights of strangers runs strong in nearly every age; in gold rush California, it reached flood proportions. The miners had taken California's physical grandeur and assimilated it; they saw themselves as titans striding across a global stage. So argued Walter Colton, the Navy chaplain-turned-Monterey-*alcalde,* who saw the emigrants' bombast and pomposity as the key to understanding their outlook on the world.

Take slavery, the great issue of the age, destined within a decade to tear the nation in two. California, with its instant population, was sure to come into the union as a new state. The question was whether it would be free or slave. The stakes were immense: in 1849 the United States was made up of thirty states, fifteen slave and fifteen free. As the state that would tip the balance, California drew all eyes. The miners saw that attention as only fitting. "They may offer to come into the Union," wrote Colton, "but they consider it an act of condescension, like that of Queen Victoria in her nuptials with Prince Albert."

The gold-seekers vehemently opposed slavery, but not out of concern for justice or equality. Despite the miners' constant talk of California as an egalitarian paradise, black men in the diggings were not allowed to sit at meals with whites. In all but the smallest camps, black miners ate at a blacks-only boardinghouse. (If there was no such site, black miners had to wait for whites to leave the table before sitting down themselves.) Those were unwritten rules. The written law was just as plain. California's first state legislature decreed, in 1850, that "no Black, or Mulatto person, or Indian shall be allowed to give evidence in favor of, or against, a white man."* Those white men, after all, occupied a spot near the pinnacle of creation.

In California, their smugness had grown beyond all bounds. These proud men "walk over hills treasured with precious ores," Walter Colton explained. "They dwell by streams paved with gold, while every mountain around soars into the heaven, circled with a diadem richer than that which threw its halo on the seven hills of Rome. All these belong to them; they walk in their midst; they feel their presence and power, and partake of their grandeur. Think you that such men will consent to swing the pick by the side of slaves? Never!"

---

*The law did not mention the Chinese, which made for a vexing case in 1854 when the state supreme court reviewed a murder conviction. A white man had been found guilty of killing a Chinese man. All the testimony had come from Chinese witnesses. In the court's eyes, this posed a riddle. Did the law rule out testimony from "all inferior races" or only from the specific inferior races it listed? Noting that the Chinese were a people "whose mendacity is proverbial," the judge quickly found his answer. Chinese witnesses didn't count. Conviction overturned.

Thus, white miners opposed slavery not because it was a moral affront to the men held in chains; they opposed it because it implied that they, working like slaves, were no better than slaves. Resentment of the slave owners' easy deal further stoked the miners' anger. Why should the owners be able to put their feet up and rake in a fortune while men in bondage did all the work? Was that fair?

No group suffered as much in the gold rush years as Native Americans. For California's Indians, the rush was a calamity. Before gold was discovered, Indians had outnumbered whites nearly ten to one. By the early 1850s, they were strangers in their own land, outnumbered two to one. Worse still, California's Indians happened to live in the greatest numbers in the very regions where gold was found. The white invasion came straight to those traditional enclaves, like a knife to the heart. These new enemies, moreover, represented a new threat rather than a familiar danger magnified. The Spanish-speaking ranchers who dominated California in pre–gold rush days had exploited the Indians, but they needed their labor. The newly arrived whites had no brakes on their mistreatment. They simply wanted the Indians gone. Soon they were.

Native Americans had known about California's gold long before the first whites arrived, but they had never paid it any heed. While searching for gold in the vicinity of the Yuba River, in November, 1848, Edward Buffum had happened on a group of Indians. (It was Buffum who went on to confront the lynch mob on Weaver's Creek.) One man, named Pule-u-le, spoke Spanish. Buffum asked if he had ever looked for gold. When he was a boy, Pule-u-le recalled, he had entertained himself by picking out pebbles of gold from larger rocks and flinging them into the river below.

White traders quickly cashed in on this indifference. One early miner saw Indians "giving handfuls of gold for a cotton handkerchief or a shirt." A trader named John Marsh packed sugar into the foothills and sold it even-up, a cup of sugar for a cup of gold. Still another brought raisins and similar treats, and a scale. He put the raisins in one pan, his Indian buyers put a matching weight of gold in the other pan, and the deal was done.

In the earliest days of the gold rush, the surest way to make a fortune was to set large numbers of Indians to work, at peon wages. "They make the most who employ the wild Indians to hunt it for them," wrote one gold-seeker, in August, 1848. "There is one man who has sixty Indians in his employ: his profits are a dollar a minute. The wild Indian knows nothing of its value and wonders what the palefaces want to do with it; they will give an ounce of it for the same weight of coined silver, or a thimble full of glass beads, or a glass of grog."

For whites in a position to exploit Indian labor, profits mounted up almost too quickly to count. One small group of miners dragooned fifty Indians to work for them and gathered 273 pounds of gold in two months. Thirteen pounds went to the Indians. "There are at this time," wrote an observer, in December, 1848, "not less than 2000 white men and more than double that number of Indians washing gold."

It didn't last. Whites late to the party fumed at the unfairness of competing with cheap Indian labor. What chance did a lone man have, or even a man working with two or three companions, against a squad of conscripted savages? The whole system was an affront to justice.

The contempt that the newcomers felt for California's Indians made matters worse. Even Alonzo Delano, who was far more broad-minded than most of his fellow emigrants, recoiled. "A more filthy and disgusting class of human beings you cannot well conceive. They are dark-skinned, nearly as dark as a negro, covered with dust, living upon acorns, wild fruit and fish. They have nothing of the noble bearing of the Indians east of the Rocky Mountains, and they seem to be only a few degrees removed from brutes."

Such dismissive ugliness was all but universal. "The Digger Indians, the natives of California, are to be ranked among the least intelligent of the human race," wrote a Unitarian minister turned gold-seeker.* "Their dwelling houses and their construction display less mechanical genius than the habitations of the beaver, or even the muskrat." The scientific literature of the day was filled with nearly identical pronouncements. Samuel George Morton, a particularly esteemed authority, spent a lifetime gathering human skulls and painstakingly measuring their volume, to see how different races stacked up. Indians had particularly small skulls and little brains, Morton claimed, in a lavish volume published in 1839 called *Crania Americana*. These supposed facts provided irrefutable proof of "the inaptitude of the Indian for civilization." Certainly such backward creatures could not be allowed to take the gold that the emigrants had come so far to find.

As early as 1849 whites joined forces to clear the Indians from the diggings. In the words of Kevin Starr, California's most acclaimed historian, "Native Americans were hunted down like so much vermin." Whites pillaged Indian villages; Indians stole cattle from whites; raids and counterraids followed one another in endless succession. Each theft or killing called for retaliation.

Israel Lord, a humane man by the standards of the day, wrote in

---

*The emigrants called the Indians Diggers because they grubbed a meager living from the soil.

his journal that "the Indians are much sinned against as well as sin-
ning," but he also predicted, without much emotion, that "these
'Diggers' are bound to be exterminated." On April 9, 1850, he
noted laconically, "A large number of armed men went up today to
shoot the Diggers."

Alonzo Delano took a similar tack. "Nine-tenths of the troubles
between the whites and Indians" could be set at the feet of the
whites, he wrote, but "the two races cannot exist in contact." This
was more measured than many judgments—"There will be safety
only in a war of extermination raged with relentless fury far and
near," the *Daily Alta California* declared in May, 1850—but the
message was the same.

From early on, some whites had shaken their heads sorrowfully
as they called for the removal of the Indians, and some had shaken
angry fists. Whether the threats came in sorrow or in anger made
little difference. In a speech to the state legislature on January 7,
1851, California's first elected governor, Peter Burnett, spelled out
the prevailing view: "A war of extermination would continue to be
waged between the two races until the Indian race becomes
extinct." Although this was dismaying news and a source of "pain-
ful regret," Burnett continued, "the inevitable destiny of the race is
beyond the power and wisdom of man to avert."

California's violence took its most gruesome form when it pitted
race against race, but the gold-seekers happily did in one another
even when they lacked any excuse at all. Hollywood has done its
best to defang the image of life in the diggings; Mark Twain captured the truth when he called gold rush California "a wild, free,
disorderly, grotesque society." Without the constraints of law or
family or women, one miner wrote, "Men assumed their natural

shape, and showed what they really were, following their unchecked impulses and inclinations." It did not make a pretty picture.

Nearly everyone in California was young, and the emigrants had left home fit and healthy. But in the diggings as on the battlefield, youth and strength proved no safeguards. Shootings and stabbings were routine, and broken bones, bashed-in skulls, and bouts of dysentery and pneumonia scarcely worth remarking. So dangerous was life in California that, beginning in January, 1849, life insurance companies refused to sell policies to anyone hunting gold.

One gold-seeker, who had turned from mining to storekeeping, cringed at first at the violence all around him. He quickly grew blasé. "Sonora is very dull compared to what it used to be," he complained in March, 1852. "We have now no fights, no murders, no rapes, no robberies to amuse us!" That tone of studied nonchalance came to be almost universal. "Nothing fatal has taken place since my last letter," wrote another miner, in September, 1852, "but there have been some awfully close shaves. One man has been shot through the cravat, one through the hat and one in the arm."

Always in the background at every camp in gold country, scarcely more noteworthy than the swinging of hammers or the thudding of picks, was the sight of someone fighting, someone falling, someone dying. "Yesterday one American shot another in the street," a miner from Pennsylvania wrote in his journal, in August, 1850, "and the occurrence was not noticed as much as a dog fight at home."

California's boosters tried to cast this every-man-for-himself isolation as a virtue. The land of opportunity was also the land of self-reliance, they declared; no shirkers need apply. "This is the worst country in the world for men of no occupation," one minister told his San Francisco congregation, in 1850, "and thank Heaven." This was as it should be, for "'if a man will not work, neither shall he eat.' This is the scriptural doctrine, and it is the California doctrine too. It is death to stand still. A man must keep moving, and that to some purpose; for there are none to help a man who will not help himself."

Such harsh creeds held no appeal for Luzena Wilson, but even she found herself unmoved by the death and mayhem all around her. Not so much inured to the violence as too exhausted to deal with it, she expended all her strength in keeping her boardinghouse afloat. "It has been a life-long source of regret to me that I grew hard-hearted like the rest," she recalled in her old age. "I was hard-worked, hurried all day, and tired out, but I might have stopped sometimes for a minute to heed the moans which caught my ears from the canvas house next to me."

This was in 1849, shortly after Wilson's arrival in Sacramento. In time she would prosper and have a chance to breathe, but in the early days she had no time for anything but work. Certainly she had no time to dally with her neighbors. "I knew a young man lived [next door], for he had often stopped to say 'Good morning,' but I thought he had friends in the town; and when I heard his weak calls for water I never thought but some one gave it.

"One day the moans ceased, and, on looking in, I found him lying dead with not even a friendly hand to close his eyes. Many a time since, when my own boys have been wandering in new countries have I wept for the sore heart of that poor boy's mother, and I have prayed that if ever want and sickness came to mine, some other woman would be more tender than I had been, and give them at least a glass of cold water."

The violence that marked California was hideous, but *every* aspect of gold rush life—the danger, the reward, the exhilaration, the suffering, the self-indulgence, the toil, the loneliness—was over the top. California in the mid-1800s was a vast experiment, in one miner's words "a picture of universal human nature boiling over."

That picture captivated enthusiasts like Jennie Megquier and Louise Clappe (who found herself unfazed by witnessing, in less than a single month, "murders, fearful accidents, bloody deaths, a mob, whippings, a hanging, an attempt at suicide, and a fatal duel"). Others saw a nightmare worthy of Hieronymus Bosch. "A residence here at present is a pilgrimage in a strange land, a banishment from good society, a living death, and a punishment of the worst kind," a gold-seeker from Illinois lamented, "and the time spent here ought to be considered as a blank period in existence, and accordingly struck from the record of one's days."

What caught every eye, both the enthralled and the appalled, was the frantic energy everywhere on display. Everyone in California craved action and distraction. Nearly anything would do. "If a terrier catches a rat or if a big turnip is brought to market, the people cluster together and scramble for a sight," marveled a miner from North Carolina. Let one man accidentally step on somebody's foot, he went on, and "it only requires one minute for the injured party to shoot the offender, two minutes for somebody else to stab the shooter, and three minutes for the whole crowd to hang the stabber."

In the diggings, the pace was just as crazed as in town. Miners lived in fear that, while they labored *here*, the real action was going on over the next hill, around the next bend, on the next river. This desperation to be up and moving reflected not the vitality of the athlete but the itch of the addict. "Our countrymen are the most discontented of mortals," Louise Clappe observed. "They are always longing for big strikes. If a claim is paying them a steady income, by which, if they pleased, they could lay up more in a month than they could accommodate in a year at home, still they are dissatisfied." Off they marched, in search of more. "There are hundreds now pursuing this foolish course, who, if they had stopped where they first camped, would now have been rich men."

Few gold-seekers saw it that way. One miner conceded that the Sierra foothills boasted all that nature could provide "to make pleasant man's stay on earth." Here was "a mild climate...soil that would raise almost any vegetable...grapes or figs, apples or potatoes; land to be had for the asking; water for irrigation accessible on every hand." And the upshot? "We were all anxious to get away. Our heaven was not at Red Mountain." Gold was the only game, and the gold was always brighter somewhere else.

As a consequence, California had ruins and abandoned towns almost from the start. "The whole population of the mining country," one newcomer observed, "is as fluctuating and unstable as the waves of the sea." In their restlessness, the miners tended to slosh hither and thither without any pattern. But at times the same rumors took hold everywhere. Then the buzz of "Have you heard?" and "Will you go?" grew from a murmur to a roar. The psychology replayed the gold rush saga in miniature. To stay put when a few men moved on was routine. But to miss out on what was about to make everyone else rich was impossible.

And so, in the summer of 1850, when word came of the greatest find of all—a golden lake, high in the mountains, immense and hidden and unimaginably rich!—men swarmed into the foothills by the thousands. Large, eager battalions abandoned their claims, even good, steady ones, and headed to the backcountry. Why settle for a bird in the hand when the birds in the bush had golden plumage that shone like the sun?

Joseph Bruff heard the story of the incredible golden lake from a young man named Gibbs, who swore he had seen it with his own eyes. Gibbs had been exploring high in the Sierra with his uncle and a group of other men. At a remote spot somewhere near the headwaters of the Feather River and the Yuba, the company happened on a lake straight out of fable. Over the years other expeditions had glimpsed it, too. At this secret lake, miners swore, sheets of gold dotted the water's surface like leaves in autumn, and Indians fished with hooks of solid gold.

In the course of a few hours, Gibbs reported, he had gathered gold nuggets ranging in size from marbles to walnuts. With no labor except bending down, just as a beachcomber might gather shells, he had collected gold worth $5,000 (in today's money, $100,000). At Gold Lake, the only question was whether the mules would collapse under the load of gold heaved onto their backs.

But the lake came with drawbacks and dangers, and they, too, smacked of fable. It was nearly inaccessible, for one thing. Not until you crested the last, high mountains, Gibbs warned, could you even see the lake nestled down below. The descent to the lake was so steep that the mules had to be *lowered down* by rope. And this country was home to fierce, hostile Indians who feared and resented the gold-seekers. Indians had attacked the Gibbs party and wounded several of them before the rest managed to flee.

One obstacle outweighed all the others: no one knew just how to find the lake again. Gibbs's uncle, a surveyor, had drawn a rough map, but someone had lost it. The geographic clues—the lake was five miles long, and three buttes rose up along it on one side— served more to tantalize than to inform.

That shaky story, in countless variant forms, sufficed to lure hordes of gold-seekers into the far corners of the Sierra. Bruff didn't believe the chatter, but a few months had gone by since he had

stumbled, half dead, into Lassen's camp. He itched to be out and
exploring. Bruff had a boyish streak almost impossible to tamp
down — he could turn a search for firewood into an adventure —
and who was to say they *wouldn't* find gold, even without a treasure
map? Bruff set out cheerily on what he called "the great Gold Lake
hunt" as part of a company that numbered twenty-three men and
thirty horses and mules.

Nearly everyone else took to the hills, too. Alonzo Delano ventured out in search of "a wonderful lake...a hundred miles back
among the mountains, towards the head of the Middle Fork of
Feather River." (Israel Lord, who scoffed at nearly everything, was
one of the few to dismiss the "Gold Lake humbug.")

In fabulously rich Downieville, on the North Fork of the Yuba
River, miners nearly drooled over the stories of Gold Lake passed
along by one half-crazed old-timer. Captain Thomas Stoddard
claimed he had been the first white man to find the lake. Before he
could gather up his fortune, Indians had driven him away. At
Downieville the captain took every opportunity to roll up his pants
and show where an arrow had plunged into his knee. "He would
often say," another miner recalled, "when we struck anything particularly rich, 'At Gold Lake we would not consider this worth
picking up.'"

Precisely where Gold Lake could be found, Stoddard refused to
say. Perhaps he had learned his lesson. Shortly before he turned up
in Downieville, he had offered to lead a small group to the lake.
On their way, they happened to pass within range of a prospector
who had climbed a hill to look around. He had assumed he was all
alone. Then the wandering prospector looked around and found,
to his "utmost surprise, [the valley] alive with at least three thousand people." These were Stoddard's few followers now grown into
an army. The prospector joined the throng.

They climbed on, day after day. At last someone spotted a lake. "That is it!" said Stoddard. "You can see now the lake with the blue water, which I have described; the three peaks and the log yonder, where I camped. There are tons of gold there."

The men stampeded, racing to find their fortune. The fleetest reached the lake's edge first, gasping for breath. Nothing! Up close, the log turned into a boulder. The three peaks turned into five. The army turned into a lynch mob. "Hang him!" "I have a rope that will hold him!" "Here's a branch that will carry him!" Stoddard escaped the mob and did not venture off on any further explorations.

By the time Bruff set off for Gold Lake, the stories about this magical spot had mostly lost their luster. Bruff happily recorded the stories in his journal anyway, lingering over the most far-fetched bits and wondering how "a person of common sense, who knows anything about the rugged country" could believe them. (He had harbored doubts about Gibbs from the start, in good measure because the young man was "wearing *earrings*.")

But wanderlust had caught hold of Bruff years before, and it gripped him still. For him, though not for many other gold-seekers, the chance to be out and exploring was lure enough. Gold was a welcome bonus, not the sole point of the exercise. While searching for his lake, Bruff happened to see a crane and a pelican one day, he noted cheerily, and a pair of bald eagles the next.

Everything caught his eye. Lava, obsidian, and "beautiful white botyroidal crystals of chalcedony" delighted him. So did the colors on a crisp morning. "The earth is tinted with the warm and rich hues of autumn. Orange and bright yellow (of plum bushes) predominate in the plains, and on the lower slopes. Dark cedars are scattered about."

Bruff took careful notes on how Indians started fires by twirling one fire-stick in a hole cut in a second stick, and how they sent smoke signals. He basked in vistas of snow-capped mountains with "light floculent clouds passing by them" and a river glinting in the distance. Even bad health could be framed as if it were a bit of fun. "This afternoon I am amused with chills fever and headache," Bruff noted on September 20, two months into his wild goose chase.

He continued unfazed even when he and a companion found themselves under attack from unseen Indians. Arrows struck within a few feet of the two men, who retreated safely to camp. Bruff brushed off the encounter except to make fun of the accent of another man in search of the lake, a Dane, who suggested that the two wanderers should "*tank* our *Got* we escaped so luckily."

On October 1, Bruff ducked out of a dispute about what route the company should follow. "I told them it was all the same to me, as every mile produced some new scenery." But perhaps even level-headed Joseph Bruff had bigger dreams than he dared admit. He had crossed the continent and nearly starved to death, after all, and his hopes when he'd set out had soared to more than a notebook full of drawings.

The weather had turned cold and wet. Bruff was still weak, and sick again, and no one had much of a plan about where to search next. On the night of October 11, he "laid down with considerable fever, slept uncomfortably, and dreamt that I was abandoned by my family, my friends, and the whole world, because I had not found a gold mine."

Every miner shared that fear. The gold-seekers had started out for California as the objects of universal envy. Brass bands sent them on their way, and everyone pictured that their return home would be even grander. Few could bear the thought of limping home, broke and pitiable. Men stayed in California year after year, digging their youth away and waiting for the payoff that would let them go home in style. They told themselves, and anyone foolish enough to ask, that all was going smoothly.

"It's hard work writing home," the New York miner Prentice Mulford confessed. "I put it off for weeks and months. It lays a load on my mind. I receive at times letters from people complaining of my neglect. I know I ought to write, but what is there to write? Nothing but the same old story: 'Hope soon to do well.'

"I have written in this strain for the last six years until I am tired and sick of it," Mulford went on. "It is of no use telling any more about the country. All that has been told. If my people only knew how much I suffered in this endeavor to be dutiful, perhaps they would not insist on my writing more than the line, 'I am still alive; yours truly.'" To live with humiliation was bad enough; to proclaim it was unbearable.

CHAPTER FIFTEEN

THE PRINCESS AND THE MANGLED HAND

WHEN THE DOORS OF history swing open, the hinges may not make a sound. When Columbus pulled ashore in the New World, Europe continued on its accustomed way for months, unaware that the globe had shifted. When Edward Matteson looked at a California hillside and imagined the power of a water cannon blasting a wall of rock, he transformed gold mining forever.

Matteson was a Connecticut miner with a knack for tinkering. His bright idea came to him not when an apple fell on his head but when a landslide nearly buried him. It was a March morning in 1853. Matteson had been digging away at a gravel hillside with a pick. The hill collapsed. Matteson scrambled to safety, emerging with his life and with a bright idea besides: what a man with a pick could do slowly and at great risk, a man directing a mighty hose could do quickly and from a distance.

By 1853, the easiest-to-get-at gold, which sat on the surface or near it, was nearly gone. Forced to move on, miners turned their gaze upward. Gold, after all, could only sit in place or tumble and fall. If today it was buried in a streambed or tucked behind a boulder in a river, then it stood to reason that yesterday—and "yesterday" might have been a million centuries ago—it was farther up the stream or higher up the hill. This was one reason the Gold Lake tales had proved irresistible. Look high enough, the miners all assumed, and you might find gold in its original, intact state, not broken up and scattered in flakes and pebbles as it was at lower elevations but in pristine and astonishing profusion.

The miners' geology was educated guesswork, and not very well educated at that, but they had grasped the big picture—once upon a time, vast geologic forces had thrust the Sierra Nevada high into the air. The huge, ancient rivers that had flowed down what was now the mountains' western flank had vanished long ago, but they had carried gold, and much of that gold was surely still there. The problem was that it lay buried under hundreds of feet of rock and gravel, and far from the nearest water. How to get at it?

With picks and shovels and blasting powder, for a start. Anywhere that a gravel outcropping showed hints of gold, or a steep canyon or a cliff edge offered a promising peek inside a mountain, miners set to work. They tore into the hills with the tirelessness of burrowing ants, but this was brutal, dangerous work. To dig to paydirt with hand tools, through tons of rock and rubble, took weeks. After all that, there might be no gold.

In the winter of 1853, at a spot called American Hill, near Nevada City, Matteson put his idea into practice. He had joined forces with a sailmaker named Anthony Chabot, who sewed a hose out of canvas, and a tinsmith named Eli Miller, who shaped a three-foot-long nozzle from a piece of sheet iron. Their idea could hardly have been simpler. Pounded by a torrent of water bursting from an enormous, high-pressure fire hose, entire hillsides of dirt and gravel would crumble away. A massive chunk of mountain would become a thick, muddy river. That rock-filled river could be directed into the enormously stretched-out, open-ended troughs called sluices, and riffles at the sluices' downstream end would catch any gold that the hillside had formerly concealed.

The scheme succeeded from the start. Before Matteson came along, miners working high in the hills with pick and shovel had faced a predicament akin to digging out gold coins hidden deep within house-sized blocks of ice and snow. Armed with Matteson's hose, "hydraulickers" could blast the ice away with ease and collect the coins at their leisure.

Everything depended on scale. Since the fire-hose streams were powered only by gravity, the plan required that immense quantities of water be pooled high in the mountains and directed downhill to the hydraulickers. In the words of one modern historian, Matteson had "devised a way to use living rivers to exhume the dead."

A river roaring downhill and then bursting from a hose made a fearsome spectacle. "No person who has not seen them in operation can have an idea of the force of these streams," a report by California's state mineralogist declared. "If a giant nozzle should be set in front of the strongest building in San Francisco and a stream turned on it, the walls would melt away in a few minutes."

The impact on the old-style miner, a loner with a pick, a pan, and a mule, was almost as devastating. In the early days, when gold could be found glittering in a streambed and dug free with a knife or even a spoon, industrial might was beside the point. But as soon as that surface gold vanished, corporations—which could muster capital and technology on an enormous scale—knocked individuals out of their way. The day of the free spirit laboring on his own was done. "It takes a mine," a newly coined proverb declared, "to run a mine."

The age of the independent miner had lasted five years.

*   *   *

As technology improved, the hoses grew ever larger and sturdier. Stitched canvas gave way to stitched canvas bound with rope, then to double-thick canvas bound with iron hoops, and finally to iron pipe. The fire hose had become a water cannon. In time the cannon barrel would stretch twenty feet in length and a foot across. Water shot out from that barrel at one hundred miles an hour. "The velocity of the water makes boulders two feet in diameter jump twenty feet in the air when it hits them," one observer gasped. "Trunks of trees lying in the mine can be made to spin like straws or be hurled away many feet distant." Anyone hit by the blast would be killed instantly.

The names of the new models—"Monitor," "Dictator," "Chief," "Little Giant"—hinted at their power. Even so, a writer from *Scientific American* exclaimed, the hoses boasted an ingenious swivel apparatus that permitted them to be "moved in any direction by a child" or a man using only one hand. "Thus one man, with perfect ease, moves as much gravel in a day as 1,000 men could with shovels and cars."

Hydraulicking was hugely effective but startlingly wasteful, akin to gathering acorns by clear-cutting a forest and then bulldozing the shaved hills. Millions upon millions of gallons of water pulverized rocky hillsides, and millions of tons of dirt and gravel formed a muddy slurry, all in pursuit of golden flecks and pebbles that weighed not tons or pounds but fractions of an ounce. The impact on the landscape was devastating. Mudslides swallowed up farms and orchards, burying them waist-deep. Sand and gravel choked the waterways that fed the Sacramento River and then the Sacramento itself, transforming clear rivers into thick, chocolate-hued streams. When snow melted in the mountains and poured downstream, the mud-clogged, gravel-dammed rivers flooded. Cattle drowned by the thousands. Farms washed away. Town dwellers lost their homes. In Sacramento, in 1862, the governor-elect had to travel to his inauguration by rowboat.

But hydraulicking took its heaviest toll in the mountains. Decades afterward the wounds had still not healed. "The hills have been cut and scalped," one horrified observer wrote in 1894, "and every gorge and gulch and valley torn and disemboweled."

At the time of that cutting and tearing, few miners had any misgivings. It took an outsider to look at the landscape and see what the bounty had cost. "This place," wrote a New York newspaperman touring gold country, "makes one think of a princess who has been captured by bandits who cut off her fingers for the jewels she wore."

No independent miner could stand up to a water cannon, any more than John Henry could outwork a steam hammer, but the story could not have gone on for long regardless of technology. The problem was numbers. "There are now thousands of men more here than will ever get paid for coming, and thousands still on the road," one Baltimore man wrote a friend on August 2, 1850. "I thought the country full to overflowing some time ago, but they still come. There are a thousand per day arriving by the overland route. They come into the country strapped and have no place to strike a lick, for all the diggings are claimed that can be worked."

Many of the gold-seekers had begun to fear early on that they had made a dreadful mistake. They had raced to California, one miner lamented, like "an excited and impatient audience into a theatre, when it is known that a favorite actor is about to perform."

Thousands of men had pushed their way through the doors, fought for seats, and settled back to enjoy the show.

But only a few liked what they saw. As early as July, 1850, Israel Lord had begun losing hope, and most of the gold-seekers felt their spirits sagging at roughly the same time. California was a scam, Lord fumed; in summer, it was "all dried and withered, blasted and scorched," and in winter, drenched and unlivable. "It is a worthless country for anything but gold," he complained, "and even for that, every day is accumulating evidence of its depreciating value."

Lord noted bitterly that he had been gone from home for a year. "A lost year and one that will never return." *What had he been thinking?* "Strange that we cannot believe without personal experience. Every pig must needs burn his nose, before he will be convinced that the swill is hot." Lord now spent his days digging for gold and his nights condemning that pursuit with the vehemence of an ancient preacher.

"Come here and see," he thundered in his journal. "Come where the restraints of social life, of Christian fraternity, of church discipline are not felt." *On second thought, stay put, but open your eyes.* "Save yourself the trouble and only cast a hasty glance into those sinks of moral pollution, those hotbeds of vice, those slaughterhouses of virtue, our great cities—and our small cities—and our villages." Then Lord doubled back again, adding a characteristically bitter twist to his diatribe. *Yes, come!* "The more fools the better—the fewer to laugh when we get back."

Countless thousands shared Lord's fury and shame (though, as noted, most of the emigrants had less trouble with California's wicked ways). They had left home and struggled their way to the far end of nowhere, and now they looked like chumps, not heroes. California was "a beautiful prison," one downcast miner lamented, and he himself was not an emperor in a realm of gold, as he had once dreamt, but merely an exile in "so pleasant a Siberia."

"You will hear many very exaggerated stories of gold diggers," Lord wrote his brother, in January, 1850. "You may rely upon it that the man who has gone back with his $20- or $30,000 did not dig it & none but a gambler can make $100,000 in a year." Statistically minded historians have confirmed that Lord had it about right. Fortunes were made in California but seldom by those wielding pick and shovel. Though incomes were far higher in California than in the rest of the United States, prices were, too. A few lucky winners aside, most miners would have done as well financially if they had stayed home working at their old trade.

By the reckoning of Rodman Paul, one of the most eminent gold rush historians, the average miner earned twenty dollars a day in 1848, sixteen in 1849, ten in 1850, eight in 1851, and six dollars a day in 1852. In the same years, the total amount of gold dug up increased year by year. That helped, but not enough. Even the biggest pie, when cut into 100,000 slices, would yield each man scarcely a mouthful.

Strangely, that turned out not to be the whole story. For many, it proved not even its most important aspect. What was different about California, the gold-seekers had thought way back before they set out, was that a man could get rich there. Most who took that bait soon gagged on it.

Many never did overcome their anger and disappointment. But a fair number who failed to find a fortune reported, to their surprise, that they had found something nearly as enticing: they had found independence. Briefly, at least, they had been their own masters.

"What glorious old times they were!" one miner recalled, years later. "Who then was so much better than anybody else, when any man might strike it rich to-morrow? Who would beg for work or truckle and fawn and curry favor of an employer... when he could shoulder pick, shovel, and rocker and go down to the river's edge?"

Like old soldiers, the ex-miners looked back on the worst but most eventful time of their lives and skipped over all the gruesome parts. From what remained they composed a kind of epitaph. They had not found a treasure, most of them, but what of it? For a few astonishing years, they had lived in a land of perfect equality and absolute independence. They had woken every morning in a shabby tent or a crude cabin and dreamed that they would fall asleep that night as rich as Croesus.

They had dared to hope.

EPILOGUE

ISRAEL LORD RETURNED HOME in 1851, as angry with California as if it had personally betrayed him. His last looks around served only to confirm his disdain (a harmless pelican was "a crooked disgusting deformity" and "a slovenly compound of stupidity and ignorance"). Humanity was even worse. A farewell peek at San Francisco revealed a "steaming, boiling, seething, reeking" abomination, Lord raged, and the gold rush itself had been less an adventure than a desecration.

Nearly home again, on a steamship from Panama, he summarized all he had seen on his westward journey: "A rushing, living tide of men and animals sweeping across the trackless deserts and wild mountains; the bowels of the earth ransacked, and the rivers turned from their courses; their banks uptorn, plundered, ravaged, deserted — villages, towns, cities rising like Aladdin's palace in a single night, vanishing at noonday, and forgotten at eventide."

He concluded his journal with one last, characteristic harrumph. "If I should get time, I will give you my reasons why I think ninety-nine out of a hundred who shall hereafter go to California are either madmen, fools — or radically unprincipled, and of course, dishonest. Meantime, I remain as ever, yours, I. S. P. Lord."

Then he put the whole dismal business behind him and resumed his medical career.

*   *   *

Alonzo Delano invested more hope and effort in the diggings than
did Israel Lord, but he reaped the same meager reward. A bit too
soft and a bit too old to sift gravel for a living, Delano had never-
theless "performed prodigies in moving rocks and throwing out
dirt," to little profit. But California appealed to him. A far less earnest character than Lord — "I haven't got to drinking, stealing, or
gambling yet, but expect to commence in a day or two," he assured
his friends back in Illinois, in 1851 — he saw early on that he was
temperamentally suited to the make-your-own-rules West.

Game for nearly anything after failing as a miner, Delano tried
every moneymaking scheme he could think of. First came a stint
painting miniature portraits of his fellow miners, at an ounce a
drawing. In three weeks he earned $400 but promptly lost it all in
real estate investments gone bad. He put money, when he had it,
into dam-building and river-dredging schemes, but spring floods
washed out his investments. He opened stores in the diggings but
ran into trouble with timing — he tended to have bare shelves when
his customers arrived, or mountains of goods at a time when all
the miners had moved elsewhere.

He found his niche as an author. Like many of his fellow gold-
seekers, Delano had arranged to send reports of life on the trail to
newspapers back east. A quick and versatile writer, he moved
smoothly from straightforward accounts of the journey over the
plains to humorous sketches of exotic California. A two-act farce
called *A Live Woman in the Mines* made the biggest splash. The title
was the plot, and the dialogue what you would expect. "Whoora!
For a live woman in the mines. What'll the boys say? They'll peel
out o' their skins for joy. A live female woman in the mines!"

Bret Harte and Mark Twain would mine the same vein with

more art, but Delano got there first. He brought his family to join him in California in 1857 and lived contentedly in a mining town called Grass Valley for another two decades, a prominent citizen and a beloved emblem of pioneer days. There he celebrated in cornball verse the eureka moment he never achieved in life:

The vein is struck! Ah, noble heart!
A thrill of joy is thine!
A purer and a better thrill
Than that produced by wine.

Those looking to dig their way to fortune seldom fared as well as Alonzo Delano's poetic hero. On the other hand, merchants, lawyers, hotel-keepers—everyone providing a service and not just a strong back—often did far better than they could have at home. For an entrepreneur like Luzena Wilson, California truly was a land of gold.

Wilson proved nearly impossible to discourage. Flush after her first hotel success and then left penniless by a flood in Sacramento and homeless by a fire in Nevada City, she and her husband had promptly rebuilt their lives. (In the Sacramento flood of 1849, Luzena had retreated to an upper floor of her hotel with her children and forty other people, while water lapped at the windows. For food, the marooned group fished for bags of onions or anything else they could snag from the water. For fire, they burned driftwood. They kept rowboats tied up at the window for scavenging expeditions.) Luzena seemed to have no doubt that she would rise again. And so she did. Her mini-empire began with still another open-air "hotel" with tree-stump chairs and a dining table slapped together from scavenged boards.

Luzena, who had a gift for viewing hardship as opportunity, marveled at her good fortune. What could be more enviable than a hotel where there was "no fussing with servants or housecleaning, no windows to wash or carpets to take up"? Soon she noted proudly that "my hotel had the reputation of being the best on the route from Sacramento to Benicia."

Over the next few years, as Luzena's hotel grew more permanent and more prosperous, she and Mason began investing in real estate. By the time of the Civil War, they were wealthy. Life ran smoothly for another decade. Then, in December, 1872, a local newspaper ran a story under the ominous headline "Unaccountable Affair." "On Wednesday of last week," it began, "Mason Wilson, one of the oldest, wealthiest, best known and most highly respected citizens of Vacaville, left home to go to Dixon on business, telling his wife that he might be gone all night."

Luzena, who was fifty-three, never saw him again. (In her account of her journey across the plains and her early days in California, dictated to her daughter in her old age, she referred to "my husband" but never called him by name.) She sold her hotel for the considerable sum of $6,000 (in today's money, $120,000) and moved to San Francisco, where she lived in comfort and style to the age of eighty-three.

For the last fourteen years she lived as a guest at the Hotel Pleasanton, a "Family and Tourist Hotel," where, after so many years, it was the task of others to wait on her.

Jennie Megquier prospered in California, though not to the same extent as her fellow hotel-keeper Luzena Wilson. On a visit home to Maine in 1851, she bought a large, well-situated piece of land with her California earnings. In 1854, on another visit, she set about building a spacious, imposing house. Her descendants would keep the house for a century. Maine held hard-to-resist temptations — this was the home of her children and two grandchildren (one named Jennie, in her honor) — but, family aside, Megquier vastly preferred California. "The very air I breathe seems so very free," she wrote from San Francisco in 1855, "that I have not the least desire to return."

She had made her latest trip to California on her own. Thomas stayed behind in Maine, in poor health and out of favor with his wife. Jennie did not spell out her grievances, but she did not hide her feelings. "I have never regretted for a moment that I left Winthrop," she wrote her daughter, Angie. "That beautiful house has no charms for me at present and should I know I would never visit it again, it would give me no sorrow as I should have the trials I have endured there." Thomas died in 1855, a continent away from his discontented wife. She seldom spoke of him again.

"I should never wish to be in Maine again," Jennie wrote Angie in 1856, and the implicit message was scarcely hidden: *and you should leave, too.* This was well-worn ground, but Jennie tried once more to tempt Angie to her. Maine was a land of petty scandal and raised eyebrows; California was "the place to enjoy life."

In San Francisco, Jennie wrote, all was hustle and bustle and commotion and energy. She could look out her window to a view of "a dozen big clippers unlading their freight" and three steamers bound for Sacramento, "and I can hear every revolution of the wheel as they pass the window." On an April day in 1856, the captain of a steamer took out his handkerchief and waved it to Jennie, who happened to be ironing. She outdid him, lifting an entire bedsheet into the air and proudly saluting back.

After the day's hard work came the night's diversions. "We dine at seven in the evening and then comes the frolic and dancing," Jennie wrote. "Shan't I miss them at home. I shall have the blues."

Jennie Megquier had once prophesied that she would "come trudging home with an apron full" of gold. Unable to coax Angie to join her in the West and unwilling to face the prospect of a life without her family, she did indeed trudge her way back to Maine, in 1856. This was her third and last round-trip across the continent. She would spend the rest of her life in Maine.

Joseph Bruff, despite his fears, was *not* abandoned by his family and friends, and lived to a venerable age. Back at home in Washington, D.C., after his two-year adventure, he returned to his work as a draftsman and never ventured off again. Bruff racked up "54 years in the service of the Government," he wrote proudly in his old age, "49 years of which steadily employed in designing and executing every description of drawing, for nearly every branch of public service... to the perfect satisfaction of my employers, and having their respect and esteem."

Dutiful to the end, he marched off to his office every day until a few months before his death, at age eighty-four. (Age offered little protection. At eighty-one, according to notes in his personnel file, Bruff was reprimanded for tardiness on five different occasions. He had arrived one and a half minutes late one morning and five minutes late on another, and "offers no excuse.") Bruff rarely mentioned his gold rush adventures. A death notice in the Washington *Weekly Star* compressed the whole life-and-death ordeal into a dozen or so words: "For the past sixty-three years Mr. Bruff has been in government employ" — the *Star*'s count was off by nine years — "and there was only one interregnum, when, in 1849, with other young men, he was stricken with the gold fever and started for California to amass a fortune. He was unsuccessful."

But Bruff did succeed in bringing home his journals and sketches. They nearly vanished before anyone had a chance to see them, and more than once they almost cost Bruff his life. Late in 1849, trapped in the snow in the Sierra and starving, he'd had to choose whether to try to make his escape. "I cannot abandon my notes and drawings," he wrote, and he stayed put. Months later, he could wait no longer. He packed up a shirt, a comb, a few matches, and his journals. He might die on the trail, he knew, but perhaps his rescuers would examine the bulky parcel in his knapsack. "Labeled my papers and drawings so that they may possibly reach my family if I am lost," Bruff wrote, and then he staggered off, to rescue or to death.

A year later, he nearly lost them again. Late on the night of May 3, 1851, San Francisco caught fire, and two thousand buildings burned to the ground. Bruff's room was ablaze, but he rescued his papers and dashed into the street. In the confusion, a horse-drawn carriage ran him down; friends dragged him and his cargo to safety. Finally, on July 17, 1851, Bruff landed in New York, his journey home nearly at its end. That night thieves ransacked his baggage and made off with "every thing of value I possessed except my books and drawings."

Today those notes and drawings are acclaimed as the best and most thorough of all the gold rush diaries. That was Bruff's judgment from the beginning. In 1850, he recalled later, "I was offered Ten Thousand dollars cash [$200,000 in today's money] for my rough sketches of the overland Travel, but declined it, for obvious reasons."

The adventurer whose wanderlust had led him across a continent died in his bed a few hundred yards from the home where he had been born.

*   *   *

As for California, the legacy of the gold rush long outlasted the
gold itself. Those who had hoped for something else — perhaps the
fever would break and the patient would return to a normal life? —
glowered in frustration. "The rush to California," declared Henry
Thoreau, in a lecture delivered in 1854, reflects "the greatest dis-
grace on mankind." The miners had worked until their bodies gave
out, but that was beside the point. "It is not enough to tell me that
you worked hard to get your gold. So does the Devil work hard."

It was the nature of that work, not its difficulty, that so riled
Thoreau. "The gold-digger in the ravines of the mountains is as
much a gambler as his fellow in the saloons of San Francisco. What
difference does it make whether you shake dirt or shake dice? . . .
The humblest observer who goes to the mines sees and says that
gold-digging is of the character of a lottery; the gold thus obtained
is not the same thing with the wages of honest toil."

It wasn't the same thing. It was much better, as everyone in California knew. Who would choose a paycheck over a jackpot? (The
difference in effort between a man working for hire and a miner
digging to make himself rich, one eyewitness in the goldfields
reported, was like that "between the agonizing, aimless movements
of the sloth and the pounce of the panther.") In any case, what
need did California have for scoldings from staid New England?
What did Boston, with its long history and its stern and disapprov-
ing ways, understand of bold, bad San Francisco, born the day
before yesterday?

"There is nothing around us older than ourselves," Hubert Bancroft proclaimed happily, in 1888. "All that we see has grown up
under our eyes. . . . We lack the associations running back for generations, the old homesteads, the grandfather and grandmother,

and uncles and aunts." Lacking such restraints, Californians could bound joyously ahead, like puppies who slip their leash. That should have brought trouble, but it did not. "Men thrived on what elsewhere would prove their destruction," wrote Bancroft. "Old maxims were as useless as broken crockery."

Save for a rainy day? Haste makes waste? Look before you leap? Bancroft scoffed. "Deliberation and caution are well enough in their place...but a good driver does not put the brakes on going uphill."

California was different, and it celebrated that difference. "In California the lights went on all at once, in a blaze," wrote the historian Carey McWilliams, "and they never have dimmed." What set California apart from other places was that it "has not grown or evolved so much as it has been hurtled forward, rocket-fashion, by a series of chain-reaction explosions."

The first detonation, triggered by the rush of people from around the globe, set the tone. From its earliest days as a state, California was cosmopolitan. In 1860, its population was 39 percent foreign-born, triple the rate in the rest of the United States. San Francisco had more daily newspapers than did London, and they appeared not only in English but in Chinese, Swedish, French, Italian, and German. California was rich, with the highest per capita income in the nation. California was rowdy. In Massachusetts in 1856, a ship captain named Kemble, who had returned from a three-year voyage on a Sunday, was sentenced to two hours in the stocks for kissing his wife on his front doorstep; this was deemed "lewd and unseemly behavior." California's founding fathers were made of different stuff.

And, from the beginning, women were rare, which gave them

bargaining power unavailable to their sisters back east. Many miners refused to wash a shirt or cook a meal, on the grounds that this was "women's work." All the better for the few women around, who could charge sky-high prices. Scarcity paid off in other ways, too. In the East, a woman in a bad marriage was often stuck; in California, she could boot a second-rate husband to the curb and try again.

Every new arrival saw at once that California was not like home. Some recoiled, as Israel Lord had. But many in that great human flood exulted in their new freedom, like residents of small towns today who flee to the big city, or teenagers who suffer through high school and then reach college and thrill at the chance to start over. California's array of natural wonders only heightened those feelings of happy disorientation. Towering mountains, an endless ocean, countless acres of rich soil, rivers strewn with gold — everything in California was out of scale, everything was biggest and boldest and best. In 1852, for example, newcomers to California saw sequoia trees for the first time. Almost unfathomably gigantic, the biggest trees soared three hundred feet into the air and measured one hundred feet around the trunk. This seemed completely unlikely, a crude spoof like a jackalope postcard today. And yet, there the trees were, further proof that California was the Land of Fable where nature had suspended all the rules.

The emigrants felt that the rules that had held them in check, back at home, had been suspended, too. A missionary named William Taylor, sent to San Francisco to civilize the gold-seekers, found himself appalled at what these new Californians had got up to with the grown-ups two thousand miles away. Taylor spent seven years preaching on San Francisco's streets and in the diggings, starting in 1849, with meager results. Though he liked and admired the miners, he noted regretfully that they seemed vastly to prefer the here and now to the prospect of bliss in the afterlife. "Many men of fine mind and good education have laid all their intellectual strength [toward] the manufacture of witticisms and vulgar sayings...and spend their evenings in detailing them for the entertainment of the fun-loving crowds," he wrote. "Very few of them are particularly anxious to go to heaven."

This indifference stemmed not from any philosophical quarrel with religion; the problem was more that the miners looked on their time in the West as an interlude in their life, a time-out from the usual strictures and creeds. They "cared nothing about California except for her gold," Taylor reported, "and hence felt but little responsibility in regard to their conduct or character." *What happens in Vegas, stays in Vegas,* nineteenth-century style.

The miners put their case to Taylor openly. "I knew I couldn't carry my religion with me through California," one man told him, "so when I left home in Missouri I hung my religious sign on my gate-post until I should return."

The twist in the tale was that many of these miners never did return. Or they gave home a try but found that, once they had basked in California's sunshine and savored its freedom, life on an Indiana farm or in a Cleveland office had lost its allure. "Many of us have gone back to the Eastern United States, attempting to make homes there, but found the attempt a complete failure," wrote one gold-seeker. "Life was a dull and commonplace routine; once accustomed to the whirl of Californian speculation and the cordiality of Californian society, we could not live without them."

A miner named William Manly, who returned home to Wisconsin in 1852 to settle down, found himself desperate for distraction. "Every day was like Sunday so far as anything going on," he wailed. After weathering a few months' peace and quiet, he set off for the West Coast again.

Nobody was bored in California. "Recklessness is in the air," wrote Rudyard Kipling, after a visit to San Francisco in the 1880s. "I can't explain where it comes from, but there it is." Kipling, only in his twenties himself, found himself surrounded by men as active and spirited as he was. "The young men rejoice in the days of their youth. They gamble, yacht, race, enjoy prize-fights and cock-fights, the one openly, the other in secret; they establish luxurious clubs; they break themselves over horse-flesh and other things, and they are instant in a quarrel. At twenty they are experienced in business, embark in vast enterprises, take partners as experienced as themselves, and go to pieces with as much splendor as their neighbors."

The observation about going broke in style was key. In California failure *was* an option; sometimes it seemed almost a requirement. Nearly all of California's rich men had risen and fallen again and again, the trajectory of their careers almost always a jagged peak-and-valley sawtooth rather than a smooth incline. This, too, set California apart. The notion in the East had always been that to fail in business was to suffer a humiliation that could last a lifetime. People stared and whispered at their fallen neighbors with an almost lascivious malice. A man's reputation as fiscally sound, nineteenth-century moralists delighted in pointing out, was akin to "a woman's chastity, which a breath of dishonor may smirch and sully forever."

But Californians seemed almost to take pride in their falls. "In any little random gathering of a dozen men in San Francisco, you will probably find some among them who have been wealthy on three or four occasions and then poor again," wrote one miner-turned-journalist. "When men fail they do not despair...they hope to be rich again."

In the newcomers' eyes, this was testimony to their nerve, not to their lack of judgment. Everyone knew the story of California's great fortunes, after all, and everyone understood that, in a land awash in money, fortune favored the bold. Or the lucky. Charles Crocker, a shopkeeper who rose to colossal riches as one of the "Big Four" railroad tycoons, put it bluntly (as, indeed, he put everything). "One man works hard all his life and ends up a pauper. Another man, no smarter, makes twenty million dollars. Luck has a hell of a lot to do with it."

Riches might arrive from any direction. Swinging a pick was seldom the best option. (Crocker had failed as a miner but prospered as a dry-goods merchant selling to other miners.) An Italian candymaker named Domenico Ghirardelli raced to California in 1849 to try his hand at mining. It didn't pan out. He opened a store and then a second one. Both burned to the ground. He started over. The new business failed. His next venture, which in time changed its name to Ghirardelli Chocolate Company, made him rich. Levi Strauss famously made his fortune by outfitting the miners not with underwear or even shovels (though he did sell both) but with newfangled, hard-to-wear-out "waist overalls." The turning point in his career—the moment when the rise from successful merchant to millionaire began—came in the summer of 1872. A fellow German Jewish immigrant named Jacob Davis wrote Strauss a letter. A tailor (and another failed miner), Davis knew Strauss because he bought cloth from him. He had news—he had come up with a better way to make sure that pant pockets didn't come undone. "The secret of them Pents"—you can hear Strauss's German-inflected English—"is the Rivits that I put in those Pockets and I found the demand so large that I cannot make them up fast enough." So it proved.

*   *   *

California found its formula early on: a coyness-be-damned scramble for money, a taste for gambling and all-in bets, a gaze directed intently at the future, an embrace of talent regardless of age or accent or pedigree. It was a recipe for change. It worked, and it still works, but it is not a simple business. The race for fortune brought a trampling of those caught in the way; the eager taking up of new ideas carried with it a vulnerability to cults and fads of every stripe. On the complicated control panel that is California, the alluring and the off-putting, the brilliant and the inane, have always been only a few knob twists apart.

The pace has seldom slowed. It would be ludicrous to claim that innovation in America always starts in California. The car, perhaps the iconic image of American technological prowess, had nothing to do with California, nor did Henry Ford, patrolling his assembly line with stopwatch in hand, bear any relation to the buccaneers who grabbed up fortunes on the West Coast. But when the *New York Times* recently referred, and merely in passing, to "the great laboratory state of California," they knew that every reader would understand. In entertainment, in free higher education, in environmental reform, in aerospace, in electronics, California more often than not shows the way. Apple, Google, Disney... the list of California-based innovators is long.

Is it coincidence that such companies thrive in a state founded by speculators with a fondness for risk taking? "The cowards never started," Californians liked to say when their state was young, and there was truth as well as self-congratulation in the remark. Just as important, the tolerance of failure that marked the gold rush years lives on today. In Silicon Valley, it has become dogma that if you *haven't* failed, you haven't tried hard enough. "You've got to be willing to fail," Steve Jobs preached. "You've got to be willing to crash and burn ... with starting a company, with whatever. If you're afraid of failing, you won't get very far."

The biggest of California's innovations was California itself. Elsewhere, "heritage" and "tradition" were hallowed words; here, they were not living links to history but dead weights. The new state beckoned the world with an invitation it had never heard, and the world came running: *Come to California, where the end of the story has not yet been written.*

ACKNOWLEDGMENTS

THE HISTORIAN G. M. Trevelyan wrote that the astonishing, compelling, almost unfathomable feature of history is "the quasi-miraculous fact that once, on this earth, once, on this familiar spot of ground, walked other men and women, as actual as we are today, thinking their own thoughts, swayed by their own passions, but now all gone, one generation vanishing into another, gone as utterly as we ourselves shall shortly be gone, like ghosts at cockcrow."

The great treat for anyone who writes about the gold rush is the chance to savor the letters and diaries of countless men and women, as actual as we are today, who confronted an opportunity like none they had ever imagined. The gold-seekers knew they had embarked on one of the great adventures in American history. They set down their thoughts at the end of exhausting marches or in snatched breaks along the way. Many of their journals vanished, but hundreds have turned up at the bottom of trunks, in cobwebbed attics, in yard sales and rubbish heaps.

My greatest debt is to the editors and librarians who lovingly preserved this other sort of gold rush treasure, first of all, and then presented it to the world. The Library of Congress, in particular, has gathered in one place nearly two hundred gold rush diaries in its "California as I Saw It" archives. All students of American history are in its debt, and to the gold rush collections at the

Beinecke Library at Yale University; the Huntington Library in San Marina, California; the Bancroft Library at the University of California, Berkeley; and the New York Public Library; as well as a myriad of smaller institutions. For guidance I turned often to Gary Kurutz, the leading authority on gold rush narratives. His generosity is a match for his scholarship.

I chose to focus on five gold-seekers. In some ways these five— Joseph Bruff, Alonzo Delano, Israel Lord, Jennie Megquier, and Luzena Wilson—were representative of gold-rushers generally. They came from different parts of the country, occupied different rungs on the social ladder, traveled different routes, harbored different ambitions, and included both sexes and a variety of ages. But, in truth, they would not do as a random sample of "typical gold-seekers." All five were American, for one thing, and two women out of five is vastly out of proportion.

They stood out for their distinctive, quirky voices and their storytelling skills. We can hear them thanks to a small group of dedicated researchers who labored mightily to honor their achievements. Georgia Willis Read and Ruth Gaines edited Joseph Bruff's journals brilliantly and diligently. Necia Dixon Liles lovingly transcribed and edited Israel Lord's manuscript diary. Polly Welts Kaufman captured Jennie Megquier's humor and vitality. Fern Henry brought context and background to the bare-bones story of the indomitable Luzena Stanley Wilson, who announced in the first paragraph of her diary that whatever her husband might think, "I would not be left behind." (Alonzo Delano told his story himself, in an account published in 1854.)

This book has been several years in the making. Like the gold-seekers themselves, I found that working in a team far surpassed struggling alone. Flip Brophy, my agent and my friend, grabbed up the idea with characteristic gusto. Liese Mayer was the first to support it. Geoff Shandler improved the manuscript with sharp questions and wry humor. Chris Jerome copyedited thoughtfully and meticulously. Ben Allen managed somehow to combine gentleness and tenacity in his supervision of the production process.

My two sons, one a novelist and the other an editor, weighed in on every decision. No writer could have better allies.

Lynn, my road-trip partner on a gold rush excursion and the best of partners on every journey, deserves more thanks than I can put in words.

NOTES

Sources for quotations and for assertions that might prove elusive can be found below. To keep these notes in bounds, I have not documented facts that can be readily checked in standard sources. Publication information is provided only for books and articles not listed in the bibliography.

LC denotes a work that can be found online in the Library of Congress archives, at http://memory.loc.gov/ammem/cbhtml/cbhome.html

Epigraph

ix *"The planter, the farmer"*: Andrew Jackson's Farewell Address, Mar. 4, 1837, available online at http://tinyurl.com/q4gwojb.

ix *"A frenzy seized"*: Bancroft, *Works*, v. 23, p. 56.

Prologue

3 *The scraps, Bruff conceded in his diary*: Read and Gaines, eds., *Gold Rush*, p. 330. Bruff ate his dinner of coffee grounds on March 30, 1850.

3 *"I will soon have plenty to eat"*: ibid., p. 342.

PART I: HOPE
Chapter One: A Crack in Time

7 *"effeminate indulgence"*: Howe, *What Hath God Wrought*, p. 505. See also Reynolds, *Walt Whitman's America*, p. 48, and Lepler, *1837*, p. 101.

8 *Henry Thoreau's brother*: Richardson, *Thoreau*, p. 113.

8 *William Henry Harrison*: Gail Collins, *William Henry Harrison* (New York: Henry Holt, 2012), pp. 121–3.

8   *"one moment warm"*: "History of the Origin, Progress, and Mortality of the Cholera Morbus," *London Medical Gazette* 44 (1849), p. 557.

8   *The cholera epidemic that hit*: Byrne, ed., *Encyclopedia of Pestilence, Pandemics, and Plagues*, p. 99.

8   *"In St Louis…"*: Cooperman, "Cholera."

9   *"to implore the Almighty"*: President Zachary Taylor on July 3, 1849. The full text can be found in *The American Quarterly Register and Magazine* 3, no. 1 (Sept. 1849), p. 74.

10   *"Being a shoemaker"*: McNeil, *Travels*, p. 3. LC.

10   *"Jane i left you"*: Johnson, *Roaring Camp*, p. 73. Johnson is quoting a miner named Nathan Chase, writing on March 5, 1852. His letters are at Yale's Beinecke Library.

10   *California is like the rest*: It was Wallace Stegner who famously wrote that California was like the rest of the United States but more so, in a *Saturday Review* essay in 1967. The essay is reprinted and discussed at http://tinyurl.com/m4pyahl.

11   *A new word, millionaire*: Clark, *Social Change*, p. 196.

11   *"furnished once a month"*: Gordon, *An Empire of Wealth*, p. 158.

11   *by 1836 the number had soared*: Shepard, *Martin Van Buren*, p. 249.

12   *The population had skyrocketed*: McPherson, *Battle Cry*, pp. 6–10.

12   *"a mere 812"*: Edward Kemble, "San Francisco: Her Prospects," *Alta California*, Feb. 1, 1849.

12   *a rollicking city of 30,000*: Garrett, "San Francisco," p. 253.

12   *"I am among the French"*: Clark, *Social Change*, p. 220, quoting Mary Ballou.

13   *"A New York merchant"*: Marryat, *Diary*, v. 2, p. 13.

13   *"regular and uniform prices"*: Burrows and Wallace, *Gotham*, p. 668.

13   *"A few are riding"*: Henry Thoreau, *Walden*, ch. 1, "Economy."

14   *"nearly four million people lived in bondage"*: Kolchin, *Slavery*, p. 242.

14   *"She does not know"*: The letter is part of the Kinsey Collection of books and artifacts relating to African American history. A full transcript, and a link to a PDF of the original, handwritten note, can be found at http://tinyurl.com/mbgkugh.

14   *"I have followed that plow"*: Larkin, *Reshaping*, p. 15.

14   *tailors went on strike*: Spann, *Metropolis*, p. 71, and Wilentz, *Chants*, p. 350.

14   *"We are flesh and blood"*: Foner, *Labor Movement*, v. 1, p. 199.

15   *"Hot corn"*: Spann, *Metropolis*, p. 70.

15   *"the horse pulling"*: Delbanco, *Melville*, p. 101.

15   *"All communities divide themselves"*: Alexander Hamilton, *Debates of the Federal Convention: 1787*.

16   *Benjamin Franklin wrote an essay rebuking*: Isaacson, *Franklin*, p. 63.

17   *"not a totally new life"*: Clark, *Social Change*, p. 220.

17 *Most were young, single, inexperienced*: Wright, "Cosmopolitan California," pt. II, p. 74.

17 *"toil had heretofore consisted"*: Perkins, *Three Years in California*, p. 76.

17 *"My little girls"*: Wyman, ed., *Letters*, pp. 23–26.

18 *some 90,000 young men*: Starr and Orsi, eds., *Barbarous Soil*. For the 90,000 figure in particular, see p. 57, and for a discussion of the gold-seekers' numbers and makeup generally, see pp. 44–85.

19 *more than 1 percent of the American population*: The figure comes from an essay by the Wake Forest University economist Robert Whaples, which in turn draws on *Wages and Labor Markets in the United States, 1820–1860* by Robert A. Margo, p. 123. See Whaples, "California Gold Rush."

19 *"I did greatly fear"*: Cooke, *Alistair Cooke's America*, p. 156.

19 *Horace Greeley famously advised*: Greeley is always credited with the advice to "Go West, young man," but the quotation has a tangled history, and Greeley may never have put it quite that way. See "Who Said 'Go West, Young Man'—Quote Detective Debunks Myths," by Fred Shapiro, editor of the *Yale Book of Quotations*, at http://tinyurl.com/le7v5sq.

20 *The name "California" came*: Holliday, *Rush for Riches*, p. 5.

20 *California's non-Indian population totaled only fifteen thousand*: Wright, "Cosmopolitan California," pt. I, p. 323.

20 *The Indian population was ten times as large*: Hurtado, *Indian Survival*, p. 100.

20 *the number who made the overland trip*: Unruh, *Plains Across*, tables I and II, p. 119.

20 *"as lonely as men left swimming"*: Stewart, *California Trail*, p. 217.

20 *"There seemed to be an unending stream"*: Johnston, *Experiences*, p. 79.

21 *A group of gold-seekers from France*: Gay, *Marshall*, p. 224.

21 *A Rochester, New York, man*: Bieber, "Mania."

21 *"California Gold Grease"*: An advertisement for the magical ointment ran in the Richmond, Indiana, *Palladium* on Feb. 7, 1849. See also the Feb. 8, 2008, lecture by Gary Kurutz, one of the best-known gold rush historians, online at http://tinyurl.com/nd3ox5w.

21 *"The rich for many years"*: McNeil, *Travels*, p. 5. LC.

21 *"not a rich country"*: Lewis, *Sea Routes*, p. 7.

22 *Barclay set out*: Johnston, *Experiences*, p. 13.

22 *"What makes you think"*: "The Gold Hunter's Farewell to his Wife," quoted in Browning, ed., *Golden Shore*, p. 147.

22 *"wholesome restraints of New England"*: E. L. Cleaveland, "Hasting to Be Rich," 1849.

23 *"You know that I am in the prime"*: White, ed., *Buck*, p. 26. LC.

24 *"We are rather poor"*: Roberts, *American Alchemy*, p. 85. See also Bonfield and Morison, *Roxana's Children*, pp. 64–77.

25   *"One June morning [in 1848]"*: Mulford, *Life,* p. 5. LC.

27   *Take every American in 1850*: Haines, Michael R., and Richard H. Steckel. *A Population History of North America,* (New York: Cambridge University Press, 2000), table A-4, pp. 702–4.

27   *"What would you do"*: Author interview with Gary Kurutz, Mar. 5, 2012. Kurutz, for many years director of the Special Collections Branch of the California State Library, is the author of an immense and indispensable work called *The California Gold Rush,* which consists of commentary on every gold rush journal and diary.

Chapter Two: "I Believe I Have Found a Gold Mine!"

29   *seventeen tons of gold:* Meldahl, *Rough-hewn Land,* p. 38. Meldahl cites the figures for several years running: 17 tons in 1849, 68 tons in 1850, 126 tons in 1851, and 135 tons in 1852. He also provides a graph (p. 39) of California's gold production from 1848 until today.

29   *a trove of gold:* Holliday, "Failure Be Damned: The Origin of California's Risk-taking Culture." This was a lecture delivered May 3, 2000, at the Milken Institute Forum.

29   *"Neither moth nor rust"*: Bernstein, *The Power of Gold,* p. 3.

30   *Warren Buffett proclaimed*: quoted on NPR, *Marketplace,* Dec. 8, 2010.

30   *a lump the size of a sugar cube*: Bernstein, *Power,* p. 3.

30   *A golden stack five hundred leaves high*: "Make Everything Golden," *Popular Science,* June, 2005.

31   *Gather up a billion atoms*: Meldahl, *Hard Road West,* p. 265.

31   *Gold for one wedding ring*: Meldahl, *Rough-hewn Land,* p. 21. (Herrington explores the same analogy and comes up with a figure of 2,000 tons, but my own rough calculation tallies with Meldahl's. See Richard Herrington, *Gold,* p. 8.)

32   *"until through ill treatment they die"*: Jackson J. Spielvogel, *Western Civilization: To 1715* (Boston: Wadsworth, 2006), p. 102.

32   *"on a plate of Japanese porcelain"*: William Morrell, *The Gold Rushes* (New York: Macmillan, 1941), p. 54.

34   *Bigler scrawled an entry*: Paul, *Discovery,* pp. 32–35. Bigler's account differs from Marshall's in some important details, notably the date and whether the discovery was made in two stages (Bigler's version) or in one (as Marshall had it).

34   *"gold badly on the brain"*: Owens, *Saints,* p. 114.

35   *"I am no ordinary gentleman"*: Lienhard, *Pioneer,* p. 155.

36   *"all the Indians I could employ"*: Owens, ed., *John Sutter,* p. 61.

37   *"The harvest of weeks"*: The startled eyewitness was California pioneer John Bidwell, who told his story in "Life in California Before the Gold Discovery," *Century Magazine,* Dec., 1890.

37   *"Gold Mine Found"*: *Californian,* Mar. 15, 1848. The newspaper can be found online at http://tinyurl.com/mtzvpmh.

38   *"we must use two v's"*: Bruce, *Gaudy Century,* p. 5.

38   *"ruralize among the rustics"*: *California Star,* Apr. 15, 1848. This edition of the *Star* is available at the California Newspaper Digital Collection. See http://tinyurl.com/q5l79kc.

38   *Kemble concluded grumpily*: *California Star,* May 20, 1848, which is online, as noted above.

39   *"Men seemed to have gone insane"*: Bieber, "Mania."

40   *California struck Young as* too *enticing:* Owens recounted the clash between Brannan and Young, based on eyewitness accounts: "We have no business in San Francisco; the Gentiles will be there soon," Young insisted. Brannan responded with complaints about Utah's desolation. Young thumped the ground with his cane. "No sir, I am going to stop right here. I am going to build a city here. I am going to build a temple here, and I am going to build a country here." See *Saints,* pp. 51–52.

41   *"one of the poorest businessmen"*: Hurtado, *Sutter,* p. xiii.

42   *"That is money"*: ibid., pp. 220–21.

42   *"Gold, gold, gold, boys"*: ibid, p. 220.

43   *Brannan waved his hat*: Bancroft, *Works,* v. 23, p. 56.

43   *"a fleet of launches"*: Kemble, *California Star,* May 20, 1848.

44   *Carts with solid, wooden, Flintstone-style wheels*: Bidwell, "Life in California," *Century Magazine,* Dec., 1890.

44   *"Still the public incredulity remained"*: Colton, *Three Years,* p. 247.

45   *"Three seamen ran"*: ibid., p. 248.

45   *"No hope of reward"*: Thomas ap Catesby Jones, in a letter to the secretary of the navy on Nov. 2, 1848, reprinted in *The American Quarterly Registry and Magazine* 2 (Mar., 1849), p. 293.

45   *"the struggle between right"*: Bieber, "Mania."

46   Fn *A sailor's life*: Read and Gaines, eds., *Gold Rush,* p. 688.

46   *In San Jose, the constable*: Boessenecker, *Gold Dust,* p. 3.

46   *"A hint to the wise"*: Bieber, "Mania."

Chapter Three: Headlong into History

47   *"both Iliad and Odyssey"*: Starr, *Dream,* p. 52.

48   *Within six months of reaching California*: Roth, "Public Health."

48   *"I took the fever"*: Wing, *Journal,* p. 3.

48   *"What seems to you mere fiction"*: Browning, ed., *Golden Shore,* p. 34, quoting Walter Colton.

49   *That meant two things*: McWilliams, *California, the Great Exception,* p. 27. This is a paraphrase of an observation by McWilliams.

49   *a hoe and spade*: Buffum, *Six Months in the Gold Mines,* p. 79.

50   *"nearly crazy with the riches"*: Wyman, ed., *Letters*, p. 26.

50   *Men told tales of barbers*: This story is from a lecture by Gary Kurutz, an eminent gold rush historian, given on Feb. 8, 2008. Online at http://tinyurl.com/nd3ox5w.

50   *"It was easier to dig"*: Carson, *Bright Gem*, p. 9.

50   *"By me soul"*: Taylor, *Eldorado*, v. 2, p. 9. LC.

50   *"gold all along the banks"*: Downie, *Hunting*, p. 49.

51   *for eleven stunning days in a row*: Federal Writers' Project, *California*, p. 477. Online at http://tinyurl.com/mz7d9p6.

51   *One of Downie's companions*: Downie, *Hunting*, p. 48.

51   *"The gold excitement spread"*: Henry, ed., *My Checkered Life*, p. 11.

52   *"the damndest scoundrel"*: Ken Burns, *The Civil War* (New York: Random House, 1994), p. 74.

53   *"embrace the earliest opportunity"*: Read and Gaines, eds., *Gold Rush*, p. 684 fn. The biographical facts come from the fine introduction to this exemplary volume.

53   *"We go as a body"*: ibid., p. xxxiii.

53   *"A jolly good fellow"*: McKee, ed., *Alonzo Delano's California Correspondence*, p. xxv.

54   *a man who had reached the age of 250*: Billington, "Words That Won the West 1830–1850." This was a lecture delivered on Nov. 18, 1963, by Billington, a historian at the Huntington Library.

54   *"I was suddenly seized with the fever"*: Delano, *Journey*, p. 14.

54   *"a nomad denizen"*: ibid., p. 13.

54   *"no love for the good town of Turner"*: Kaufman, ed., *Apron Full of Gold*, p. xiv.

55   *"labored in Winthrop twelve years"*: ibid., p. xvi.

55   *a woman's bonnet blowing in the breeze*: Letts, *California Illustrated*, p. 89, introduces his story as "an anecdote almost universally told," but Gary Kurutz, an authority on gold rush history, presents the story as bizarre but factual. See Kurutz, "Popular Culture on the Golden Shore," in Starr and Orsi, eds., *Barbarous Soil*, p. 296.

56   *"Asses, asses all"*: Liles, ed., *Journey*, p. 124.

57   *"They've left me here to starve and die"*: ibid., p. 120.

57   *"A Christian man who went to California"*: ibid., p. 387.

57   *"the mountainous billows"*: McNeil, *Travels*, p. 9.

58   *"There is sometimes in the American metaphors"*: Marryat, *Diary*, p. 151.

58   *"He can't see through a ladder"*: Martineau, *Society in America*, v. 1, p. 250.

58   *"Oh, if we could kiss"*: Roberts, *American Alchemy*, p. 194.

58   Fn *This was a prudish age*: Bonfield and Morison, *Roxana's Children*, p. 66.

59   *"At 4 this morning"*: Merrill and Kirk, eds., *From Ohio to California*, p. 302.

59   *"plain American which cats and dogs can read!"*: The line is from Marianne Moore's poem "England." Edward Hirsch discusses Moore and the "plain American" voice in *How to Read a Poem* (New York: Harcourt Brace, 1999), p. 11.

60   *"the trials I have endured"*: Kaufman, ed., *Apron*, p. xix.

60   *"a rather unmated couple"*: Read and Gaines, eds., *Gold Rush*, p. xx.

60   *Attributed to "Isaac Lord"*: Liles, ed., *Journey*, p. xi.

60   *"Our servants have run"*: Colton, *Three Years*, p. 248.

61   *"Interesting Narrative of the Voyage"*: reprinted in Browning, ed., *Golden Shore*, p. 10.

62   *"You reckon by acres"*: ibid, p. 27.

63   *"a reptile marking his path"*: Stashower, *Beautiful Cigar Girl*, p. 111.

63   *"a decrepit, licentious, stupid"*: Mindich, *Just the Facts*, p. 47.

63   *The New York* Sun *reported*: Goodman, *The Sun and the Moon*, pp. 217–32. The articles themselves can be found at http://tinyurl.com/m6j9s3d.

64   *The first-ever crossing of the Atlantic*: Goodman, *Sun and the Moon*, pp. 233–44.

64   *"industrious fleas, educated dogs"*: Minnigerode, *Fabulous Forties*, p. 225.

65   *"a smaller than life man"*: Merry, *Polk*, p. 13.

66   *"any goose who could talk"*: Jackson, *Gold Dust*, p. 64.

67   *The Mint's one-word telegram*: Roberts, *American Alchemy*, p. 20.

67   *"The El Dorado of the old Spaniards"*: Browning, ed., *Golden Shore*, p. 45.

67   *"moved the whole nation"*: Langworthy, *Scenery*, p. iii.

67   *"Hurrah for California"*: Browning, ed., *Golden Shore*, p. 164.

PART II: JOURNEY
Chapter Four: Swarming from All Over

71   *"at 9 A.M. sharp, by order"*: Read and Gaines, eds., *Gold Rush*, p. xlii.

73   *"When we talked it all over"*: Henry, ed., *My Checkered Life*, p. 11.

75   *"I'm going where there is plenty more"*: White, ed., *Franklin Buck*. Buck described the scene in a letter of Jan. 17, 1849. LC.

75   *half-hour-long snowball fight*: McCollum, *California*, p. 46.

76   *On the island of Nantucket*: Bieber, "Mania."

76   *In New York a young lawyer*: This was George Templeton Strong, quoted in Roberts, *American Alchemy*, p. 6.

76   *"From Maine to Texas"*: The historian was Hittell, *San Francisco*, p. 130.

77   *"I saw a colored man"*: Lapp, *Blacks in Gold Rush California*, p. 21.

77   *He could bear any hardship*: David DeWolf, quoted in Elisha Perkins, *Gold Rush Diary*, p. 152. For more on DeWolf, see Lorenz, "Scurvy," p. 488, and "Captain David DeWolf," *History and Reminiscences from the Records of Old Settlers Union of Princeville and Vicinity*," p. 109, online at http://tinyurl.com/keubruk.

77   *"the trader [who] closed"*: Bancroft, *Works*, v. 23, p 118.

77   Fn *One gold-seeker composed a song*: James Pierpont wrote "The Returned Californian" (quoted here) in 1852 and "Jingle Bells" in 1857.

78   *Ralph Waldo Emerson focused*: Emerson, *The Conduct of Life*, p. 224.

78   *They gleefully recited a poem*: The poem, by Daniel March, is called *Yankee Land and the Yankee*. It is book length and online at http://tinyurl.com/ nj8emkq.

79   *"Any man's son may become the equal"*: Trollope, *Manners,* p. 171. Six decades later, English visitors were still complaining about American presumption. Rudyard Kipling found hotel clerks particularly irritating. "When that resplendent individual stoops to attend to your wants," Kipling wrote, "he does so whistling or humming or picking his teeth, or pauses to converse with someone he knows. These performances, I gather, are to impress upon you that he is a free man and your equal." See Kipling, *From Sea to Sea,* p. 439.

79   *"There was scarcely one"*: Taylor, *Eldorado,* p. 1.

79   *"What an innocent, unsophisticated"*: Mulford, *Life,* p. 9.

80   *"Few could conquer with Pizarro"*: McWilliams, *California,* p. 27.

80   *"no useless trumpery"*: Palmer, *Journey,* p. 126.

81   *Alonzo Delano packed*: Delano, *Correspondence,* p. 84. LC.

81   *"on bacon and flour"*: Henry, ed., *My Checkered Life,* p. 11.

82   *one-fifth of the soldiers*: Lorenz, "Scurvy," p. 475.

82   *"noise and din"*: Fairchild, *Letters,* p. 6. LC.

82   *"one funeral after another"*: Cooperman, "Cholera."

83   *"miserable, dull, unbuilt, unpainted"*: Liles, ed., *Journey,* p. 19.

83   *"not very well done"*: ibid., p. 17.

83   *"a biped five feet four inches tall"*: ibid., p. 18.

84   *One Philadelphia woman noted*: Drinker, *Journal,* pp. 263, 288. Online at http://tinyurl.com/kyd3dhy.

84   *"neither shaves nor shears"*: Helper, *The Land of Gold,* p. 180.

84   *"As far as we could see"*: Read and Gaines, eds., *Gold Rush,* p. 7.

85   *One favorite tale related*: Billington, "Words."

85   *Did you hear about the diamond*: Both newspaper stories were reprinted in Browning, ed., *Golden Shore,* pp. 75, 151.

85   *"a capital weapon to kill a bear"*: Reid, *Overland,* p. 26.

86   *"many a man whose legs"*: Kip, *California Sketches,* p. 16. LC.

86   *"The markets are filled"*: Ingalls, *Journal,* p. 11.

86   *"West of that stream"*: Frink, *Journal,* p. 57.

87   *"the place where civilization ended"*: Cooke, *America,* p. 177.

87   *"Our ignorance of the route was complete"*: This was John Bidwell, who told his story in "The First Emigrant Train to California," *The Century Magazine,* Nov., 1890.

88   *"We are now on the Platte"*: Tamsen Donner's letter is online at http://
      tinyurl.com/n5cswck.

89   *Bronco Charlie Miller*: "Pony Express Arrives," *New York Times*, May 15, 1932.

89   *An emigrant named Ezra Meeker*: Meeker, who was born in 1830, lived to
      age ninety-eight. He drove a car (with the cover of his ox wagon fastened to
      the roof) along the route of the Oregon Trail in 1915, at age eighty, and he
      flew the route in a Fokker T-2 airplane in 1924, at age ninety-four. See
      http://tinyurl.com/mfcw3mq.

Chapter Five: A Day at the Circus

90   *"The crowd at the ferry"*: Read and Gaines, eds., *Gold Rush*, p. 3.

90   *"Our first campfire was lighted"*: Henry, ed., *My Checkered Life*, p. 12.

90   *"I had read and heard"*: ibid., p. 12.

91   *"Gracious God! What a scene"*: Pearce, "Captivity," p. 16.

91   *"I felt my children the most precious"*: Henry, ed., *My Checkered Life*, p. 12.

91   *"They sent back word"*: ibid.

92   *"friendly, of course"*: ibid.

92   *By the tally of the historian John Unruh*: Unruh, *Plains Across*, p. 185.

92   *"The timber continued"*: Delano, *Journey*, p. 21.

93   *"we feel like mere specks"*: Frink, *Journal*, p. 28.

94   *"loves his wife more than gold"*: Joseph Banks quoted in Scarnehorn, ed.,
      Buckeye Rovers, p. 17.

94   *"Every mode of travel"*: Wyman, ed., *Letters*, p. 95.

94   *"Some drive mules"*: Liles, ed., *Journey*, p. 18.

94   *Wheelbarrow man:* Wyman, ed., *Letters*, p. 108, and Unruh, *Plains Across*,
      p. 107.

95   *"Happiness for Voltaire"*: Simon Schama, "A Whiff of Dread in the Land of
      Hope," *New York Times*, Sept. 15, 2002.

95   *"our own innocent ignorance"*: Webster, *Gold-Seekers*, p. 33. LC.

95   *"It is fun to see them"*: Fairchild, *Letters*, p. 14.

96   *"Hell, west & crooked*: Vincent Geiger, quoted in Potter, ed., *Overland Jour-
      nal*, p. 77.

96   *"wild as the deer on the prairie"*: Webster, *Gold-seekers*, p. 35.

96   *"Owing chiefly to some difficulty"*: Dundass, *Journal*, p. 8.

97   *The mules "had not given their consent"*: Reid, *Overland*, p. 33.

98   *"who have never dug a rood"*: Roberts, *American Alchemy*, p. 6.

99   *"the servile trade of quill-driving"*: Luskey, *Clerks*, p. 69. William Perkins
      used the same phrase in describing one of his own, pre-California jobs. See
      Three Years in California: William Perkins' Journal, p. 162.

99   *"showing rags to the ladies"*: Fairchild, *Letters*, p. 42.

99   *In Mark Twain's Hannibal*: The passage is from "The Boys' Ambition,"
      chapter 4 of *Life on the Mississippi*.

100 *"As we wended our way"*: Thompson, *Reminiscences,* p. 6.

101 *"Once in line"*: Mattes, *Platte River Road,* p. 55.

101 *"we either had to stay poking behind them"*: ibid.

101 *"Our train consisted only of six wagons"*: Henry, ed., *My Checkered Life,* p. 12.

102 *"like fine hail"*: Mattes, *Platte River Road,* p. 94, quoting Ezra Meeker.

102 *The novelist Willa Cather*: Cather's observation was from a newspaper interview in 1913. See http://tinyurl.com/kpz4ncu.

103 Fn *"the butter gathers in lumps"*: Liles, ed., *Journey,* p. 21.

104 *"the swamps, stagnant waters, reptiles"*: Lewis, *Sea Routes,* frontispiece.

105 *"Nine men occupied a space"*: McCollum, *California,* p. 87. LC.

105 *One singularly unlucky traveler*: Dolly Bates told her story in Bates, *Incidents on Land and Water.* LC.

106 *"You must not believe half"*: Kaufman, ed., *Apron,* p. 7.

106 *"Sunday night, lonesome as death"*: ibid., p. 1.

106 *"It is a long route"*: ibid., p. 7.

107 *"a splendid steamship"*: ibid., p. 11.

107 *"We found benaners"*: Lewis, *Sea Routes,* p. ix.

107 *"Duff, plum duff"*: DeCosta, quoted in Lorenz, "Scurvy," p. 482.

108 *"Mine were generally of the hardened species"*: Mulford, *Life,* p. 56.

108 *"It might be mule"*: Liles, ed., *Journey,* p. 360.

109 *"oppressive almost beyond endurance"*: Perkins, *Three Years,* p. 81.

110 *"The old year ended in scarcity"*: Rapport, *1848,* p. 37.

112 *"The gold excitement here"*: Wright, "Cosmopolitan California," pt. II, p. 66.

113 *A new song*: *London Sunday Times,* Jan 6, 1849, reprinted in Browning, ed., *Golden Shore,* p. 133.

113 *"Nothing in Norway's condition"*: Wright, "Cosmopolitan California," pt. II, p. 67.

114 *"it abounds with wine and money"*: Jackson, *Gold Rush,* p. 36.

114 *"Money is in great plenty"*: Whipple, *The Challenge,* p. 63.

114 *Steerage was so overcrowded*: Corbett, *Poker Bride,* p. 8.

114 *In a single two-day span*: Wright, "Cosmopolitan California," pt. I, p. 330.

Chapter Six: An Army on the March

115 *"The force of the wind"*: Delano, *Journey,* p. 27.

117 *"Distance gained—nothing"*: ibid., p. 31.

117 *"for without firing a shot"*: ibid., p. 38.

117 *As lost as "the children of Israel"*: ibid.

117 *"being unaaccustomed to labor"*: ibid., p. 32.

118 *"a company of Christians"*: Ingalls, *Journal,* p. 15.

118 *"as if a mighty army"*: Delano, *Journey,* p. 46.

119 *"Love is hotter here"*: Unruh, *Plains Across,* p. 397.

119   *"Many a Green 'un trembled"*: Wyman, ed., *Letters*, p. 48.

119   *"the most beautiful prairie"*: Liles, ed., *Journey*, p. 20.

119   *"To see and feel it in all its beauty"*: Ingalls, *Journal*, p. 15.

120   *"All the storms which I ever before"*: Reid, *Overland*, quoting Niles Searls, a fellow passenger.

120   *"The thunder and lightning were continuous"*: Liles, ed., *Journey*, p. 26.

121   *"It is necessary to rouse"*: ibid., p. 23.

121   *"We left a dead man"*: Liles, ed., *Journey*, p. 15.

122   *"He called himself T. R. Waring"*: ibid., p. 23.

122   *"Every steamer was impregnated"* with the disease: Thissell, *Plains*, p. 8.

124   *"the scum of the city"*: Burrows and Wallace, *Gotham*, p. 591, quoting John Pintard.

125   Vibrio cholerae *"converts the human body"*: Johnson, *Ghost Map*, p. 38.

125   *With the rise of giant, filthy, slum-infested cities*: ibid., p. 41.

125   *"the gold rush was to cholera"*: Groh, *Gold Fever*, p. 28.

126   Fn *"The past is a foreign country"*: Gregory Cochran's remark is from an Edge.com forum on explanations in science. See http://tinyurl.com/86b8uzj.

126   *"Dear me! What insipid water!"*: Steele, *Summer Journey*, p. 210.

126   *a diet of bacon covered in cayenne pepper*: Foreman, ed., *Marcy*, p. 85.

127   *"Have passed a great many graves"*: Liles, ed., *Journey*, p. 28.

127   *"Passed a number of graves"*: ibid., p. 24.

127   *"The meat is better than venison"*: ibid., p. 25.

127   *"One of the oddest little creatures"*: Thissell, *Plains*, p. 53.

128   *"In a moment all was excitement"*: Liles, ed., *Journey*, p. 30.

128   *A young carpenter named Reuben Shaw*: Shaw, *Plains*, pp. 50–52.

129   *"The casualties of buffalo hunting"*: Read and Gaines, eds., *Gold Rush*, p. 24.

129   *"a slaughter yard, dotted all over with skeletons"*: Unruh, *Plains Across*, p. 386.

129   *"We frequently see half-eaten corpses"*: Liles, ed., *Journey*, p. 34.

130   *the gold-seekers and those who followed*: This is a paraphrase of a passage on p. 75 of Keith Meldahl's *Hard Road West*.

130   *"The locusts of Egypt"*: Johnston, *Experiences*, p. 79.

130   *"We found the bodies of nine Sioux"*: Stansbury, *Exploration*, pp. 43–46.

131   *"the worst river to ford"*: Morton and Watkins, *Nebraska*, p. 94.

131   *"fearful to look at"*: Frink, *Journal*, p. 67.

132   *"The frantic driver shouted"*: Henry, ed., *My Checkered Life*, p. 13.

132   *Joseph Bruff saw a wagon*: Read and Gaines, eds., *Gold Rush*, p. 25.

133   *"No loved one near"*: Thissell, *Plains*, p. 28.

133   *"Another of our company died"*: Fairchild, *Letters*, p. 26.

134   *"Passed a camp of 5 wagons"*: Read and Gaines, eds., *Gold Rush*, p. 39.

134   *"Custom made us regard"*: Henry, ed., *My Checkered Life*, p. 14.

Chapter Seven: Let Us Glory in Our Magnificence

135 *"The worst hills this side of the Missouri"*: Liles, ed., *Journey*, p. 33.

136 *"Here you saw the minarets of a castle"*: Delano, *Journey*, p. 73.

136 *"If a man does not feel like an insect then"*: Perkins, *Diary*, p. 46.

137 *"The evening was wet"*: Liles, ed., *Journey*, p. 72.

137 *"If a man has a mean streak"*: ibid.

137 *"this long, weary, and vexacious journey"*: Delano, *Correspondence*, p. 16.

137 *"no situation so trying"*: Reid, *Overland*, p. 97. Another emigrant described the dissension on a cross-country journey, in 1858, where "everything went lovely for a while, but the men soon became cross and ill-natured. The day the butter gave out, two men quarreled over the last morsel, drew their guns, and bloodshed was prevented only by the prompt interference of [two other men]." See George Thissell, *Crossing the Plains in '49*, p. 28.

137 Fn *"Grown men are apt to become children"*: Reid, *Overland*, p. 97.

138 *"If I ordered a halt at 5 o'clock*: Liles, ed., *Journey*, p. 426.

138 *"At home I saw my neighbors"*: Lewis, *Sea Routes*, p. 15.

138 *"One of the first things I plan"*: ibid., p. ix.

139 *"Poor fellow," wrote Ingalls*: Ingalls, *Journal*, p. 28.

139 *To his horror, Delano found*: Delano, *Journey*, p. 63.

140 *"nothing but the huts of savages"*: Langworthy, *Scenery*, p. 54.

140 *"Oh, what a treat"*: Meldahl, *Hard Road West*, p. 76.

140 *"some of the hills look like a mine"*: Liles, ed., *Journey*, p. 46.

141 *"thick as snowflakes"*: Webster, *Gold-seekers*, p. 49.

141 *"The mosquitoes swarm by the millions"*: Thissell, *Crossing the Plains*, p. 25.

141 *"They are very great pests"*: Liles, ed., *Journey*, p. 47.

142 *"Bear Creek...was a famous breeder of chills"*: Mark Twain, *Life on the Mississippi*, ch. 55.

142 *"Oh, from down on the Wabash"*: Delano, *Journey*, p. 262.

142 *"Chills and fevers were believed part"*: Billington, "Words."

142 *"my old companions, chill and fever"*: Delano, *Journey*, p. 256.

142 *"one man in California who ever had a chill"*: Billington, "Words."

143 *"For this blessed mission"*: Stephanson, *Manifest Destiny*, p. xi.

143 *"so ferocious and bloodthirsty"*: Roberts, *American Alchemy*, p. 67.

144 *Abraham Lincoln would frame*: This was Lincoln's "Second Lecture on Inventions and Discoveries," delivered on Feb. 11, 1859. See http://tinyurl .com/cwurcaz.

144 *"self-made" was not yet a synonym*: The argument in this paragraph and the next derives from Cawelti, *Apostles of the Self-Made Man*, pp. 41–46.

145 *"The farm boy who embarked"*: Billington, "Words."

145 *"America's national adolescence"*: David Kennedy, in his introduction to Howe, *What Hath God Wrought*, p. xiii.

145 *"In the States," one visiting Scotsman observed*: Borthwick, *Three Years in California*, p. 106.

146 *"Let us glory in the magnificence"*: Rydell, "Cape Horn Route," p. 159.

146 *"any quantity of speeches"*: Liles, ed., *Journey*, p. 48.

146 *"the singular and romantic bluffs"*: Read and Gaines, eds., *Gold Rush*, p. 31.

147 *Imploring him to "hurry up"*: ibid., p. 27.

147 *The death was "sudden and astounding"*: ibid.

148 *"It is the most beautiful spot"*: Kaufman, ed., *Apron*, p. 12

148 *"The air was filled with the music"*: ibid., p. 15.

148 *"a bed of slime"*: Bancroft, *California Inter Pocula*, p. 159.

149 *"It is composed of about fifty"*: Marryat, *Mountains and Molehills*, ch. 1.

150 *"A returning Californian had just reached"*: Taylor, *Eldorado*, p. 12.

150 *The boatmen were "naked or [wearing] nothing"*: Kaufman, ed., *Apron*, p. 14.

150 *"not inconveniently burdened with clothing"*: Grant, *Memoirs*, p. 71.

151 *"Would to God I could describe"*: Kaufman, ed., *Apron*, p. 28.

151 *"They would come and look at me"*: ibid., p. 15.

151 *"the monkies were howling"*: Matt, *Homesickness*, p. 67.

152 *"Among all the miserable places"*: Weber, ed., *Schliemann*, p. 81. Online at http://tinyurl.com/kv394mb.

153 *"travellers murdered on the road"*: ibid., p. 38.

153 *"the most delightful in the world"*: Kaufman, ed., *Apron*, p. 14.

154 *"A mule took the liberty"*: ibid., p. 30.

154 *"just room for the beast"*: ibid., p. 16.

154 Fn *"they equally shoot or stab them"*: Weber, ed., *Schliemann*, p. 38.

154 *"there are a great number of churches"*: Kaufman, ed., *Apron*, p. 31.

154 *"Cats, dogs, and rats trooped through"*: ibid., p. 19.

155 *"hundreds of us were attacked"*: ibid., p. 81.

155 *"we have not suffered"*: Kaufman, ed., *Apron*, p. 20.

155 *"The town was overrun"*: ibid., p. 31.

155 *"looked less like civilization"*: ibid., p. 21.

156 *"Every man that goes to the mines"*: ibid., p. 32.

156 *"In about one year, you will see"*: ibid., p. 25.

Chapter Eight: A Rope of Sand

157 *"our incessant journeying"*: Delano, *Journey*, p. 75.

157 *"Day after day, week after week"*: Henry, ed., *My Checkered Life*, p. 13.

158 Fn *"A woman is nobody"*: Robert James Maddox, *American History: Pre-Colonial through Reconstruction* (New York: McGraw Hill, 2000), p. 128.

158 *"Home is the palace"*: Reverend Joshua N. Danforth, *Gleanings and Groupings from a Pastor's Portfolio* (New York: A. S. Barnes, 1852), p. 1, online at http://tinyurl.com/nyfljsd.

158   *"The Victorian structure of domestic power"*: West, "Family Life," p. 35.

158   *"My health at present is rather feeble"*: Drury, ed., *Diaries of Mary Walker*, p. 9. The footnote citing Mary Walker's diary entry is from p. 227.

159   *She set their wagon on fire*: West, "Family Life," p. 36.

159   *" for the first time in our lives"*: Delano, *Journey*, p. 64. Future laundry ventures only confirmed Delano in his dislike. "Of all miserable work," he wrote on July 17, "washing is the meanest; and no man who has crossed the plains will ever find fault with his wife for scolding on a washing day." See *Journey*, p. 141.

159   *a "cruel and fiendish murder"*: Delano, *Journey*, p. 124.

160   *"The Devil seems to take full possession"*: Liles, ed., *Journey*, p. 79.

161   *"the wretch was swung into eternity"*: Thompson, *Reminiscences*, p. 6.

161   *"a rope of sand"*: Langworthy, *Scenery*, p. 40.

161   *"I immediately convened the company"*: Read and Gaines, eds., *Gold Rush*, p. 34.

161   *"great dissension in the company"*: ibid., p. 51.

162   *"No one would ever suspect"*: Ingalls, *Journal*, p. 28.

162   *"ascent of the Capitol hill"*: Unruh, *Plains Across*, p. 44.

162   *"perfectly stupid and childish"*: Read and Gaines, eds., *Gold Rush*, p. 59.

162   *"In a musing mood"*: Delano, *Journey*, p. 116.

163   *"crowded like Pearl Street or Broadway"*: Langworthy, *Scenery*, p. 73.

164   *"The whole country is one vast sand bed"*: Liles, ed., *Journey*, p. 60.

165   *"Our faces, hair, and clothes"*: Delano, *Journey*, p. 122.

165   *"All is dry, dry, dry"*: Liles, ed., *Journey*, p. 60.

165   *"You seldom see a bird"*: Banks, *Buckeye Rovers*, p. 63.

166   *"Green River presents the most romantic"*: Ingalls, *Journal*, p. 29.

166   *"like a curved silver thread"*: Read and Gaines, eds., *Gold Rush*, p. 71. Bruff's drawing of the descent is on p. 537.

166   *"the most romantic and beautiful valley"*: Liles, ed., *Journey*, p. 67.

167   *"For more than two months"*: Delano, *Journey*, p. 130.

167   *"When we commenced the journey"*: Ingalls, *Journal*, p. 33.

167   *"You may think you have seen mountains"*: Holliday, *Rush for Riches*, p. 108.

168   *"Men & oxen suffering much"*: Read and Gaines, eds., *Gold Rush*, p. 71.

168   *"innumerable large black mice"*: ibid., p. 77.

168   *a small piece of apple pie*: ibid., p. 81.

168   *"only needed lemon syrup"*: ibid., p. 91.

169   *"Bull would come up"*: ibid., p. 612.

169   *"Weary, weary, weary"*: Delano, *Journey*, p. 141.

169   *"We began to see many traveling on foot"*: ibid., p. 145.

170   *"Here we are yet"*: Kaufman, ed., *Apron*, p. 24.

170   *worthy of Molly Bloom*: ibid.

171   *"in flocks so large they look like a cloud"*: ibid., p. 22.

171   *"We killed two scorpions"*: ibid.

171   *"One of the party shot him"*: ibid., p. 23.

172   *"scarce light enough to see the rats and spiders"*: ibid., p. 140.

174   *"I am now writing the last letter"*: ibid., p. 33.

Chapter Nine: Gone!

175   *"nothing but horse broth"*: Ingalls, *Journal*, p. 40.

176   *"The reader should not imagine"*: Shaw, *Across the Plains*, p. 135.

176   *a temperature of 140 degrees*: Reid, *Overland*, p. 128.

176   *"In the creek we found"*: Langworthy, *Scenery*, p. 125.

176   *"For about ten days the only water"*: Cole, *Early Days*, p. 101.

177   *"Our dreams are of water"*: Barry, ed., "John Hawkins Clark," pp. 282–83.

177   *"One of the men had got crazy"*: Stewart, *California Trail*, p. 265.

177   *"the parched and dry alkaline crust"*: Delano, *Journey*, p. 169.

177   *"Suppose dry ashes and fine sand were mixed"*: Reid, *Overland*, p. 115.

178   *"It is a dreary barren spot"*: Dundass, *Journal*, p. 49.

178   *"like ducks on a pond"*: Reid, *Overland*, p. 120.

178   *"On leaving home it looked like a hardship"*: Delano, *Journey*, p. 171.

178   *"The appearance of emigrants has sadly changed"*: Ingalls, *Journal*, p. 40.

179   *"We have absolutely used up"*: Reid, *Overland*, p. 128.

179   *"a great rent in the earth"*: Shaw, *Across the Plains*, p. 137.

179   *"Sand!!! Hot!!!"*: Stewart, *California Trail*, p. 266.

180   *"It was a forced march"*: Henry, ed., *My Checkered Life*, p. 27.

181   *"a scene more horrid"*: Ingalls, *Journal*, p. 44.

182   *"While we were yet five miles"*: Henry, ed., *My Checkered Life*, p. 28.

182   *"Men were seen to rush up"*: Owen Coy, *The Great Trek*, p. 203.

182   *"We buried our faces"*: Fey et al., *Emigrant Shadows*, p. 124.

183   *"as steep as the roof of a house"*: Ingalls, *Journal*, p. 48.

183   *"Just ahead," wrote one dismayed traveler*: Coy, *Great Trek*, p. 203.

183   *"It made one's flesh creep"*: Meldahl, *Hard Road West*, p. 259.

184   *"creep upward upon their knees"*: Langworthy, *Scenery*, p. 161.

184   *"I do not think it possible"*: ibid., p. 165.

184   *"By the side of such a grove"*: ibid., p. 173.

184   *Eleazer Ingalls waxed philosophical*: Ingalls, *Journal*, p. 48.

185   *"Already we began to forget"*: Henry, ed., *My Checkered Life*, p. 28.

Chapter Ten: Marooned

186   *"I had determined to take a northern route"*: Read and Gaines, eds., *Gold Rush*, p. 140.

186   *he wrote a proud note*: ibid., p. 144.

187   *the goldfields were only 110 miles ahead*: Unruh, *Plains Across*, p. 353.

188   *"a dead ox, swelled up"*: Read and Gaines, eds., *Gold Rush*, p. 148.

188   *"it seemed to be the River of Death"*: Thornton, *Oregon and California*, p. 179.

188   *"monstrous, unmeaning, vacant, lustrous"*: Liles, ed., *Journey*, p. 104.

189   *Some of the fallen animals*: Cole, *Overland Travel*, p. 108.

189   *The stink hung so heavy*: Liles, ed., *Journey*, p. 117.

189   *"By actual measurement"*: ibid., p. 126.

189   *"The selfishness of my men"*: Read and Gaines, eds., *Gold Rush*, p. 157.

189   *"Held a meeting to inflict penalties"*: ibid., p. 164.

190   *The ascent was "pretty steep"*: ibid., p. 174.

190   *"What a scene from here"*: ibid., p. 185.

191   *"To admire is a long way behind me"*: Liles, ed., *Journey*, p. 147.

192   *"The company very anxious"*: Read and Gaines, eds., *Gold Rush*, p. 194.

192   *he had "brought them to this point"*: ibid., p. 207.

193   *"We pitched our tent"*: ibid., p. 209.

193   *"Thin with hunger"*: ibid., p. 212.

193   *A group of emigrants had purposely set fire*: ibid., p. 214.

194   *"You came for me!"*: ibid., p. 221.

194   *"An aged, grey headed man"*: ibid., p. 224.

194   *"Alas for the sick & helpless"*: ibid., p. 228.

195   *"many a poor, wet, tired, and ragged hombre"*: ibid., p. 234.

196   *"Unsuccessful hunt today"*: ibid., p. 231.

196   *"Quite ill tonight"*: ibid., p. 239.

196   *It was a thundering shame*: ibid., pp. 242, 248.

197   *"Unless succor is sent me"*: ibid., p. 250.

197   *"strong gales and snow"*: ibid., p. 255.

197   *"I & the child are doomed, perhaps"*: ibid., p. 262.

198   *"All wet, and confusion"*: ibid., p. 265.

198   *"An extremity has come"*: ibid., p. 266.

198   *"we enjoyed our pipes"*: ibid., p. 271.

199   *"So we have a Christmas dinner"*: ibid., p. 273.

199   *"Poyle and myself are too weak"*: ibid., p. 276.

200   *"WILLIAM, Infant son of LAMBKIN"*: ibid., p. 285.

200   *"pain in back very bad"*: ibid., p. 309.

200   *"old hunter, and used to a rough life"*: ibid., p. 288.

200   *"A series of circumstances & misfortunes"*: ibid., p. 685.

201   *"About 7 p.m. my comrade returned"*: ibid., p. 309.

201   *"I am now in a snap truly"*: ibid., p. 324.

203   *"Made a fire"*: ibid., p. 335.

204   *"I will soon have plenty to eat"*: ibid., p. 342.

PART III: REALITY
Chapter Eleven: First Peeks at the Golden Land

207   *"The sight of his white shirt"*: Henry, ed., *My Checkered Life*, p. 28.

208   *"I'll give you five dollars"*: ibid., p. 29.

209   Fn *"all kinds of animals"*: Wyman, ed., *Letters*, p. 140.

209   *"The present of this city"*: Woods, *Sixteen Months*, p. 47. LC.

209   *"Imagine a long room"*: Henry, ed., *My Checkered Life*, p. 39.

210   *"Every new-comer in San Francisco"*: Taylor, *Eldorado*, p. 57.

211   *"You speak to an acquaintance"*: ibid., p. 112.

212   *Taylor watched a dozen men*: ibid., p. 60.

212   Fn *Con men knew these stories*: Barker, ed., *Memoirs*, p. 143.

212   *"hurry and skurry"*: Barker, ed., *Memoirs*, p. 200.

212   *"It is impossible to witness this excess"*: Taylor, *Eldorado*, p. 114.

212   *"People seem to be very near crazy"*: Kaufman, ed., *Apron*, p. 38.

213   *"The most busy streets in New York"*: ibid., p 39.

213   *"There never was a place"*: ibid., p. 42.

213   *Thomas wrote to a friend*: ibid, p. 43.

213   *"People lived more in a week"*: Borthwick, *Three Years*, p. 49.

213   *"A man, on coming to California"*: Taylor, *Eldorado*, v. 2, p. 64.

214   *"You are right in thinking"*: White, ed., *Franklin Buck*, p. 233.

214   *"gigantic temptations" lurked*: This passage and the other quotations from Farley come from "The Moral Aspect of California: A Thanksgiving Sermon," by Charles A. Farley (delivered Dec. 1, 1850).

215   Fn *A miner named Vicente Pérez Rosales*: Barker, ed., *Memoirs*, p. 145.

215   *His task was to exchange*: Lavender, *New Beginnings*, p. 158.

215   *Like barbers who found gold*: Barker, ed., *Memoirs*, p. 143.

215   *great numbers of young men*: Wyman, ed., *Letters*, p. 27.

216   *"the returned gold diggers were there"*: McCollum, *California*, p. 122.

216   *"Wrapped in rags were nuggets"*: Barker, ed., *Memoirs*, p. 135.

216   *"The immigrants would stop in amazement"*: Downie, *Hunting*, p. 14.

216   *Lord was "struck all aback"*: Liles, ed., *Journey*, p. 198.

217   *"Everyone must do something"*: Kaufman, ed., *Apron*, p. 37.

217   *624 miners for every 1,000 people*: Whaples, "California Gold Rush."

217   *"All were in a hurry"*: McCollum, *California*, p. 159.

217   *"Now is the time for making money"*: Barker, ed., *Memoirs*, p. 123.

218   *"as jolly as a clam at high water"*: Starr, *Barbarous Soil*, p. 175.

218   *"a cellar in the earth"*: Taylor, *Eldorado*, p. 58.

218   *One man cornered the market*: The candle wick and barley examples are both from Taylor, *Eldorado*, v. 2, p. 57.

218   *"by scraping on a squeaky fiddle"*: Barker, ed., *Memoirs*, p. 254.

218   *chickens for $25 each*: Lewis, *Sea Routes*, p. 94.

219   *"We did not get much gold"*: James Horner, "Adventures of a Pioneer," p. 573.

220   *Aboard the clipper ship* America: Haskins, *Argonauts*, p. 47.

221   *"I had never earned over one dollar"*: McNeil, *Travels*, p. 20.

221   *"As for the prospects of mining"*: Delano, *Correspondence*, p. 20.

221   *"Here were real, live miners"*: Perkins, *Three Years*, p. 92.

222 *"Four or five men were working"*: Borthwick, *Three Years*, p. 111.

222 *"You hear of men"*: Delano, *Correspondence*, p. 30.

223 *"Now I will tell you what we have done"*: Wyman, ed., *Letters*, p. 78.

223 *"The labor of gold-digging"*: Buffum, *Six Months*, p. 180.

223 *"hardest work at home"*: Perkins, *Three Years*, p. 162.

224 *"It was altogether a scene"*: Borthwick, *Three Years*, p. 113.

224 *A gold-seeker named Prentice Mulford*: Mulford, *Life*, p. 105. Mulford reached the goldfields only in 1856, but many of his descriptions of the miners' routine and their frame of mind apply to the pioneer days as well.

225 *"a dog with a sore foot"*: Clappe, *The Shirley Letters*, p. 54. Louise Clappe, a brilliant writer better known by her pseudonym, Dame Shirley, described life in the diggings in letters to her sister.

225 *"scaring the Hogs out of my kitchen"*: Ballou, "Hogs in My Kitchen," pp. 42–46.

226 *In a camp called Indian Bar*: Clappe, *The Shirley Letters*, pp. 37–39.

Chapter Twelve: Hard Times

228 Fn *"It is no uncommon thing"*: Borthwick, *Three Years*, p. 36.

230 *"A mighty river taken up in a wooden trough"*: Clappe, *Letters*, p. 162.

230 *Mercury by the ton*: Meldahl, *Rough-Hewn Land*, p. 38, and. Alpers et al., "Mercury Contamination," online at http://tinyurl.com/mbqun8c.

230 Fn *"pale, cadaverous faces"*: Brechin, *Imperial San Francisco*, p. 61.

230 *"like immensely long slimey sea-serpents"*: Borthwick, *Three Years*, p. 111.

231 *"Prying up and breaking huge rocks"*: Perkins, *Three Years*, p. 162.

232 *"We work from five in the morning"*: Fairchild, *Letters*, p. 77.

232 *"a party of gentlemen sit playing poker"*: Perkins, *Three Years*, p. 217.

232 *"The fever and uncertainty of mining"*: Henry, ed., *My Checkered Life*, p. 81.

233 *"I have seen a thousand dollars"*: Perkins, *Three Years*, p. 190.

233 *"It was strength, absolute brute force"*: Delano, *Journey*, p. 242.

233 *"They told about the heaps of dust"*: The song was "The Returning Californian," by James Pierpont.

233 *"There seems to be but one way"*: Delano, *Correspondence*, p. 24.

234 *"The miseries of a miner"*: Bancroft, *California Inter Pocula*, p. 228.

234 *"I have myself seen dozens"*: Perkins, *Three Years*, p. 186.

235 *"Weather-beaten tars"*: Taylor, *Eldorado*, v. 2, p. 9.

235 *"only knew the difference"*: Borthwick, *Three Years*, p. 194.

235 *In Coloma, two miners*: John Caughey, *The California Gold Rush*, p. 35.

235 *One grizzled loner*: Taylor, *Eldorado*, p. 10.

236 *"They were dancing when I went to sleep"*: Clappe, *Letters*, p. 93.

236 *Gambling was "a perfect mania"*: Liles, ed., *Journey*, p. 193.

237 *"The character of the pioneers"*: Henry, ed., *My Checkered Life*, p. 59.

237 *"stewed beans and flapjacks"*: Shaw, *Across the Plains*, p. 151.

238   *"Cramp is so common"*: Liles, ed., *Journey*, p. 229.

238   *"I've lived on swine"*: The lyrics to "The Lousy Miner" can be found in full in Paul, *California Gold: The Beginning of Mining*, p. 89.

239   *"Each squalid death"*: Kevin Starr, *Dream*, p. 55.

239   *"drawn up into a kind of ball"*: Reid, *Overland*, p. 150.

239   Fn *"The sensitiveness of the bodies"*: Kenneth Carpenter, *The History of Scurvy and Vitamin C* (New York: Cambridge University Press, 1988), p. 5.

240   *"Whole camps were sometimes buried"*: Bancroft, *Works*, p. 231, fn 27.

240   *"The bottom of the river is covered with gold"*: Liles, ed., *Journey*, p. 431.

241   *"The whole current of the river"*: Langworthy, *Scenery*, p. 203.

241   *"I have often been in a position"*: ibid., p. 204.

241   *"Rained all night long"*: Liles, ed., *Journey*, p. 170.

242   *"the Methodist church turned around"*: Borthwick, *Three Years*, p. 41.

242   *"The river seemed as if it had suddenly arisen"*: ibid., p. 268.

243   *"If he could blow a fife"*: Levy, *Elephant*, p. 108.

243   *"If I was a real Captain"*: ibid., p. 109.

243   *"Oh, what was your name in the states?"*: Kowalewski, ed., *Gold Rush*, p. 204.

243   *"It is all the same whether you go to church"*: Kaufman, ed., *Apron*, p. 43.

243   *"The glorious Fourth was ushered in"*: Downie, *Hunting*, p. 13.

244   *"There, sin is stealthy"*: Farley, "Thanksgiving Sermon."

244   *"I have seen purer liquors"*: Helper, *Land of Gold*, p. 68.

245   *"a lot of badges running off"*: Wisconsin Historical Society, http://tinyurl.com/qchyj7z.

245   *"Gambling, drinking, and houses of ill fame"*: Fairchild, *Letters*, p. 71.

245   Clothed in *"nature's robes"*: Kurutz, "Popular Culture on the Golden Shore," in Starr and Orsi, eds., *Barbarous Soil*, p. 293.

245   *"It is fitted up like a palace"*: Liles, ed., *Journey*, p. 284.

246   *"She greeted me with a fascinating smile"*: Perkins, *Three Years*, p. 250.

246   *"Every man thought every woman"*: Henry, ed., *My Checkered Life*, p. 71.

246   *"unfortunates who make a trade"*: Clappe, *Letters*, p. 21.

247   Some were *"quite shameless"*: Levy, *Elephant*, p. 163.

247   one shocked Philadelphia native wrote: Marston, ed., *Records of a California Family*, p. 170. LC.

247   *"Look — a back door stands ajar"*: Roberts, *American Alchemy*, p. 209.

Chapter Thirteen: At Ease in a Barbarous Land

248   *"I am right glad to hear"*: Kaufman, ed., *Apron*, p. 120.

248   *"Will you not bring back?"* Starr, *Dream*, p. 69.

249   *"In San Francisco," she wrote excitedly*: Kaufman, ed., *Apron*, p. 120.

249   *"The churches are very well attended"*: ibid., p. 56.

249   *"I suppose she thinks I am very wicked"*: ibid., p. 68.

249   *"There is no such thing as slander"*: ibid., p. 56.

249   *"You would be astonished"*: ibid., p. 65.

250   *"Your Father thinks it is no place"*: ibid., p. 45.

250   *"it is not proper for respectable ladies"*: ibid., p. 128.

251   A *"shrinking, timid, frail thing"*: Clappe, *Letters*, p. 157.

251   *"I have slept on tables"*: ibid., p. 173.

251   *"in that transcendental state of intoxication"*: ibid., p. 195.

251   *"I* like *this wild and barbarous life"*: ibid., p. 198.

251   *"I will give a dollar"*: Kaufman, ed., *Apron*, p. 68. For Megquier's nightmare, see p. 71.

251   *"I get up and make the coffee"*: ibid., p. 69.

252   *"I cast my thoughts about me"*: Henry, ed., *My Checkered Life*, p. 68.

253   *"Everybody had money"*: ibid., p. 69.

253   *"At one time I must have had"*: ibid., p. 71.

253   Fn *Married women in the early 1800s*: The judgment that "the husband and the wife are one" was a paraphrase of a slightly more cumbersome observation by the eminent English jurist Sir William Blackstone, *Commentaries on the Laws of England*. See v. 1, ch. 15.

254   *"Sparta could not hold a candle to it"*: Delano, *Correspondence*, p. 59.

254   *"bending over the wash-tub"*: Delano, *Journey*, p. 243.

254   *"Smith and Brown, whom I had brought across"*: ibid., p. 244.

255   *"Oh, doom me not to slave and toil"*: Liles, ed., *Journey*, p. 224.

255   *"Every man is his own porter"*: Taylor, *Eldorado*, p. 56.

255   *"not to labor was degrading"*: Borthwick, *Three Years*, p. 371.

256   *"LABOR IS RESPECTABLE"*: Taylor, *Eldorado*, v. 2, p. 67.

256   *"It was one intense scramble"*: Borthwick, *Three Years*, p. 66.

Chapter Fourteen: Taking the Bread from American Miners

257   *"grisly bears"*: Langworthy, *Scenery*, pp. 64, 66.

258   *The word "racism"*: Robert Miles, *Racism* (New York: Routledge, 1989), p. 42.

258   *"copper-hued Kanakas"*: Taylor, *Eldorado*, p. 118.

258   *"Their hats are made of stiff splints"*: Langworthy, *Scenery*, p. 182.

258   *"making coffee for the French people"*: Hanna, ed., "Hogs in My Kitchen."

259   Fn *"The Frenchmen are at it again"*: Liles, ed., *Journey*, p. 332.

259   *"I, for one, contend"*: Liles, ed., *Journey*, p. 243.

259   *"It's a shame"*: Fairchild, *Letters*, p. 99.

260   *"a grasping and avaricious spirit"*: Taylor, *Eldorado*, p. 103.

260   *"all those who were not American citizens"*: Perkins, *Three Years*, p. 30.

260   *two hundred men shouting "Hang them"*: Buffum, *Six Months*, p. 84.

261   Chinese men *"generally work in diggings"*: Langworthy, *Scenery*, p. 184.

261 *"A dozen armed white men"*: ibid., p. 182.

262 *"They may offer to come into the union"*: Colton, *Three Years,* p. 375.

262 *In all but the smallest camps*: Borthwick, *Three Years,* p. 164.

262 *"no Black, or Mulatto person"*: The 1850 law was quoted in *The People v. George Hall,* California Supreme Court, October, 1854, which is also the source for the footnote at the bottom of the page. See http://tinyurl.com/mvw2sen.

263 *Indians had outnumbered whites*: Albert Hurtado, *Indian Survival on the California Frontier,* pp. 120–24.

263 *In November, 1848, Edward Buffum*: Buffum, *Six Months,* p. 44.

264 *"giving handfuls of gold"*: Carson, *Bright Gem of the Western Seas,* p. 4.

264 *John Marsh packed sugar*: Lavender, *Beginnings,* p. 158.

264 *"They make the most"*: Browning, ed., *Golden Shore,* p. 58.

264 *"There are at this time"*: ibid., p. 157.

264 *"A more filthy and disgusting"*: Delano, *Correspondence,* p. 28.

265 *"among the least intelligent"*: Langworthy, *Scenery,* p. 218.

265 *"the inaptitude of the Indian"*: Stephen Jay Gould, *The Mismeasure of Man* (New York: Norton, 1996), pp. 82–93.

265 *"Native Americans were hunted down"*: Starr and Orsi, eds., *Barbarous Soil,* p. 6.

266 *"the Indians are much sinned against"*: Liles, ed., *Journey,* p. 159.

266 *"bound to be exterminated"*: ibid., p. 220.

266 *"Nine-tenths of the troubles"*: Delano, *Journey,* p. 320.

266 *"There will be safety only in a war"*: "Our Indian Policy," *Daily Alta California,* May 29, 1850. A PDF of the story is available at http://tinyurl.com/mtrybzc.

266 *"A war of extermination"*: Horsman, *Race and Manifest Destiny,* p. 279.

266 *"a wild, free, disorderly, grotesque"*: Mark Twain, *Roughing It,* ch. 16.

266 *"Men assumed their natural shape"*: Borthwick, *Three Years,* p. 67.

267 *life insurance companies refused*: Shepherd B. Clough, *A Century of American Life Insurance* (Westport CT: Greenwood Press, 1970), p. 85.

267 *Sonora is very dull*: Perkins, *Three Years,* p. 314.

267 *"Nothing fatal has taken place"*: White, ed., *Franklin Buck,* p. 106.

267 *"Yesterday one American shot another"*: Christman, *One Man's Gold,* p. 178.

267 *"This is the worst country in the world"*: Farley, "Thanksgiving Sermon."

268 *"It has been a lifelong source of regret"*: Henry, ed., *My Checkered Life,* p. 47.

269 *"a picture of universal human nature"*: Borthwick, *Three Years,* p. 91.

269 *"murders, fearful accidents, bloody deaths"*: Clappe, *Letters,* p. 145.

269 *"A residence here at present"*: Langworthy, *Scenery,* p. 222.

269 *"If a terrier catches a rat"*: Helper, *Land of Gold,* p. 179.

269 *"Our countrymen are the most discontented"*: Clappe, *Letters,* p. 118.

270 *"to make pleasant man's stay on earth"*: Mulford, *Life,* p. 142.

270 *"The whole population of the mining country"*: Langworthy, *Scenery*, p. 196.

271 *Joseph Bruff heard the story*: Read and Gaines, eds., *Gold Rush*, pp. 404–6.

272 *Alonzo Delano ventured out in search*: Delano, *Journey*, p. 332.

272 *"Gold Lake humbug"*: Liles, ed., *Journey*, p. 261.

272 *Stoddard claimed he had been the first*: Downie, *Hunting*, p. 178.

273 *"a person of common sense"*: Read and Gaines, eds., *Gold Rush*, p. 406.

273 *"beautiful, white botyroidal crystals"*: ibid., p. 419.

274 *On the night of October 11*: ibid., p. 442.

275 *"It's hard work writing home"*: Mulford, *Life*, p. 118.

Chapter Fifteen: The Princess and the Mangled Hand

277 *Matteson put his idea into practice*: Kelley, *Gold versus Grain*, p. 27.

278 *"living rivers to exhume the dead"*: Brechin, *Imperial San Francisco*, p. 33.

278 *"If a giant nozzle should be set"*: Holliday, *Rush for Riches*, p. 272.

279 *As technology improved, the hoses grew*: Kelley, *Gold versus Grain*, p. 31.

279 *"The velocity of the water"*: Brechin, *Imperial San Francisco*, p. 36.

279 *a writer from* Scientific American *marveled*: "Hydraulic Gold Mining in California," *Scientific American*, May 17, 1879, p. 314.

280 *the governor-elect had to travel*: Brechin, *Imperial San Francisco*, p. 48.

280 *"The hills have been cut and scalped"*: John Muir, *The Mountains of California*, ch. 15, online at http://tinyurl.com/14yh6of.

280 *"a princess who has been captured"*: J. S. Holliday cited this remark in his lecture "Failure Be Damned: The Origin of California's Risk-taking Culture," delivered May 3, 2000, at the Milken Institute Forum.

280 *"There are now thousands of men"*: Wyman, ed., *Letters*, p. 125.

280 *"an excited and impatient audience"*: Helper, *Land of Gold*, p. 101.

281 *"all dried and withered"*: Liles, ed., *Journey*, p. 265.

281 *"the swill is hot"*: ibid., p. 236.

281 *"Come here and see"*: ibid., p. 239.

281 *"the fewer to laugh"*: ibid., p. 275.

281 *California was "a beautiful prison"*: Reid, *Overland*, p. 163.

282 *"You may rely upon it"*: Liles, ed., *Journey*, p. 430.

282 *most miners would have done as well*: Clay and Jones, "Migrating to Riches."

282 *By the reckoning of Rodman Paul*: Paul, *Gold: Beginning*, p. 120, and more details in appendix B, pp. 349–52.

282 *the total amount of gold dug up*: ibid., p. 118.

282 *"What glorious old times they were!"*: Mulford, *Life*, p. 98.

Epilogue

285 *"a crooked, disgusting deformity"*: Liles, ed., *Journey*, p. 351.

285 *"steaming, boiling, seething, reeking"*: ibid., p. 346.

285 *"A rushing, living tide of men and animals"*: ibid., p. 386.

285 *"If I should get time"*: ibid., p. 415.

286   *"performed prodigies in moving rocks"*: Delano, *Journey*, p. 280.

286   *"I haven't got to drinking"*: Delano, *Correspondence*, p. 130.

287   *"The vein is struck"*: Delano, "The Idle and Industrious Miner," online at http://tinyurl.com/k7w34wm.

288   *"no fussing with servants or housecleaning"*: Henry, ed., *My Checkered Life*, p. 97.

288   *a local newspaper ran a story*: ibid., p. 147.

289   *"The very air I breathe"*: Kaufman, ed., *Apron*, p. 141.

289   *"I have never regretted for a moment"*: ibid., p. 143.

289   *"I should never wish to be in Maine again"*: ibid., p. 148.

289   *California was "the place to enjoy life"*: ibid., p. 158.

289   *"a dozen big clippers"*: ibid.

290   *"We dine at seven"*: ibid., p. 166.

290   *"54 years in the service of the government"*: Read and Gaines, eds., *Gold Rush*, p. xxvi.

290   *Bruff was reprimanded*: "J. Goldsborough Bruff," Library of Congress, Prints and Photographs Division, online at http://tinyurl.com/mfu3vtm.

290   *"For the past sixty-three years"*: Read and Gaines, eds., *Gold Rush*, p. 31.

291   *"I cannot abandon my notes"*: ibid., p. 214.

291   *"Labeled my papers and drawings"*: ibid., p. lxiv.

291   *"every thing of value I possessed"*: ibid., p. 522.

291   *the best and most thorough*: This is the verdict of Gary Kurutz, whose imposing and authoritative *California Gold Rush* discusses each firsthand account. See Kurutz, p. 87.

291   *"I was offered Ten Thousand dollars cash"*: Read and Gaines, eds., *Gold Rush*, p. lxv.

292   *"The rush to California"*: Henry Thoreau, "Life Without Principle," online at http://tinyurl.com/d9x965.

292   *"the agonizing, aimless movements of the sloth"*: Taylor, *California Life Illustrated*, p. 278.

292   *"There is nothing around us older"*: Bancroft, *California Inter Pocula*, p. 300.

293   *"In California the lights went on all at once"*: McWilliams, *California, The Great Exception*. Carey McWilliams's book, originally published in 1949, is brilliant and far-seeing, and I have drawn on it often.

293   *In 1860, its population*: Nugent, *Into the West*, p. 58.

293   *San Francisco had more daily newspapers*: McWilliams, *California, The Great Exception*, p. 58.

293   *California was rich*: ibid., p. 59.

293   *a ship captain named Kemble*: Alice Morse Earle, *The Sabbath in Puritan New England* (New York: Scribner's, 1891), p. 247.

294   *bargaining power unavailable to their sisters*: Lavender, *Beginnings*, p. 236, and Starr and Orsi, eds., *Barbarous Soil*, p. 163.

294 *white people in California saw sequoia trees*: Kurutz, "Popular Culture on the Golden Shore," in Starr and Orsi, eds., *Barbarous Soil*, p. 307.

295 *"Many men of fine mind"*: Taylor, *California Life Illustrated*, p. 284.

295 *"Life was a dull and commonplace routine"*: Hittell, *The Resources of California*, p. 15.

295 *"Every day was like Sunday"*: Manly, *Death Valley in '49*, ch. 15.

296 *"Recklessness is in the air"*: Kipling, *From Sea to Sea*, p. 436.

296 *A man's reputation as fiscally sound*: Sandage, *Born Losers*, p. 31. Sandage was quoting from an essay on bankruptcy in *Merchants' Magazine and Commercial Review* 4 (1841). See p. 31.

296 *"In any little random gathering"*: Hittell, *Resources*, p. 333.

297 *"One man works hard all his life"*: Lewis, *The Big Four*, p. 53.

297 *"The secret of them Pents"*: Evans, *They Made America*, p. 111.

298 *"the great laboratory state of California"*: Bill Keller, "A Jury of Whose Peers?," *New York Times*, Sept. 13, 2013.

298 *"The cowards never started"*: Joaquin Miller, a writer once famous as "the poet of the Sierras," seems to have been the first to praise the emigrants along these lines. In 1881 he wrote, "The cowards did not start to the Pacific Coast in the old days; all the weak died on the way." See Miller, "Old Californians," *The Californian* 3, no. 13 (Jan., 1881), p. 48. Over the years Miller published slight variations on his comment in various poems and articles (and Robert Heinlein, the science fiction writer, composed a pithier version, in 1945, that came to be well known).

298 *"You've got to be willing to fail"*: Steve Jobs. See http://tinyurl.com/7bejt68.

BIBLIOGRAPHY

Hundreds of diaries and journals, once hidden in the rare book rooms of the nation's best libraries, have lately been digitized. New collections come online almost daily. It is now possible to type a few keystrokes and call up, for example, the very first newspaper stories reporting the discovery of gold in California. Wherever possible, I have cited works in their easiest-to-find form. The Library of Congress has done especially fine work in making its collection available. "LC" denotes a work available in the online archive at http://memory.loc.gov/ammem/cbhtml/cbhome.html

FIRST-PERSON ACCOUNTS:

Barker, Malcolm E., ed. *San Francisco Memoirs 1835–1851: Eyewitness Accounts of the Birth of a City* (San Francisco: Londonborn, 1994).

Barry, Louise, ed. "Overland to the California Gold Fields in 1852. The Journal of John Hawkins Clark," *Kansas Historical Quarterly* 11, no. 3 (Aug., 1942).

Bates, Mrs. D. B. *Incidents on Land and Water, or Four Years on the Pacific Coast* (Boston: French, 1857). LC.

Bidwell, John. "Life in California Before the Gold Discovery," *Century Magazine*, Dec., 1890.

Borthwick, John David. *Three Years in California* (Edinburgh: William Blackwood, 1857).

Buffum, Edward. *Six Months in the Gold Mines: From a Journal of Three Years' Residence in Upper and Lower California 1847–8–9* (Philadelphia: Lea and Blanchard, 1850). LC.

Carson, James. *Bright Gem of the Western Seas: California, 1846–1852* (Lafayette, CA: Great West Books, 1991). LC.

Christman, Florence Morrow, ed. *One Man's Gold: The Letters and Journals of a Forty-niner, Enos Christman* (New York: McGraw-Hill, 1930). LC.

Clappe, Louise A. K. S. *The Shirley Letters: Being Letters Written in 1851–1852 from the California Mines by "Dame Shirley"* (Salt Lake City, UT: Peregrine Smith, 1983).

Cole, Gilbert. *In the Early Days Along the Overland Travel in Nebraska Territory, in 1852* (Kansas City, MO: Hudson, 1905).

Colton, Walter. *Three Years in California* (New York: S. A. Rollo, 1859). LC.

Delano, Alonzo. *California Correspondence* (Sacramento: Sacramento Book Collectors Club, 1952). LC.

———. "The Idle and Industrious Miner." (Sacramento: James Anthony, 1854). Online at http://tinyurl.com/k7w34wm.

———. *On the Trail to the California Gold Rush* (Lincoln: University of Nebraska Press, 2005). LC.

Downie, William. *Hunting for Gold* (San Francisco: California Publishing, 1893).

Drinker, Elizabeth. *Extracts from the Journal of Elizabeth Drinker, from 1759 to 1807* (Philadelphia: Lippincott, 1889).

Drury, Clifford Merrill, ed. *On to Oregon: The Diaries of Mary Walker and Myra Eels* (Lincoln: University of Nebraska Press, 1963).

Dundass, Samuel. *The Journal of Samuel Rutherford Dundass: Crossing the Plains to California in 1849* (Fairfield, WA: Ye Galleon, 1983).

Farnham, Elijah. "From Ohio to California in 1849: The Gold Rush Diary of Elijah Bryan Farnham," *Indiana Magazine* 14, nos. 3–4 (Sept.–Dec., 1950).

Foreman, Grant, ed. *Marcy and the Gold-Seekers: The Journal of Captain R. B. Marcy with an Account of the Gold Rush over the Southern Route* (Norman: University of Oklahoma Press, 1939).

Frink, Margaret. *Journal of the Adventures of a Party of California Gold-seekers* (Fairfield, WA: Ye Galleon, 1988).

Gernes, Phyllis, ed. *Daily Journal 1852–60 of Stephen Wing* (Garden Valley, CA: Phyllis Gernes, 1982).

Gordon, Mary McDougall. *Overland to California with the Pioneer Line: The Gold Rush Diary of Bernard J. Reid* (Stanford, CA: Stanford University Press, 1983).

Grant, Ulysses. *Personal Memoirs of Ulysses S. Grant* (New York: Cosimo, 2007).

Hanna, Archibald, ed. *"I Hear the Hogs in My Kitchen": A Woman's View of the Gold Rush* (New Haven, CT: Yale University Press, 1962). This is Mary Ballou's account of her days running a boardinghouse in the diggings.

Haskins, Charles. *The Argonauts of California* (New York: Fords, Howard, & Hulbert, 1890).

Helper, Hinton. *The Land of Gold: Reality versus Fiction* (Baltimore: Henry Taylor, 1855). LC.

Henry, Fern, ed. *My Checkered Life: Luzena Stanley Wilson in Early California* (Nevada City, CA: Carl Mautz, 2003).

Horner, James. "Adventures of a Pioneer," *Improvement Era* 7, no. 2, 1904.

Ingalls, Eleazer Stillman. *Journal of a Trip to California by the Overland Route Across the Plains in 1850–1* (FQ Books, 2010). Online at http://tinyurl/lqv2dgb.

Johnston, William G. *Experiences of a Forty-niner* (Pittsburgh, 1892).

Kaufman, Polly Welts, ed. *Apron Full of Gold: The Letters of Mary Jane Megquier from San Francisco 1849–1856* (Albuquerque: University of New Mexico Press, 1994).

Kemble, Edward. "San Francisco: Her Prospects," *Alta California,* Feb. 1, 1849.

Kip, Leonard. *California Sketches, with Recollections of the Gold Mines* (Los Angeles: Kovach, 1946). LC.

Kipling, Rudyard. *From Sea to Sea: Letters of Travel* (New York: Doubleday, 1915).

Langworthy, Franklin. *Scenery of the Plains, Mountains, and Mines, or A Diary Kept upon the Overland Route to California.* (Ogdensburgh, NY: Sprague, 1855). Online at http://tinyurl.com/krpba43.

Letts, John. *California Illustrated* (New York: R. T. Young, 1853). LC.

Lienhard, Heinrich. *A Pioneer at Sutter's Fort: 1846–1850* (Los Angeles: The Calafia Society, 1941). LC.

Liles, Necia Dixon, ed. *A Doctor's Gold Rush Journey to California. By Israel Shipman Pelton Lord* (Lincoln: University of Nebraska Press, 1995).

Manly, William. *Death Valley in '49: The Autobiography of a Pioneer* (San Jose, CA: Pacific Tree and Vine, 1894). LC.

Marston, Anna Lee, ed. *Records of a California Family: Journals and Letters of Lewis C. Gunn and Elizabeth Le Breton Gunn* (San Francisco: Johnck and Seeger, 1928). LC.

Marryat, Frank. *Mountains and Molehills* (New York: Harper, 1855). LC.

Marryat, Frederick. *A Diary in America: With Remarks on Its Institutions* (New York: W. H. Colyer, 1839), 2 volumes.

Mattes, Merrill, and Esley J. Kirk, eds. "From Ohio to California in 1849: The Gold Rush Journal of Elijah Bryan Farnham," *Indiana Magazine of History* 46, no. 3 (Sept., 1950).

McCollum,William. *California as I Saw It* (Los Gatos, CA: Talisman, 1960). LC.

McNeil, Samuel. *McNeil's travels in 1849, to, through and from the gold regions, in California* (Columbus, OH: Scott & Bascom, 1850). LC.

Mulford, Prentice. *Prentice Mulford's Story: Life by Land and Sea* (New York: Needham, 1889). LC.

Palmer, Joel. *Journey of Travels over the Rocky Mountains* (Cincinnati: James, 1847).

Perkins, Elisha. *Gold Rush Diary* (Lexington: University of Kentucky Press, 1967).

Perkins, William. *Three Years in California: William Perkins' Journal of Life at Sonora, 1849–1852,* with introduction and annotations by Dale Morgan and James Scobie (Berkeley: University of California Press, 1964).

Pierce, Hiram. *A Forty-niner Speaks* (Oakland, CA: Keystone-Inglett, 1930). LC.

Potter, David M., ed. *The Overland Journal of Vincent Geiger and Wakeman Bryarly* (New Haven, CT: Yale University Press, 1945).

Read, Georgia Willis, and Ruth Gaines, eds. *Gold Rush: The Journals, Drawings, and Other Papers of J. Goldsborough Bruff* (New York: Columbia University Press, 1949).

Ring, Bob, Al Ring, and Steven Ring. *Detour to the California Gold Rush: Eugene Ring's Travels in South America, California, and Mexico 1848–1850* (Tucson, AZ: U.S. Press, 2008).

Royce, Sarah. *Frontier Lady: Recollections of the Gold Rush and Early California* (New Haven, CT: Yale University Press, 1932).

Sawyer, Lorenzo. *Way Sketches, Containing Incidents of Travel Across the Plains from St. Joseph to California in 1850* (New York: Eberstadt, 1926).

Scarnehorn, Howard, ed. *The Buckeye Rovers in the Gold Rush* (Athens: Ohio University Press, 1965). This book includes the diary of John Banks.

Schafer, Joseph, ed. *California Letters of Lucius Fairchild* (Madison: State Historical Society of Wisconsin, 1931). LC.

Shaw, Reuben. *Across the Plains in '49* (New York: Citadel, 1967).

Stansbury, Howard. *Exploration and Survey of the Valley of the Great Salt Lake of Utah, Including a Reconnaissance of a New Route Through the Rocky Mountains* (Philadelphia: Lippincott, 1852).

Steele, Eliza. *A Summer Journey in the West* (New York: J. S. Taylor, 1841).

Taylor, Bayard. *Eldorado, or Adventures in the Path of Empire* (New York: Putnam, 1850), 2 volumes. LC.

Taylor, William. *California Life Illustrated* (New York: Carlton & Porter, 1858).

Thissell, George. *Crossing the Plains in '49* (Oakland, CA, 1903).

Thompson, William. *Reminiscences of a Pioneer* (San Francisco, 1912).

Thornton, Jesse Quinn. *California and Oregon in 1848* (New York: Harper, 1864).

Webster, Kimball. *The Gold-Seekers of '49* (Manchester, NH: Standard, 1917). LC.

White, Katherine A., ed. *A Yankee Trader in the Gold Rush: The Letters of Franklin A. Buck* (Boston: Houghton Mifflin, 1930). LC.

Woods, Daniel. *Sixteen Months at the Gold Diggings* (New York: Harper, 1851). LC.

Wyman, Walker D., ed. *California Emigrant Letters* (New York: Bookman, 1952).

HISTORIES

Alpers, Charles, et al. "Mercury Contamination from Historical Gold Mining in California," November, 2005, United States Geological Survey Fact Sheet 2005-3014 Version 1.1. Online at http://tinyurl.com/mbqun8c.

Bancroft, Hubert. *California Inter Pocula* (1888). Online at http://tinyurl.com/l6ycxp3.

————. *The Works of Hubert Howe Bancroft*, v. 23 *(History of California)*, (San Francisco: A. L. Bancroft, 1882).

Bernstein, Peter. *The Power of Gold: The History of an Obsession* (New York: John Wiley, 2000).

Bieber, Ralph. "California Gold Mania," *The Mississippi Valley Historical Review* 35, no. 1 (June, 1948).

Billington, Ray. *Words That Won the West, 1830–1850* (Foundation for Public Relations Research and Education, 1964). This is the transcript of a lecture delivered on Nov. 18, 1963, by Billington, a frontier historian then at the Huntington Library.

Boessenecker, John. *Gold Dust and Gunsmoke: Tales of Gold Rush Outlaws, Gunfighters, Lawmen, and Vigilantes* (New York: John Wiley, 1999).

Bonfield, Lynn, and Mary Chase Morison. *Roxana's Children: The Biography of a Nineteenth Century Vermont Family* (Amherst: University of Massachusetts Press, 1995).

Brechin, Gray. *Imperial San Francisco: Urban Power, Earthly Ruin* (Berkeley: University of California Press, 1999).

Brown, Daniel James. *The Indifferent Stars Above: The Harrowing Saga of a Donner Party Bride* (New York: William Morrow, 2009).

Browning, Peter, ed. *To the Golden Shore: America Goes to California—1849* (Lafayette, CA: Great West Books, 1995).

Bruce, John. *Gaudy Century: The Story of San Francisco's Hundred Years of Robust Journalism* (New York: Random House, 1948).

Burrows, Edwin G., and Mike Wallace. *Gotham: A History of New York City to 1898* (New York: Oxford University Press, 1998).

Byrne, Joseph, ed. *Encyclopedia of Pestilence, Pandemics, and Plagues* (Westport, CT: Greenwood Press, 2008).

Caughey, John. *The California Gold Rush* (Berkeley: University of California Press, 1948).

Cawelti, John. *Apostles of the Self-Made Man* (Chicago: University of Chicago Press, 1965).

Chartier, JoAnn, and Chriss Enss. *With Great Hope: Women of the California Gold Rush* (Guilford, CT: Two Dot, 2000).

Chen, Jack. *The Chinese of America* (New York: Harper & Row, 1980).

Clark, Christopher. *Social Change in America: From the Revolution to the Civil War* (Chicago: Ivan Dee, 2006).

Clay, Karen, and Randall Jones. "Migrating to Riches: Evidence from the California Gold Rush," *The Journal of Economic History* 68, no. 4 (December, 2008).

Cleaveland, E. L. "Hasting to Be Rich: A Sermon, Occasioned by the Present Excitement Respecting the Gold of California, Preached in the Cities of New Haven and Bridgeport, Jan. and Feb. 1849" (New Haven, CT: J. H. Benham, 1849).

Clough, Shepherd B. *A Century of American Life Insurance* (Westport, CT: Greenwood Press, 1970).

Conlin, Joseph R. *Bacon, Beans, and Galantines: Food and Foodways on the Western Mining Frontier* (Reno: University of Nevada Press, 1986).

Cooke, Alistair. *Alistair Cooke's America* (New York: Knopf, 1974).

Cooperman, Jeannette. "Take Care, and Don't Take the Cholera," *St. Louis Magazine,* July, 2010.

Corbett, Christopher. *The Poker Bride: The First Chinese in the West* (New York: Atlantic Monthly Press, 2010).

Courtwright, David T. *Violent Land: Single Men and Social Disorder from the Frontier to the Inner City* (Cambridge, MA: Harvard University Press, 1996).

Coy, Owen. *The Great Trek* (Los Angeles: Powell, 1931).

Curran, Harold. *Fearful Crossing: The Central Overland Trail Through Nevada* (Las Vegas: Nevada Publications, 1982).

Danforth, Reverend Joshua N. *Gleanings and Groupings from a Pastor's Portfolio* (New York: A. S. Barnes, 1852). Online at http://tinyurl,com/nyfljsd.

Delbanco, Andrew. *Melville: His World and Work* (New York: Random House, 2006).

DeVoto, Bernard. *Across the Wide Missouri* (Boston: Houghton Mifflin, 1947).

Emerson, Ralph Waldo. *The Conduct of Life* (Boston: Ticknor and Fields, 1860).

Evans, Harold. *They Made America: From the Steam Engine to the Search Engine* (New York: Little, Brown, 2004).

Farley, Charles A. "The Moral Aspect of California: A Thanksgiving Sermon" (New York: Henry Spear, 1850).

Federal Writers' Project. *California: A Guide to the Golden State* (New York: Hastings, 1939).

Fey, Marshall, R. Joe King, and Jack Lepisto. *Emigrant Shadows: A History and Guide to the California Trail* (Virginia City, NV: Western Trails Research Association, 2002).

Foner, Philip. *History of the Labor Movement in the United States: From Colonial Times to the Founding of the AFL* (New York: International, 1972).

Garrett, Lula May. "San Francisco in 1851 As Described by Eyewitnesses," *California Historical Society Quarterly* 22, no. 3 (Sept., 1943).

Gay, Theressa. *James W. Marshall: The Discoverer of California Gold* (Georgetown, CA: Talisman, 1967).

Goodman, Matthew. *The Sun and the Moon: The Remarkable True Account of Hoaxers, Showmen, Dueling Journalists, and Lunar Man-bats in Nineteenth Century New York* (New York: Basic Books, 2008).

Gordon, John Steele. *An Empire of Wealth: The Epic History of American Economic Power* (New York: HarperCollins, 2004).

Groh, George. *Gold Fever* (New York: William Morrow, 1966).

Herrington, Richard, et al. *Gold.* (London: Natural History Museum, 1999).

Hill, William E. *The California Trail: Yesterday and Today* (Boise, ID: Tamarack, 1993).

"History of the Origin, Progress, and Mortality of the Cholera Morbus," *London Medical Gazette* 44 (1849).

Hittell, John. *A History of the City of San Francisco* (San Francisco: A. L. Bancroft, 1878).

———. *The Resources of California* (New York: Widdleton, 1874).

Holliday, J. S. "Failure Be Damned: The Origin of California's Risk-taking Culture." This was a lecture delivered on May 3, 2000, at the Milken Institute Forum.

———. *Rush for Riches: Gold Fever and the Making of California* (Berkeley: Oakland Museum of California and the University of California Press, 1999).

———. *The World Rushed In: An Eyewitness Account of a Nation Heading West* (New York: Simon and Schuster, 1981).

Horsman, Reginald. *Race and Manifest Destiny* (Cambridge, MA: Harvard University Press, 1981).

Howe, Daniel Walker. *What Hath God Wrought: The Transformation of America, 1815–1848* (New York: Oxford University Press, 1997).

Hurtado, Albert. *Indian Survival on the California Frontier* (New Haven, CT: Yale University Press, 1988).

———. *John Sutter: A Life on the North American Frontier* (Norman: University of Oklahoma Press, 2006).

Isaacson, Walter. *Benjamin Franklin: An American Life* (New York: Simon and Schuster, 2003).

Jackson, Donald Dale. *Gold Dust* (Edison, NJ: Castle Books, 2004).

"J. Goldsborough Bruff," Library of Congress, Prints and Photographs Division. Online at http://tinyurl.com/mfu3vtm.

Johnson, Steven. *The Ghost Map: The Story of London's Most Terrifying Epidemic and How It Changed Science, Cities, and the Modern World* (New York: Riverhead, 2006).

Johnson, Susan Lee. *Roaring Camp: The Social World of the California Gold Rush* (New York: Norton, 2000).

Jones, Peter. *The 1848 Revolutions* (London: Longman, 1991).

Kelley, Robert L. *Gold versus Grain: The Hydraulic Mining Controversy in Caliornia's Sacramento Valley* (Glendale, CA: Arthur H. Clark, 1959).

Kolchin, Peter. *American Slavery 1619–1877* (New York: Hill and Wang, 1993).

Kowalewski, Michael, ed. *Gold Rush* (Berkeley, CA: Heyday, 1997).

Krech, Shepard, III. *The Ecological Indian: Myth and History* (New York: Norton, 1999).

Kurutz, Gary. *The California Gold Rush: A Descriptive Bibliography of Books and Pamphlets Covering the Years 1848–1853* (San Francisco: Book Club of California, 1997).

Lapp, Rudolph. *Blacks in Gold Rush California* (New Haven, CT: Yale University Press, 1977).

Larkin, Jack. *The Reshaping of Everyday Life 1790–1840* (New York: Harper & Row, 1988).

Lavender, David. *California: Land of New Beginnings* (Lincoln: University of Nebraska Press, 1972).

Lepler, Jessica M. *1837: Anatomy of a Panic* (Ann Arbor, MI: Proquest, 2007).

Levy, JoAnn. *They Saw the Elephant: Women in the California Gold Rush* (Norman: University of Oklahoma Press, 1992).

Lewis, Oscar. *The Big Four* (New York: Knopf, 1938).

———. *Sea Routes to the Gold Fields: The Migration by Water to California in 1849–52* (New York: Knopf, 1949).

Limerick, Patricia Nelson. *The Legacy of Conquest: The Unbroken Past of the American West* (New York: Norton, 1987).

———. *Something in the Soil: Legacies and Reckonings in the New West* (New York: Norton, 2000).

Lorenz, Anthony J. "Scurvy in the Gold Rush," *Journal of the History of Medicine* 12, no. 4 (October, 1957).

Luskey, Brian. *On the Make: Clerks and the Quest for Capital in Nineteenth Century America* (New York: New York University Press, 2010).

Mackay, Charles. *Extraordinary Popular Delusions and the Madness of Crowds* (New York: Farrar, Straus and Giroux, 1932).

"Make Everything Golden," *Popular Science*, June, 2005. Online at http://tinyurl.com/kfzsa9x.

Martineau, Harriet. *Society in America*, v. 1 (New York: Saunders and Otley, 1837).

Marvin, Judith, Julia Costello, and Salvatore Manna. *Northern Calaveras County* (Charleston, SC: Arcadia, 2007).

Matt, Susan J. *Homesickness: An American History* (New York: Oxford University Press, 2011).

Mattes, Merrill. *The Great Platte River Road: The Covered Wagon Mainline via Fort Kearny to Fort Laramie* (Lincoln: University of Nebraska Press, 1987).

McPherson, James. *Battle Cry of Freedom: The Civil War Era* (New York: Oxford University Press, 1988).

McWilliams, Carey. *California: The Great Exception* (Berkeley: University of California Press, 1949).

Meldahl, Keith. *Hard Road West: History and Geology Along the Gold Rush Trail* (Chicago: University of Chicago Press, 2007).

———. *Rough-hewn Land: A Geologic Journey from California to the Rocky Mountains* (Berkeley: University of California Press, 2011).

Merry, Robert W. *A Country of Vast Designs: James K. Polk, the Mexican War and the Conquest of the American Continent* (New York: Simon and Schuster, 2009).

Mindich, David T. Z. *Just the Facts: How "Objectivity" Came to Define American Journalism* (New York: New York University Press, 1998).

Minnigerode, Meade. *The Fabulous Forties, 1840–1850* (Garden City, NY: Garden City, 1924).

Morris, Roy, Jr. *Lighting Out for the Territory: How Samuel Clemens Headed West and Became Mark Twain* (New York: Simon and Schuster, 2010).

Morton, Julius, and Albert Watkins. *History of Nebraska from the Earliest Explorations of the Trans-Mississippi Region* (Lincoln, NE: Western Publishing, 1918).

Muir, John. *The Mountains of California* (New York: Century, 1894).

Newell, Olive. *Tail of the Elephant; The Emigrant Experience on the Truckee Route of the California Trail, 1844–1852* (Nevada City, CA: Nevada County Historical Society, 1997).

Nugent, Walter. *Into the West: The Story of Its People* (New York: Knopf, 1999).

Owens, Kenneth, ed. *Gold Rush Saints: California Mormons and the Great Rush for Riches* (Norman: University of Oklahoma Press, 2005).

———. *John Sutter and a Wider West* (Lincoln: University of Nebraska Press, 1994).

Paul, Rodman. *California Gold: The Beginning of Mining in the Far West* (Lincoln: University of Nebraska Press, 1947).

———. *The California Gold Discovery: Sources, Documents, Accounts and Memoirs Related to the Discovery of Gold at Sutter's Mill* (Georgetown, CA: Talisman, 1966).

Pearce, Roy Harvey. "The Significances of the Captivity Narrative Author," *American Literature* 19, no. 1 (March, 1947).

Pessen, Edward. *Riches, Class, and Power: America Before the Civil War* (New Brunswick, NJ: Transaction, 1990).

Rapport, Mike. *1848: Year of Revolution* (New York: Basic Books, 2008).

Reynolds, David S. *Walt Whitman's America: A Cultural Biography* (New York: Vintage, 1996).

Richardson, Robert. *Henry Thoreau: A Life of the Mind* (Berkeley: University of California Press, 1986).

Roberts, Brian. *American Alchemy: The California Gold Rush and Middle-Class Culture* (Chapel Hill: University of North Carolina Press, 2000).

Roberts, Sylvia Alden. *Mining for Freedom: Black History Meets the California Gold Rush* (Bloomington, IN: Universe, 2008).

Rosenberg, Charles E. *The Cholera Years* (Chicago: University of Chicago Press, 1962).

Roth, Mitchel. "Cholera, Community, and Public Health in Gold Rush Sacramento and San Francisco," *Pacific Historical Review* 66, no. 4 (Nov., 1997).

Rydell, Raymond. "The Cape Horn Route to California, 1849," *The Pacific Historical Review* 17, no. 2 (May, 1948).

Sandage, Scott. *Born Losers: A History of Failure in America* (Cambridge, MA: Harvard University Press, 2009).

Schlissell, Lillian. *Women's Diaries of the Westward Journey* (New York: Schocken, 1982).

Schudson, Michael. *Discovering the News: A Social History of American Newspapers* (New York: Basic Books, 1978).

Shepard, Edward. *Martin Van Buren* (Boston: Houghton, Mifflin, 1892).

Spann, Edward. *New Metropolis: New York City 1840–1857* (New York: Columbia University Press, 1983).

Starr, Kevin. *Americans and the California Dream, 1850–1915* (New York: Oxford University Press, 1973).

Starr, Kevin, and Richard J. Orsi, eds. *Rooted in Barbarous Soil: People, Culture, and Community in Gold Rush California*. This collection of essays was published as a special issue of *California History*, v. 79, no. 2 (Summer, 2000).

Stashower, Daniel. *The Beautiful Cigar Girl: Mary Rogers, Edgar Allan Poe, and the Invention of Murder* (New York: Berkley Books, 2006).

Stellman, Louis J. *Sam Brannan: Builder of San Francisco* (Fairfield, CA: James Stevenson, 1996).

Stephanson, Anders. *Manifest Destiny: American Empire and the Empire of Right* (New York: Hill and Wang, 1995).

Stewart, George R. *The California Trail* (Lincoln: University of Nebraska Press, 1962).

Stillson, Richard Thomas. *Spreading the Word: A History of Information in the California Gold Rush* (Lincoln: University of Nebraska Press, 2006).

Thoreau, Henry. *Walden* (New York: Thomas Crowell, 1910).

Tong, Benson. *Unsubmissive Women: Chinese Prostitutes in Nineteenth-Century San Francisco* (Norman: University of Oklahoma Press, 1994).

Trollope, Frances. *Domestic Manners of the Americans* (New York: Dover, 2003).

Twain, Mark. *Life on the Mississippi* (New York: Harper & Brothers, 1883).

———. *Roughing It* (Hartford, CT: American, 1872).

Unruh, John D., Jr. *The Plains Across: The Overland Emigrants and the Trans-Mississippi West, 1840–60* (Urbana: University of Illinois Press, 1979).

Weber, Shirley H., ed. *Schliemann's First Visit to America, 1850–1851* (Cambridge, MA: Harvard University Press, Gennadeion Monographs, 1942). Online at http://tinyurl.com/kv394mb.

West, Elliot. "Family Life on the Trail West," *History Today*, Dec., 1992.

Whaples, Robert. "California Gold Rush." Online at http://tinyurl.com/6vnxoxm.

Whipple, A. B. C. *The Challenge* (New York: Morrow, 1987).

Wilentz, Sean. *Chants Democratic: New York City and the Rise of the American Working Class, 1788–1850* (New York: Oxford University Press, 1984).

Wright, Doris Marion. "The Making of Cosmopolitan California: An Analysis of Immigration 1848–1872," *The California Historical Society Quarterly* 19 (Part I, Dec., 1940; Part II, March, 1941).

INDEX

ABOUT THE AUTHOR

EDWARD DOLNICK is the author of *The Clockwork Universe, The Forger's Spell, Down the Great Unknown, Madness on the Couch,* and the Edgar Award–winning *The Rescue Artist.* A former chief science writer at the *Boston Globe,* he has written for *The Atlantic Monthly,* the *New York Times Magazine,* and many other publications. There are over 130,000 copies of his books in print. He lives with his wife in rural Virginia, in the foothills of the Blue Ridge Mountains.